Isabella Greenway

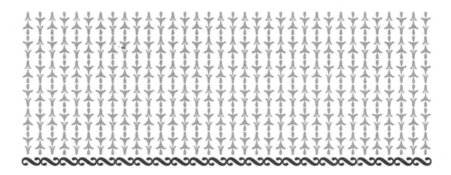

Isabella Greenway

An Enterprising Woman

KRISTIE MILLER

THE UNIVERSITY OF ARIZONA PRESS • TUCSON

THE UNIVERSITY OF
ARIZONA PRESS

© 2004 The Arizona Board of Regents
All rights reserved
First issued as a paperback edition 2005

www.uapress.arizona.edu

Library of Congress Cataloging-in-Publication Data appear
on the last printed page of this book.

Publication of this book is made possible in part by a grant
from the Southwestern Foundation.

Manufactured in the United States of America on acid-free,
archival-quality paper containing a minimum of 30% post-
consumer waste and processed chlorine free.

16   15   14   13   12   9   8   7   6   5

For My Mother

Bazy Tankersley

Chatelaine of the
Quarter Circle
Double X Ranch

CONTENTS

PART TWO

ILLUSTRATIONS

Illustrations

ACKNOWLEDGMENTS

I am most grateful to my mother, Bazy Tankersley, who gave me the idea for this book—one of her *many* excellent ideas. I owe her my first intriguing glimpse of Isabella Greenway: a woman who lured Franklin D. Roosevelt up to a ranch on a mountain six miles from a small town I'd never heard of.

I could never have written this book without the help of Patty Doar, who generously shared books and letters and photographs, conversations and trips, and the hospitality of Isabella's famous Inn. I am thankful to Jack Greenway, who agreed to let me interview him just two months before he died; to David Breasted; and to the late Mary Marvin Breckinridge Patterson, Isabella's cousin, who all gave me important insights into Isabella and her family.

I drew on the work of earlier biographers of Isabella Greenway. I am deeply indebted to Blake Brophy, Avan Probst, and Robert E. Miller for having broken the ground I tilled.

I am blessed with wise and wonderful colleagues who gave me invaluable ideas and paid me the compliment of honest criticism: Stacy Cordery, Bruce Dinges, John Gable, Melanie Gustafson, Barbara Guth, David Holtby, Pamela Reeves Kilian, Bob McGinnis, Nell Minow, and Judy Nolte Temple. Special thanks to my daughter, Ellen Twaddell, for reading more drafts than anyone else.

Acknowledgments

For assistance in mining the Greenway and Roosevelt papers I want to thank Susan Berry of the Silver City Museum; Robert Parks and the archivists of the Franklin D. Roosevelt Library; Deborah Shelton and Arnem Benneian of the Arizona Historical Society Archives, as well as Rose Byrne and Riva Dean; Jim Sutherland of the Cantigny Foundation and Eric Gillespie of the First Division Museum; and the staff of Dinsmore Farm.

I am grateful to Steve Cox, Patti Hartmann, Al Schroder, and Christine Szuter of the University of Arizona Press for their faith and patience and to Mary Rodarte for meticulous editing.

Thanks to Anne Adams, Andrea Caplan, Michael Kilian, Linda Kleczewski, Ruth Little, Mark Miller, Pete Miller, Bob Mohr, Gail Parsons, George Rosenberg, Anne Sturm, Joanna Sturm, Sandy Twaddell, Tiffany Wolfe, and the wonderful Washington Biography Group under the mentorship of Marc Pachter for guidance, care, and comfort.

And special thanks to my dear husband, T. L. Hawkins, for his insistent reminders that there is more to life than books.

INTRODUCTION

The 1932 Democratic National Convention opened in Chicago on June 27. The Republicans had just departed, after gloomily nominating Herbert Hoover, in this, the second year of the Depression. Democrats, arriving eleven days later, were enthusiastic as they had not been for years; almost any Democratic nominee could be sure of election. They descended upon the Windy City in droves, partisans of many eager candidates, fired up to repeal Prohibition. Hotels were packed, Michigan Avenue seethed with humanity, and the air shook with the sound of fifes and drums.[1]

Among this throng of vivid personalities, the *New York Times* reported, Isabella Greenway of Arizona was "the most-talked-of woman at the National Democratic Convention today." Twelve years after women had won the right to vote, she was something of a political phenomenon: She had seen to it that her state's delegates were pledged to Franklin D. Roosevelt, the front-runner but by no means the assured nominee. She was going to second his nomination. And she herself was slated to receive an honorary vice-presidential nomination. By the end of the convention, she had prompted the switch of the California delegation that swept FDR to victory.

"Who is this Mrs. Greenway?" the *Times* wondered. "The most colorful woman in the United States," was the answer. They noted that her color was natural, too: "No rouge, no lipstick, no salon specialist's 'set' to her curly brown hair. Her cheeks have a healthy glow that comes of cow-ranching and flying over mountains in airplanes." When she sat down in a restaurant for dinner, she and her young son were mobbed by reporters and photographers. Her home town Tucson newspaper crowed that she had put Arizona on the "convention map." Political humorist Will Rogers promised her his vote, and Alice Roosevelt Longworth, Theodore Roosevelt's notoriously sharp-tongued daughter, was heard to exclaim: "Isabella is one of my few enthusiasms."[2]

Who *was* Isabella Greenway and how had she come to play a leading role among the Democrats in Chicago?

Twenty years before, she had been homesteading on a remote mountain near Silver City, New Mexico. She was twenty-six years old, she had two small children and a husband suffering from tuberculosis. They made their home in a scattering of Adirondack tents, semipermanent structures with wooden floors and canvas sides, in the desert where, Isabella gamely insisted, a "well-applied quart" of water could be stretched quite far. She home-schooled her children until high school, laughing that she had to "make up my mind if the sixth continent is the 'quotient' and if the difference is obtained by dividing Australia."[3] When America entered World War I, Isabella organized women in a Land Army to harvest crops while the men were away fighting.

Isabella had, in addition to courage and executive ability, an amazing capacity to find the adventure and joy in any situation. Eleanor Roosevelt, who met Isabella when they were in their teens and remained her close friend for fifty years, wrote of Isabella's time in New Mexico: "When I think of the endless care that went into the upbringing of two children in the same house with a man who was slowing dying of tuberculosis, I marvel at the fact that Isabella was able to create the impression that . . . anyone who was not living that kind of life was missing something."[4]

Isabella Greenway's spirited response to her many misfortunes was a factor in her political success. Widowed twice, she turned to public service, using her grief to fuel accomplishment. After helping win Roosevelt's nomination in Chicago, Isabella ran for Congress to represent the entire state of Arizona. She served in Washington for three hectic years, working with the Roosevelts to construct the New Deal and bringing critical relief programs to her state.

Remarkably good-looking, at home in southern tobacco country, western ranches, or New York salons, shrewd, energetic and idealistic, Isabella Selmes Ferguson Greenway King was, as her obituary in the *New York Times* reiterated, "one of the more colorful personalities who flashed into prominence in the political upheaval that brought Franklin Delano Roosevelt to the presidency."[5] More than that, Isabella Greenway left two important legacies: She was the first of a number of remarkable women in Arizona politics, and she founded the Arizona Inn. Seventy-five years later, it is still recognized as one of the best hotels in the world.

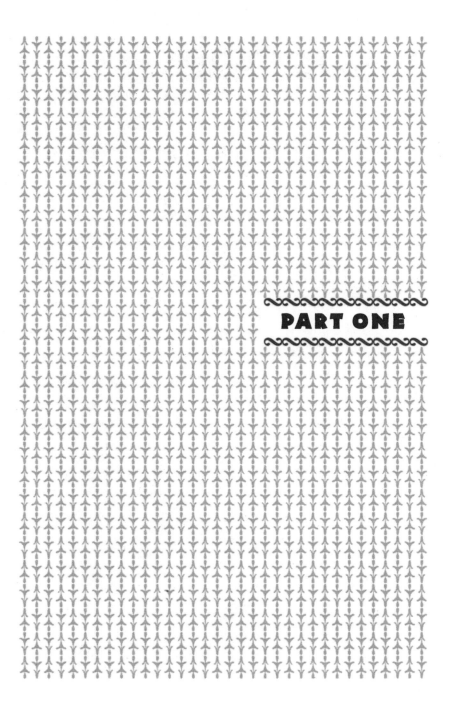

PART ONE

"Time of Gray Sorrow"

ISABELLA'S BEGINNINGS in the Badlands of the Dakotas determined the course of her life. Theodore Roosevelt used to say that if he had never lived in the Badlands, he would never have become president.[1] If Isabella Selmes had not met Roosevelt in the Badlands, her life, too, would have been completely different. The Roosevelts were a clannish family, and they made Isabella one of their tribe, admiring her effervescent spirits, strength of character, and a dedication to public service much like their own.

Theodore Roosevelt and Tilden Selmes both arrived in the Dakota Territory in 1883. Tilden Selmes, whose forebears had been early settlers in the Massachusetts Bay Colony, was educated at Yale and went on to read law. He had come into his inheritance as a young man on the death of his father in 1870, and was living in Boston with his widowed mother next to the Alcott family, immortalized in *Little Women*. But he found life in New England stultifying, so, like many men in the latter half of the nineteenth century, he went west in search of adventure and opportunity.[2] The Dakota

Territory was the new frontier. With the buffalo disappearing, and the arrival of the railroads, shrewd businessmen calculated that they could fatten cattle on the rich grass and ship them to eastern markets.

Passing through Minnesota, Selmes met Charles Flandrau, an ambitious attorney who was pursuing a career in territorial and state politics in St. Paul. Til fell in love with his lively, auburn-haired daughter Martha, known as Patty, and they became engaged. She was as eager as he to make their fortune by ranching. Patty was no stranger to rural life, having grown up on her aunt Julia Dinsmore's Kentucky farm in Boone County, just south of Cincinnati. Patty's mother, Isabella Dinsmore Flandrau, had died shortly after the birth of her second child, Sarah, known as Sally. Flandrau's hectic life made it hard for him to tend to two little girls, so, promising to provide for their financial security, he sent them to live with his wife's sister in Kentucky. Julia Dinsmore had inherited the family farm in 1872, when her father died, and managed its operation for more than fifty years, growing tobacco, corn, wheat, and hay. She never married, though her poetry suggests that she had an understanding with a Confederate soldier who died during the War.[3]

Flandrau remarried and proved to be far more generous to his new wife, Rebecca, and their two sons, Blair and Charlie, than to his daughters. Tellingly, Patty called her aunt and foster-mother "Own Mommy," "Owny" or "Ma," reserving for Rebecca the dutifully formal title "Mother." Flandrau constantly urged on Patty the need for economy, although he spent lavishly on his new family. After Patty's engagement to Tilden Selmes in 1883, Flandrau wrote her sternly: "As usual you want money . . . if you don't learn to deny yourself some things, and live within your means, you will see the day that you will tear your hair out in regret for your extravagance." He approved of their plans to begin in North Dakota, where Tilden had invested all his money in a ranch; Flandrau insisted that they would value comfort and luxury more after they had earned it. Six days after their wedding, Tilden and Patty were in the Dakota Territory, in a small wooden house on the banks of the Heart River near Mandan. Patty quickly took to life on the ranch, despite its rigors. She wrote Julia about chasing antelope on horseback, and ridiculed friends visiting from the East: "Such tenderfeet! They were almost killed by a ride down to the lower ranch." Still, she loved the excitement of city life; on a visit to St. Paul at Christmas, Til reported to Julia that the young men were lining up to dance with his lovely wife and that Patty seemed to enjoy it all the more for having been so isolated.[4]

Early on, the Selmeses met Theodore Roosevelt in the Mandan hotel. He was a flamboyant figure in a wide cowboy hat, fringed buckskin shirt, leather chaps, and boots with silver spurs.[5] He had come to the Dakotas for adventure; Theodore's real life was in the East, where he was a rising politician in New York state politics, living with his young bride, the beautiful Alice Lee. But in the winter of 1884, he suffered a double calamity when both his mother and his wife died on Valentine's Day, his mother of typhoid fever, and Alice of kidney disease, two days after giving birth to a daughter named after herself. Roosevelt left little Alice in the care of his sister Anna and fled westward to seek solace in the bleak landscape that seemed a reflection of his stricken soul.

Roosevelt enjoyed visiting Til Selmes and the vivacious Patty on his occasional trips to Mandan. For two years following his wife's death, Roosevelt had made almost no mention of women in his frequent letters home to his sister Anna. But after a visit to the Selmeses in August 1886, he wrote, "Mrs. Selmes is really to my mind a singularly attractive woman. She is, I think, very handsome, though not with regular features; . . . she is very 'séduisante'—like most Kentucky girls. She is very well read, has a delicious sense of humor and is extremely fond of poetry."[6]

Tilden Selmes had become an influential member of the community as president of the First National Bank at Mandan and, by

1885, as attorney for the Northern Pacific Railroad. He needed the outside income; ranching was proving more difficult than he had anticipated. Roosevelt spent the inheritance from his mother to build a comfortable ranch house, but the Selmeses had only what Patty called a "shanty" on their spread; they had to spend the winter in rented rooms in Mandan. Til's law partner dissolved their relationship and began to pester him for money. Til worried and suffered from headaches. In the summer of 1885, Patty moved out to the ranch to save money, and Til joined her only on weekends. Once he came in midweek, just to spend the night: "Forty miles for a kiss," Patty mused to Aunt Julia. When she had married, Patty admitted, "I did not know what a brave, tender, pure, good man" he was, "but I do now."[7]

They were expecting their first child in March. Til grew increasingly anxious about his wife, alone on the ranch, so Patty returned to Julia's farm. Childbirth was a difficult time for women, with a mortality rate more than thirty times higher than today.* Patty's father, solicitous for once, wrote her "[Y]ou must keep up your courage, take all the exercise you can, and I will promise you just as safe an outcome of your approaching crisis as your mother had when she underwent the same tribulation with you." Considering that Patty's mother had died shortly after giving birth to her second child, this may have been small consolation. Til stayed on in Mandan, hoping to work his way free from his debts by the winter.[8]

Isabella Dinsmore Selmes was born on March 22, 1886. Patty survived, although her delivery was a difficult one. She wryly remarked that God must not have been paying attention when He designed women's anatomy for bringing children into the world. Isa-

---

*In 1915, the first year for which national figures are available, sixty-one women died per ten thousand live babies born, vs. two per ten thousand today. Maternal mortality rates were no doubt higher in the nineteenth century. Ehrenreich and English, *For Her Own Good*, 112.

bella would be an only child, an "onliest only child," as she put it, having no cousins either. Patty's father made light of her ordeal, looking to the future: "Now all you have to do is to make a good, sound, sensible woman of her and we will have something to be proud of." Til had an offer to go back to St. Paul as an attorney for $1500 a year but was persuaded by his father-in-law not to give up the advantages of life in a new country. It was to be a fatefully wrong decision.[9]

In July, when Isabella was four months old, Patty took her back to Mandan, accompanied by Julia Loving, known in the family as Mammy, an African American woman whose family had come north to Kentucky with Julia Dinsmore's parents. She would become Isabella's other mother. Soon after their arrival, Isabella was presented to Theodore Roosevelt. One afternoon, Theodore took an outing with Patty and baby Isabella along the bank of the Big Heart River. Roosevelt was secretly quite tenderhearted about children, although he was apt to take a gruffly mocking tone toward them: He once compared his own infant Alice to "a trilobite of pulpy consistency and shadowy outline." But he admitted to Anna, "I miss . . . darling Baby Lee [his daughter Alice Lee] dreadfully. . . . I am really hungry to see her." So when Isabella wriggled out of one of her knitted booties, Roosevelt picked it up and put it in his buttonhole. He wore the little badge until they started back toward town, when he gently put the bootie back on Isabella's foot.[10]

But the young widower was less taken by the baby than by the baby's mother. Biographer David McCullough summed up Roosevelt's reaction to Patty: "[U]nquestionably she impressed him as few women ever had or ever would (he was to refer to her as time went on as 'the wonderful Mrs. Selmes'), but the fact that there was a Mr. Selmes would . . . have precluded any thought of a romantic involvement." Roosevelt turned his attention instead to Edith Carow, a childhood friend. On a trip east in November 1885, he had asked her to marry him. But, tormented by the thought of disloyalty to his beloved first wife, he wanted to keep their engagement secret for a year.[11]

Before Roosevelt returned from the Dakotas to his fiancée in early October 1886, he paid a final visit to the Selmeses and confided his secret engagement to Patty. "I hope she is all that is lovely," Patty wrote Julia. "He is one of the nicest men I ever knew." Back east, Roosevelt wrote a cautionary article on ranching for *Century* magazine, warning that the current overstocking would spell ruin in a hard winter: "[I]t is merely a question of time as to when a winter will come that will understock the ranges by the summary process of killing off about half the cattle throughout the Northwest."[12]

As the beautiful fall weather gradually gave way to something more ominous, the Selmeses were left to battle the elements alone. In early November, Patty wrote Julia that the wind was rising: "the trees, once bent by it, have never raised their heads. . . . The chickens can't walk across the yard and everything loose in the place is flap[ping] against the fence." At the end of the month, Tilden had to leave on a four-week business trip. Patty wrote to her mother-in-law, Sarah Selmes, wondering what effect the isolation and storms would have on her character. "I can only hope," she mused grimly, "that it will not end in my having to be caged for the public good." Patty was depressed during Tilden's frequent absences to do the legal work that brought in cash to keep his ranch running. But she consoled herself with Isabella, who was beginning to show glimmers of intelligence and humor. However, even Isabella's baby charms were not proof against the onslaught that awaited.[13]

That fall produced ominous signs: Muskrats' fur was uncommonly long; beavers were storing huge amounts of willow branches; Arctic owls appeared. Then, in November, weeks ahead of time, the storms started. Snow and wind pelted the plains. Drifts mounted a hundred feet high and covered the grass, leaving only a few strands of sage sticking above the snow. The cattle froze and they starved. Some even suffocated, buried by snow as their feet froze fast in the ice. It was the worst winter on record in the Great Plains. Patty wrote to her mother-in-law, "all my time and strength has been taken up with the struggling to keep warm. . . . The mercury has been flitting around from 20 to 40 below zero for two weeks." Isabella, who was growing apace, "would walk if the floors were not too cold for her to stand on."[14] Til was still gone, trying cases in the West.

The cold, when it finally broke that spring, was followed by a huge thaw and floods. Ranchers calculated their losses: on average, three-quarters of their herds. Roosevelt, when he returned, called the situation a perfect "smashup"; he had ridden for three days without seeing a live steer. But he had another life in the East. He could absorb his ranching losses, large though they were. And he had gained something more valuable than mere money—health and composure. TR later described this period as "the romance of my life." But Tilden Selmes would not have so described it. It broke him. He struggled with debt for years, and his family later believed that this struggle fatally weakened his health. But his family reaped a legacy in their association with Roosevelt.[15]

Theodore Roosevelt and the Selmeses had been tempered by the same fire, and Roosevelt's admiration of them formed the basis for a lifelong friendship. Patty was one of a mere handful of women on the frontier. She shared with Roosevelt not only the frontier hardihood but his intellectual interests. The connection she had made to Roosevelt was renewed and strengthened later in New York, and it shaped Isabella's life to the end of her days.

By Isabella's first birthday, her mother was packing to leave the ranch for good. Although their cattle business was finished, Til could still practice law. He began to look for a position in St. Paul, where he took rooms with Franklin Warner Cutcheon, another young lawyer. Patty hoped Til would go into partnership with Cutcheon, but Cutcheon was already working for Patty's father, by now a judge. Furthermore, the two young men were poles apart temperamentally: Where Tilden was prodigal and carefree, Frank was careful to the point of stuffiness. Instead, Til joined another lawyer. Patty and Isabella retreated to Dinsmore Farm until he could afford to send for them.[16]

When Patty rejoined her husband in the autumn, she found that living near her father did nothing to improve their financial prospects. Julia cautioned her, "You can't make anything, poor child, so your part must be to keep expenses down." However, the fun-loving Patty continued with a busy schedule of dinners, theater, and dances, rationalizing that her social contacts would help her husband get ahead. Julia observed regretfully, "Unfortunately neither you nor Til seem to have any idea of how to live with economy." Isabella bid fair to inherit her mother's social graces. At Christmas, Patty reported to her sister Sally that Isabella, at twenty-one months, had greatly enjoyed their holiday visitors: "You should have seen her last night standing on the table letting them kiss her hand with a queenly grace peculiar to her self."[17]

Patty's failure to economize was critical, as Til's practice was not faring well. He complained that although his little firm had plenty to do and sent out a great many bills, they could get no money, as everyone was hard up. The crisis in southern and western agriculture that would culminate in the Panic of 1893 had already begun. The Selmeses were in debt, and Patty confessed, "It takes all the courage I have to keep Til from getting desperate."[18]

Isabella was a solace; though not yet two, she had become very talkative. She endeared herself to her grandfather, overcoming her aversion to his beard and consenting to kiss him. The following summer of 1888, Til wanted to keep Patty with him in Minneapolis, so they sent two-year-old Isabella to stay with her great-aunt Julia at Dinsmore Farm, where the two forged a long-lasting bond. She was accompanied by Julia Loving, her "Mammy," whom she later described as "big, dark, intelligent . . . and hideously temperamental."

Martha Dinsmore Selmes (Patty) with Isabella, c. 1890

Isabella's earliest memory was of falling into the fountain in the park while trying to fish out a piece of gum. Mammy sent her to bed for the entire day on bread and milk. But Mammy's sternness was born of love, and she called the baby "Dimp" for Dimples.[19]

By the end of the year, Til's business picked up a little, but bill collecting was still hard, and Patty complained she never saw Til except at meals and on Sundays. He looked tired all the time and suffered from "rheumatism" in his back. But he was Isabella's hero, especially after she had seen him in a scuffle with some tramps who tried to ambush him when he gave them food. She always remembered what he taught her to pray: "Dear God, make me good and brave and true."[20]

Tilden Russell Selmes with Isabella, early 1890s

When Isabella was four, another important figure entered her life. Frank Cutcheon, the lawyer Patty had hoped would go into business with her husband, now moved in with the Selmeses. Patty was glad to have his help with household expenses. She hoped the arrangement was mutually beneficial, because he seldom seemed entirely well or happy. He captivated Isabella with a doll from Paris and soon won the heart of Patty's sister as well. Frank and Sally became engaged in January 1890 and married a year later. Patty may have been a little jealous: "Instead of marrying a man much more extravagant and careless than herself as I did, she has married one the like of which for details and managing I have never seen. . . .

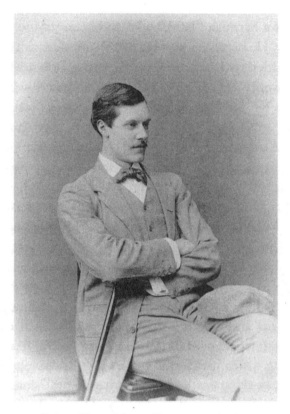

Robert Harry Munro Ferguson, early 1890s

When you are calling there, he dusts the tables, and a speck on the carpet makes him ... unhappy." In short, she remarked to Julia, "We never had anything like him in our family before."[21]

By the spring of 1890, Til finally managed to pay off the Mandan debts. That fall, he and Patty joined Theodore Roosevelt on one of his annual treks to the Badlands. Til hadn't been well, and Patty hoped the trip would do him good. She herself had a wonderful time, despite the lack of game. "The more I see of our dear Theodore the better I like him," she wrote Julia. And this time, "He had a very nice Scotchman out with him, a Mr. Ferguson from Fifeshire." Robert H. Munro Ferguson, twenty-two, was the sixth child and third son of a Scottish "laird," who had been sent to America to earn a living. He became a partner of TR's in the ranching venture. Tall and slender, with blue eyes and dark hair, Bob made a hit with Patty, just twenty-nine herself. At Christmas, he visited them in St. Paul, where he met little Isabella. He was more taken with her mother; on a hunting trip with Roosevelt in February, he wrote Patty that he hoped she would join them the following winter.[22]

Isabella had her own diversions. By the spring of 1891, when she was five, she had learned to read and to skate, the latter a grand passion with her, although she spent most of her time "prostrate on the ice," as Patty noted in a letter to Ferguson. The following year, Ferguson wrote to inquire about Isabella's skating prowess, but he was still more interested in Patty, asking for her photograph. Patty described Bob to Julia as "Dear, worldly, sporty, gentle Ferguson."[23]

By 1894, things at last began to look up for the Selmeses. Til was in good spirits and working hard. He was now assistant counsel with the legal department of the Northern Pacific Railroad in St. Paul, earning a steady income. In the fall, Roosevelt, by then in Washington working for the Civil Service Commission, came west, stopping in St. Paul to see Patty. He found her as charming as ever, he reported to Ferguson, who had gone on a six-month trek north of the Churchill River and west of Hudson Bay to make a survey. They all planned to go to Alaska together the following summer.[24]

It was not to be. In February 1895, Til began to suffer from severe stomach pains. He could eat nothing but ice cream, and his weight dropped from 167 to 132. Patty took him to Boone County, where she hoped a few weeks of rest and riding would restore his health. The winter was bitter cold, Til was bedridden most of the time, and Patty exerted herself nursing and entertaining him. Isabella, at school in St. Paul with Mammy, spent her ninth birthday without her parents, although the Flandraus tried their best to make it festive. That very day, Til went to a hospital in Cincinnati, where he was diagnosed with an ulcer.[25]

His condition continued to worsen, and at the end of April, they traveled to Baltimore for a consultation at the Johns Hopkins Hospital. Theodore Roosevelt drove over from Washington to visit. Doctors performed an exploratory operation, to make the horrifying discovery that Til had inoperable cancer of the liver. "My poor children—Lord love them," Julia mourned in her diary. Theodore was shocked to learn that Til had been given only six more months to live. He wrote Ferguson: "The good fellow had been told his doom. He is very brave and cheerful, and is as honest and sweet as ever." Patty, he said, was living in "a mere nightmare of horror. I can imagine nothing more terrible or awful." He did not have to imagine her pain; he knew firsthand about loss. He visited often, impressed by how "thoroughly manly" Tilden was in the face of such crushing news. Compounding the tragedy was a wire Til had received just before the operation, informing him that the Northern Pacific Railroad legal department had offered him a promotion. "After all the years of brave, hard struggle, success seemed to be just within his grasp," Roosevelt noted gloomily to Bob. Til saw it in a better light. He thought his efforts had made a man of him. Patty observed that he was so philosophical through it all that she felt ashamed not to be braver herself. Til recuperated in Baltimore for a month, diverting himself by reading Ferguson's account of his long Canadian trip, the last thing of any length he ever read. At the end of May, Tilden Selmes went back to Dinsmore Farm to die.[26]

Isabella puttered around the farm in blue-jean overalls and Julia's sunbonnet, a delight to her grieving parents. Somehow the nine-year-old understood how important she was to their spirits. Mammy wrote Isabella's grandmother, Sarah Selmes, that neither of Isabella's parents had "ever seen a tear in her eye since she came." The child was not always so stoic. "She cries and talks to me at night but no one seen or hear her but me." Patty, too, did her best to keep up her husband's spirits, taking horseback rides with him through the beautiful summer countryside. It was, Julia noted in her diary, a heartbreakingly gorgeous June, the rosebushes burdened with blooms. In July, though, the weather turned oppressively hot. Til was failing fast. On July 31, he said good-bye to his family and died the following morning, just after dawn. Isabella locked herself in his ground-floor bedroom, refusing to come out until the next day. Til was buried in the little family plot on a hill overlooking the house.[27]

After his death, Patty was at first too exhausted and heartbroken to think of the future. She wrote her stepmother that she was still waking up every hour thinking that Til needed her. "I wish I could go some where alone—where I could be as entirely old, hopeless and sad as I feel," she admitted. "It seems as if the struggle Til and I made was useless except for the love in it all, which only leaves me lonelier now." They had been married twelve years. Theodore Roosevelt wrote to let her know how completely he understood her loss. "Well, we've both *had* it, and how infinitely better that is than never to have had it at all. We have striven, and lived, and known happiness as well as sorrow; you have had a hard life, but you have faced it nobly and undauntedly; and there is something in that, when all is said and done."[28]

Patty tried to rally at least a little for Isabella's sake. Tilden had left his widow a life insurance policy that yielded the slender income of $50 a month. Patty begged the Flandraus to let her send Isabella to them with Mammy for her schooling, so that she herself could stay in Boone for the winter, curing hams to bring in a little extra money. She wanted to avoid St. Paul, where everything reminded her of her vanished home and desolated life. She was not really happier in Boone, but at least there she did not have to hide her feelings from strangers. Patty found only two things could dull the edge of her depression, she wrote her brother Charlie: "One you take out of a glass, the other comes from a long physical strain." At Boone, she could resort to both.[29]

Isabella had a good life in St. Paul. She had grown close to her grandfather, meeting him every morning at breakfast with a flower for his buttonhole. She took music, French, and dancing lessons, and looked forward to the winter when she could skate. The girl appeared content, but she was close to her mother and must have sensed her unhappiness. She later wrote, "I think my interpretation was not that Father had left me, but that he had left me a responsibility—my Mother." Aunt Julia observed that a photo taken on Isabella's tenth birthday had "a thoughtful look that shows me that poor little It is getting acquainted with this world of ours and some of its ways."[30]

The following year when Theodore Roosevelt came through on his way to the Dakotas, he failed to see Patty, although she was back in St. Paul with Isabella for the start of school. Too late, he realized what his visit would have meant to the lonely widow and wrote regretfully: "I could at least have given the comfort which would come from talking with one who deeply sympathizes with you, who appreciates and in some measure understands you, and who feels a very deep affection for you and for the memory of your husband." He concluded, "I would give much if I could only help you in your time of gray sorrow." When he visited the ranch in the summer of 1897 he wrote again: "I shall think of you very often, riding over the immense rolling plains, with their mat of short, sun-scorched grass: for it has always seemed to me that we two *felt* those plains as no one else."[31]

Roosevelt's nostalgia for the ranch was swept away by the events of 1898. The Cuban independence movement had been gathering momentum for several years, and the sympathies of the American people, played on by the Hearst and Pulitzer papers, were solidly with the rebels. When the American battleship *Maine*, bent on a vague "good will" mission, mysteriously exploded in Havana harbor, America was outraged. On April 25, President William McKinley asked Congress to declare war. Roosevelt, who by then was assistant secretary of the Navy, promptly volunteered to lead a regiment of cavalry organized by Leonard Wood, the 1st U.S. Volunteer

Cavalry, known as the Rough Riders. He recruited Bob Ferguson, advising the Scot to bring a rubber blanket and his plaid. Another recruit, Aunt Julia informed Patty, was their cousin David Goodrich, then at Harvard, who left college to join the unit forming in San Antonio, Texas. Roosevelt signed up a number of college men, among them Yale graduate John Campbell Greenway, famous on the Ivy League football and baseball fields.[32]

During the brief duration of the war, Bob Ferguson wrote frequently and vividly to Roosevelt's sister Corinne Roosevelt Robinson. He noted of their trip to Cuba that "nearly 1000 souls crowded on a 3000 ton vessel—and no sanitary arrangements whatever or even ventilation for the troops crammed into holds." But he claimed he felt very hearty. Roosevelt had lent him a copy of Thackeray's *Vanity Fair,* and Bob reported: "Becky made me laugh more than ever—after reading nothing but tactics." He also wrote Corinne about her brother's military exploits: "No hunting trip has equalled it so far in Theodore's eyes.... TR moved around in the midst of shrapnel explosions, like Shadrach, Meshach & Co.—in the midst of the fiery furnace—unharmed by the fire." Roosevelt himself wrote Patty Selmes a glowing account of his regiment: "I have always felt that it was a shame for the cow-puncher to pass away without being given a chance to show what splendid stuff there was in him as a fighting man ... and incidentally, the young men of the universities and the clubs have shown their grit in just the same way."[33]

Roosevelt made special mention of Patty's cousin Dave Goodrich, her friend Ferguson, and John Greenway, who had been the first commissioned officer to reach the top of San Juan Hill on July 1. Roosevelt called Goodrich and Greenway his "right and left bowers during the worst days of the fighting and the siege." In nearly every photo of TR with the Rough Riders, Greenway, conspicuous in his rakishly tilted hat, is to his right. Ferguson, TR reported to Patty, had earned a promotion on the field of battle to

Rough Riders Ferguson, Goodrich, and Greenway

lieutenant. "I wish you could have seen him, in his gentle, quiet way, going everywhere with me and everywhere I sent him, with literally complete indifference to the Spanish bullets." After the war, Roosevelt's three favorite veterans would continue to keep in close touch. Bob Ferguson wrote his mother that surrender had come just in time. Those who had come through the fire unscathed faced a second enemy: disease. Malaria, yellow fever, and dysentery had already broken out; tuberculosis lay in wait.

Meanwhile, Patty and Isabella continued their quiet lives half a continent away. On Dinsmore Farm that summer, Isabella worked beside the tenants' children to sucker and worm her great-aunt's tobacco plants, meeting their challenge of biting a big beaded green worm in half. Back in St. Paul, the twelve-year-old pursued her studies, including drawing, for which she showed considerable talent. Patty was at Boone, doing a brisk business in hams and bacon, too busy to join Isabella for Christmas. On December 25 she wrote her daughter, "I have thought of you all day, and just about dusk walked up to the graveyard to see your father's grave and think of him and you." It was becoming increasingly difficult for Patty to be a long-distance mother to a girl now approaching her teens. Rebecca urged Patty to give up the meat business and stay in St. Paul, although she admitted Patty could have full confidence in Mammy. Though they were separated, Isabella was very sensitive to her mother's moods. The girl had begged for permission to go to evening skating parties over the holiday, but Patty had refused, saying she did not need to be worrying about her daughter when they were apart. Isabella, crushed by her mother's tone, accused herself of being thoughtless, selfish, and worrisome. Patty vowed it would be her last year in the ham business.[34]

The new century brought new opportunities for Patty. She was invited to chaperone the daughters of the Northern Pacific Railroad magnate, James J. Hill, on a trip to Europe. Isabella insisted she go: "*Your pleasure is mine*'—that is our motto. Never forget it. . . . This is a chance that only comes once in a lifetime." Isabella assembled several mementos as an antidote to loneliness: a locket with her mother's hair, a picture of grandmother Isabella Flandrau, a railroad pass made out to her from her father. When she felt blue, "I just get these out and think what the people that they came from would say to me if they knew what I was unhappy about." She had learned early to take care of herself. She also looked out for her mother. She warned Patty, "Don't be lonesome, you know what I mean," a caution not to drink.[35]

Patty stopped off on her return in June to visit with the Roosevelts at their home in Oyster Bay, Long Island. Ten days later, at the Republican National Convention in Philadelphia, TR was nominated for vice president on the ticket with incumbent President William McKinley. McKinley's first vice-president had died in office, and TR, now governor of New York, enjoyed a national reputation because of his wartime exploits. Patty's stay may have encouraged her to think of wider horizons for Isabella; she wanted her daughter to pursue her interest in drawing, hoping it might be a way to earn her living. The Cutcheons were now living in New York, where they had moved in 1898. New York appealed even more strongly to Patty after she returned to St. Paul, where she found it irksome to live under the same roof as her stepmother. "I would give my hope of Heaven to have two rooms of my own where I could have my child and my friends to myself," she wrote Julia. Meanwhile, Isabella, now fourteen, had become very popular; Patty complained that she had to be very stern to keep the boys from coming over all the time.[36]

Doubtless to Patty's great relief, the Cutcheons invited her to bring Isabella to live with them in the fall of 1901. Mammy would be coming, too, so the Cutcheons bought a large new house for their expanding family. Judge Flandrau, though reluctant to lose his little companion, agreed to pay for Isabella's schooling. Now over seventy and in poor health, he missed her sorely. Isabella, too, was often homesick. She confided to her Uncle Blair: "New York I don't think is nice. One minute I think that in time it will be fine and the next I am crying at the idea of all the months in the horrid place before I can go to Boone."[37]

Her uncle Frank Cutcheon took the place of her grandfather as father-surrogate. Arm-in-arm, "Unc" walked Isabella to school, first to Miss Chapin's and later to Miss Spence's. Isabella recalled, "Mine was a special importance in having Uncle take me to school when Fathers rarely brought their girls. Through Central Park I stumbled, hanging on to this man, month after month and year after year, while he tried to explain the fundamentals of Latin and my day's homework." Unc laughed at her heedlessness and called her his Goosegirl. Since he and Sally never had children of their own, he loved having what he called a "ready-made daughter." Later Isabella summed it up: "Uncle became MY Uncle inevitably and soon."[38]

Patty, too, was having a dizzying first year in New York. Her old

Frank Cutcheon, early 1890s

friend Theodore Roosevelt had been suddenly elevated to the presidency, when President McKinley was shot on September 6 by an anarchist and died a week later. Soon thereafter Patty received a letter from Washington "all done in black a half an inch deep. It was from Theodore asking me to come over and see how I liked the White House." Edith Roosevelt extended a special invitation to their daughter Alice's exclusive debutante party. After the dance, Mrs. Selmes and the president sat in the cabinet room and talked. It was a far cry from their beginnings at the Mandan Hotel. Having, as she put it, "mortgaged the house" to buy clothes for this event, Patty amortized her investment in the spring of 1902 by indulging in a whirl of dinners and luncheons, hoping to make useful contacts for

Isabella. She became an intimate friend of Theodore Roosevelt's sister, Corinne Roosevelt Robinson, whom she addressed as "Beloved." Another close friend was Theodore's cousin Susie Parish.[39]

Isabella was having some social success of her own. At a formal lunch, she wrote her mother, she had felt intimidated until a sympathetic older man assured her he had once felt the same way. She later learned he was socially prominent and, an even better recommendation, a friend of "Mr. Ferguson" and their cousin Dave Goodrich. She was learning about society, but Isabella had less success at school. However, she worked diligently at her art, sketching portraits of everyone in the house. Isabella by now had reconciled herself to New York, but she was happy to escape to Boone for the summer with Mammy, while Patty went to St. Paul to care for her ailing father. "Dear Ma," Patty wrote Aunt Julia, "try and teach Isabella all the beautiful things you taught me, the only things I have really worth having: to love nature, good literature, poetry. . . . I consider sending her to Boone to you so much more worthwhile than to Miss Spence or Miss Chapin." Aunt Julia tried most to impress on Isabella the need to be frugal, hoping to succeed where she had failed with Patty. She was so successful that Isabella wrote her mother in some alarm about their financial situation. Patty, ever the grasshopper, answered, "I wouldn't worry about the Poor House. If we go we'll go together and it won't be so bad. . . . You must . . . try and draw well enough to earn both our livings, if it is necessary some day."[40]

Time in the country, away from the demands and distractions of the city, made Isabella introspective. Musing by her father's gravesite, she decided that she should dedicate her life to making life easier for others. Uncle Frank was a good role model. A tender letter from her prompted an outpouring from him: "There's just one thing in life that wears and satisfies and that's the love and devotion of those to whom you have given your own affection. Pretty much everything else is plate-ware. . . . Real, true love of the sort that does not calculate . . . is as inestimable as it is rare and as rare as it is desirable."[41]

That fall, Isabella's social success loomed far larger in Patty's letters home than did her academic progress. "Kiddy is getting to be a problem," she wrote Aunt Julia; her beauty was the talk of the artists of New York. This put Patty in the somewhat galling position of being merely the mother of a beautiful girl. Aunt Julia must have counseled Isabella against letting her head be turned by the attention, for Isabella wrote to assure her that she did not put much stock in her looks, as they were "only the kind that last while I am seventeen . . . just pink cheeks and a generally round look that all goes when I am older. I should be very sorry if I thought you imagined I was so conceited as to . . . rely on a nice face in any way." In June 1903, she attended her cousin Dave Goodrich's wedding in Albany, a splendid affair with a lavish breakfast under tents and dancing afterwards. Goodrich was attended by fourteen ushers, including fellow Rough Riders Bob Ferguson and John Greenway. Patty reported to Julia that Isabella "had more attention than anyone in sight. . . . Men were chasing around asking who she was and to be presented." The mother of the bride said, perhaps with some bitterness, that Isabella had "taken Albany by storm."[42]

Patty was determined to take Isabella to France for the summer, eager for her beautiful and talented daughter to have every possible chance at this critical period in her life. Julia Dinsmore, trapped on her father's farm, had never had a chance, and Patty herself had not had it, but, she told Julia, "I have made up my mind that to the last cent and the last effort Isabella shall have it. . . . After that she has to do the rest herself." She also planned to take Mammy. Mammy wrote Julia, "You may think, as I did at first, that it is a foolish extravagance taking me, but there will be times that Isabella will be glad that I am there. I need not speak plainer, as you will understand." She, too, knew about Patty's drinking problem. Judge Flandrau provided $1500 for the trip; he was fortunate, he reasoned, in having not only four wonderful children, but also a "granddaughter *I can bet on.*"[43]

They sailed for England a week after the Goodrich wedding, Isabella equipped with paints and paper and brushes. They traveled with Theodore Roosevelt's cousin Susie and her husband Henry Parish, visiting England, Holland, France, Germany, Switzerland, and Austria. Isabella later observed that the "phenomenal spectacle of a very large colored woman and a very gay young girl" drew attention wherever they went. Mammy, who had profited from Isabella's French lessons far more than her young charge, attracted even more attention by making cutting remarks in that language when she thought the crowds too rude. Back in England before sailing for home, they visited Salisbury and Exeter Cathedrals. Their beauty impressed Isabella, but "what almost breaks my heart are the long lists of soldiers . . . that were killed in the Boer War," she wrote her great-aunt Julia.[44]

Their trip was cut short by cables from St. Paul that Judge Flandrau had suffered a stroke and died. Susie Parish helped the distraught Patty exchange her tickets for an earlier passage and find mourning clothes. Back home, Patty had another shock: Her father had left her a relatively small legacy of $10,000 and nothing at all to her sister Sally. Everything else went to Rebecca. Frank wisely offered to invest Patty's money for her, remitting only the income. Despairing of Isabella's learning economy from her mother, he gave the girl a monthly allowance of $50, to teach her how to handle her accounts. More than ever, the family fortunes depended on Isabella.[45]

At the start of 1904 Patty confided to Julia that she had resolved to stop drinking. She proudly reported that she had not taken a drop since September, but without it, she realized, "What a struggle life is! And I get so dead sick of it sometimes." She envied the Roosevelts "their exultation of living." Isabella, in spite of having had an alcoholic parent, was also cheerful and optimistic, perhaps due to the influence of such steadying souls as her great-aunt Julia and her uncle Frank Cutcheon.[46]

Isabella celebrated a happier milestone, attending her first formal dinner at the home of the Parishes, in honor of Susie's niece, Eleanor Roosevelt. Eleanor had returned from her schooling in England the year before and was living with her aunt and uncle, as her parents had died when she was young. Soon after she arrived back in New York, Eleanor was introduced to Isabella by Bob Ferguson, her uncle Theodore Roosevelt's Rough Rider comrade and Badlands partner. Although Eleanor was more than a year older, she was immediately impressed by the younger girl. She later recalled that "Isabella, though still at school, was already the talk of New York." Isabella was equally smitten, remembering Eleanor as "slender, graceful, [with] gorgeous golden hair to her knees, eyes that crinkled with friendship and a certain humor peculiarly her own." The two young women were on the point of making their debut in society, Eleanor that year and Isabella the year after. The debut marked a woman's coming of age and eligibility for marriage. Isabella understood the seriousness that underlay the gaiety: Many of the girls had "major home problems which precluded a carefree approach, but . . . no matter how serious-minded we were, we realized that to appear to be having fun was a part you played." Her family understood the stakes as well. Sally remarked to Julia that she expected Isabella would have a social triumph if they could get her enough good clothes. After the disappointment of Judge Flandrau's will, the family's calculated investment in Isabella's future put pressure on the young girl to make a good marriage, not only to secure her own future but to keep her mother from succumbing to drink and despair. It was a real-life Edith Wharton novel.[47]

Isabella came to the end of her formal schooling that year. She did not actually graduate and later recalled, "I was discovering life and not exploring dead languages and convinced myself that Latin was not a subject for young girls to anguish over and that ultimately

Isabella Selmes

headmistresses would come to this realization. Alas, they did not in time for me to graduate." More valuable to Isabella than formal education was her acquaintance with the Roosevelts. The Cutcheons had bought a fifty-four-acre farm, Locust Valley, not far from the sprawling Roosevelt home, Sagamore Hill, on Long Island, and Isabella spent the summer going back and forth between the two places. She made friends not only with Eleanor but also with another of TR's nieces, "Corinnie" Robinson, the daughter and namesake of Patty's "Beloved" Corinne Roosevelt Robinson. Through them, and because of her beauty and charm, Isabella became a fa-

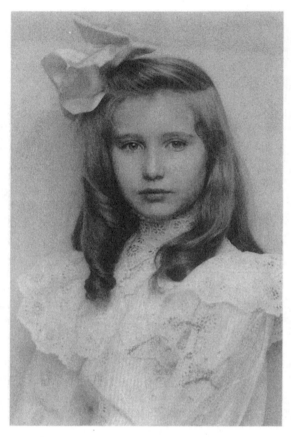

Olivia Cutting, 1902, two years before meeting Isabella

vorite of many of their social set. She became especially close to a younger girl, Olivia Cutting, daughter of William Bayard Cutting, a wealthy railroad executive and philanthropist and a member of what Louis Auchincloss called the Brownstone Aristocracy.[48]

Before the debutante season opened officially at the end of November 1904, Julia advised Isabella on the coming ordeal: "You will find a competition carried to an extent as cruel as in business, and you will find Vanity Fair far from what it seems, but I hope you will have sense enough to hold your own in the struggle and luck to enjoy what fun is in it." Susie Parish gave Isabella her debut reception on December 12 at what they called a "letting out" tea. Celebrated as a belle, the likes of whom had not been seen for many years, Isabella's sweetness of character recommended her even more than her stunning good looks. By the end of December, Patty wearily reported to Isabella's Grandmother Selmes that the girl had been home for dinner only once in five weeks.[49]

CHAPTER TWO ∾∾∾∾∾∾∾∾∾∾∾∾∾∾∾∾∾∾∾

"O'er the Border and Awa'"

ISABELLA MAY HAVE ENJOYED the whirl of activity, but she knew that the real purpose of her debut was to make a good marriage for financial security and that the financial outlay for her ball gowns was a tremendous risk. However, even to herself, she preferred to pretend that it was all being done for her amusement. She reflected in her diary: "I shall always be grateful to Mother for having given me this winter's experience. To have held and weighed in one's own hand a very good thing is an ever lasting happiness, for it prevents our over estimating its value afterwards, as those so often do who have never handled it." But even a happy outcome would have its downside: If she married, she would leave her mother. Breakfast in bed together was one of their greatest pleasures: "A cup of coffee with nice warm odors coming off it. . . . Toast with a cover over it. Fruit of some kind and a little bacon. And we are so unselfish. Mother feeds me the last bit of bacon on a piece of toast. When we can, we take a long time to our breakfast and talk a great deal." She added wistfully, "I often think any devotion, after the

∾∾∾∾∾∾∾∾∾∾∾∾∾∾∾∾∾∾∾∾∾∾∾∾∾∾∾∾∾∾∾∾∾∾∾

kind Mother gives me, would seem tame, and sometimes it seems a pity . . . suppose I should marry. No one could spoil me as Muddy does."[1]

She also appreciated the care her Mammy took of her. When Julia Loving brought up the breakfast things, the first thing Isabella would say was, "Do you love your child? Did anyone I like write me a letter?" Mammy kept a vigilant eye on her baby. She opened Isabella's letters, read them and marked them. "She knew I would not read them anyway," Isabella observed, "and she did not think it fair to the young men. When I had callers of whom she did not wholly approve (she had her favorites) she would appear in a large white apron and announce firmly that it was time to dress for dinner." In spite of, or perhaps because of living in the midst of Vanity Fair, Isabella retained an introspective outlook, confiding to her diary that "There seems little doubt in my mind that it is people that we are put here for."[2]

On January 9, 1905, Isabella attended the ninth of Mrs. William Brockhurst Astor's famous balls, the largest and most important ball of the winter. At eleven o'clock, six hundred guests passed through a foyer filled with poinsettias and Easter lilies, palm trees and roses, then assembled for dancing in an immense ballroom, its walls covered with paintings by Corot, Deschamps, and Millet. Supper was served in an ebony and gold dining room, followed by more dancing and, later, more food. This, too, was like a scene from an Edith Wharton novel; in fact, four days later, Edith Wharton invited the young belle to dine with her. Julia Dinsmore longed to know how Mrs. Wharton seemed "outside of a binding," but Isabella left no record of her impressions.[3]

Isabella had more serious pursuits as well. Less than a week later, she attended a meeting of the newly formed Junior League at the home of young Corinne Robinson, whom Isabella admired as someone who was fun but also serious and able. When they drove together to balls, Corinne would bring along a book by Jack Lon-

Patty and Isabella. On the back Isabella wrote:
"Who is the breath of your nostrils?
Am I the apple of your Adam?"

don and read aloud to Isabella because she worried they might be in
danger of forgetting about the problems of the world. Eleanor
Roosevelt and Mary Harriman, daughter of railroad financier E. H.
Harriman, were also founding members of the welfare society, organized to help poor immigrants adjust to their new life. Corinne's
mother foresaw the benefit of their social work, telling Isabella:
"The highest ambition in the social life ... is to be absolutely at
home in all sets." She candidly added: "You have many more possibilities of reaching that than Corinne, for you have the beauty that
appeals to a certain element in the 'smart set.' " These qualities
would serve Isabella well as a politician, too.[4]

Isabella also had a whirl in Washington. Near the end of January she and Corinne spent several days at the White House for a series of teas, dinners, and dances. They were accompanied by Mammy, who had nursed President Roosevelt through an asthma attack back in his ranching days. "People are wild about our child," Julia Loving reported to Julia Dinsmore with satisfaction. Mammy was hard-pressed by Isabella's popularity, though: "I have not had time to say that my soul is my own." Meanwhile, Patty was praying that they would be able to hold out until Lent, the end of the social season.[5]

In early February Isabella attended a dance in honor of Eleanor Roosevelt. Eleanor had not taken at all to the social scene; she pre-ferred to go home early. Girls' popularity was gauged by the num-ber of little favors given to them by men who wanted them as dance partners; Eleanor noted sadly that her aunt Susie Parish always had far more than she herself. Nevertheless, Eleanor had attracted the attention and kindled the love of her distant cousin, Franklin Roosevelt. They had become secretly engaged in the fall of 1903—a secret engagement to appease FDR's redoubtable mother, who possibly was hoping to break off the match. A year later, though, they were still engaged. Eleanor confided some of her anxiety about the situation to Isabella, writing her later "to thank you many times over for your kindness and patience of last night. You were very, very sweet to me, and I only hope that someday I may have the chance to help you, dear, as much as you helped me." She added, "I'm feeling quite sane again so you need worry no more about me." Eleanor and Franklin announced their engagement officially at the beginning of December 1904. Isabella, who knew how serious her young friend was apt to be, fervently hoped Eleanor would "be as happy as you are good and sweet and true." Eleanor basked in Isa-bella's understanding and sympathy: "I wonder if you do know how much your affection means to me. There are very, very few people, dear, on whom I count as I do on you," she wrote.[6]

The Roosevelt wedding took place at the Parishes' house on the afternoon of March 17, 1905. Isabella was one of Eleanor's six bridesmaids; all but one other girl were members of the family. Theodore Roosevelt gave away the bride, his niece, exclaiming, "Nothing like keeping the name in the family, eh Franklin?" The president, as his daughter Alice had noted, "liked to be the bride at every wedding and the corpse at every funeral," and he completely upstaged the young couple. So the newlyweds left him in a throng of admirers and slipped away with Isabella to call on Bob Ferguson, who was sick. Isabella had grown close to Bob, whom she had seen often throughout her debutante season. The young girl felt secure with the attractive and worldly older man. In April, after the debutante season ended, Isabella fled to Boone to recuperate, but Bob did not let her forget him. As the season warmed, so did their correspondence. In an early letter, Isabella enclosed a little pin of her father's in the shape of a red heart. She urged Bob to wear it "just for luck and because it's red like my little heart." He wrote back to his "Dearest Little Red Heart." The pin must have been offered as a pledge and signaled an understanding, for he now wrote, "Will [your mother] ever think me good enough for you? . . . I'm not, nor ever shall be. I weep to think of it, but love you all the more, dearie."[7]

The next day he honorably wrote to make plain what the drawbacks of accepting him might be: "The presumption of my dreaming that some day I might take care of such a little sweetheart and make her even partly happy or keep the smallest of life's troubles away from her makes me feel dreadfully foolish!" He looked forward to her strengthening and bettering him. But he was afraid "that I should so grow to depend on that little firm hand, [that] I should become a burden in my old age to this little child . . . that leads me." He noted that she had already had more than her fair share of trouble and warned her, "You don't quite know me yet, dearest, or how unsociable I am and little fond of crowds or of big places. The smaller the little corner and the fewer and dearer those that are in it, the happier life looks to me."[8]

He urged her, in considering his offer, to be rational, steady, and wise. She promised to try, but confessed that "the steady, wise Isabella . . . would be very much disgusted if she knew all her formality had been upset by an impulsive unsteady little red thing. Never tell her about it." She closed, "From a little red heart who is really much more sincere than all the steady well-controlled Isabellas in the world." Still, there were days she had doubts, and she wrote plaintively, "I . . . wish so that you were here and could tell me what it all means." She had answered one letter "Dear Mr. Fergie," using the name the Roosevelt children used with him; she was, after all, their contemporary, not his. Eighteen years older than Isabella, Bob was far closer in age to her mother. But he objected, and afterwards her letters began "Dear Bob."[9]

He was almost twice her age, 37 to her 19, and he sometimes addressed her as "Darling Child." Perhaps she looked for an older, wiser man, since she had been deprived so young of her father. Patty, too, wrote Bob as if they were both the caretakers of a younger person. He was planning a visit to Boone but was suffering from pain in his ribs. They had been strapped with tape, and he had been ordered to bed. Patty begged him not to come, suggesting that Isabella's long social season had taken a toll on her. "I have kept her in bed the last three days and I want you to help me get her back to where she ought to be in health and strength," she wrote him. Bob, chastened, apologized for troubling Isabella when she was not well and strong: "I am almost aghast at the idea of proposing to care for and shield you through life's troubles, when here at the very start you have taken my burden and load on your little slender shoulders. How you might despise me, and yet you're too loving and gentle, Red Heart, to do it."[10]

Patty finally relented, noting that they could all come to a better understanding by spending some quiet time together, and Bob came to visit Isabella at Dinsmore Farm. He continued poorly, with a cold and chest pain, known as pleurisy. But he assured Isabella that his "sickness and depression all vanish when compared with some glimpses of very absolute happiness." Perhaps because adult children of alcoholics have a strong need to take care of people, Isabella may have seen his health problems as an opportunity for the nurturing at which she was already so skillful.[11]

Bob had an ally in Mammy, who wrote Isabella that she would approve if Isabella accepted Mr. Ferguson but added, "remember that it was I who loved you first." Frank Cutcheon, too, thought Isabella would be lucky to marry Bob. His biggest ally, though, was Theodore Roosevelt's sister Anna Roosevelt Cowles. Bob had met Theodore through Anna, who was a friend of Bob's sister. For many years Bob had been like a son to Anna, suggesting amusing activities and acting as her host when she was in New York. She herself had married late and urged them not to wait: "Happiness should not be put aside and postponed. Take it and keep it when it is there to have."[12]

Bob returned to New York, where he worked as manager of the vast real estate holdings of the John J. Astor trust, a position for which he had been enthusiastically recommended by Theodore Roosevelt. Isabella also returned, while Patty stayed behind to help Julia with the farm. Patty missed her daughter very much, perhaps because she realized that their special days together were about to come to an end: "I don't think I ever knew how much I loved you until the last three months," she wrote, "or what a valuable possession it is to have for your very own the human soul and body which suits and satisfies you most and best in all the world."[13]

Isabella had been invited to a house party by her friend Laura Chandler in upstate New York. Bob was worried that she might reveal their secret to her girlfriends there, but she assured him that Laura and Corinne had no notion of how things stood between them and were actually planning to set her up with someone else. "You must write and say you are sorry you offended your child or thought for a moment she was anything like a chatter box about some things," she wrote Bob indignantly. No one suspected the unlikely match. The men at his office thought he might be interested in Patty, she wrote her mother, but "howl at the idea of daughter." Patty knew they wanted to marry; Bob had been thinking of a September wedding, but even this plan was subject to change. "I think if Bob knew his mind on any subject for two days at a time I might be a well woman," she wrote Isabella crossly.[14]

Unbeknownst to Patty, Bob was pressuring Isabella to be married at once so she could go with him to Scotland, where he planned to spend the summer taking a health cure. If they were thinking of a wedding in September, he wrote her, "why not now? It will be so far simpler and more reasonable. . . . Mother would not have the strain of making up her mind to it. We could just tell her of it the day before. . . . It would mean all the world to me to take you home now. I should be ever so proud of you, darling, and so happy, and health and everything would come of themselves." For him, it would be romantic and sacred. Anna Cowles had offered her cottage at Farmington, Connecticut, for their honeymoon; her support would ensure social approval. "Darling, be dear and trustful and I'll try to be all I should for ever after," he promised. His importuning letters upset Isabella, who worried that a sudden marriage would hurt not only her mother but other people as well. She also thought that Bob should get well before they married. Finally, she agreed that he should consult Patty as soon as she arrived in New York, again placing herself in the hands of her elders.[15]

They exchanged more letters. Isabella was beginning to weaken, but she could not forget Patty: "I'm all she has. . . . You must make Mother feel that I will do exactly as she wants. . . . It may be hard, Bob, but it means my happiness absolutely." Bob, however, did not let up; Sally, he informed Isabella, was now in agreement, too.

Chapter Two

"There is no real difficulty, sweetest heart, except your own mind is asked to do a very sudden thing. . . . Don't think of any preparation at all. That would spoil it all. Others will take care of that for us. Let it be just all love and happiness for the time, with no thought of the morrow. Come, darling, just come, little soul of mine." Isabella agreed that he could telegraph her to come back to Long Island, ostensibly to see her mother when she arrived, though she admonished: "You had better consider Mother's feelings by not telegraphing until you have seen her. In that way she will not feel that matters were practically settled before she arrived. I know it could hurt her if she did." But Patty delayed, and Bob threatened, "If there is any complication, sweetheart, I shall be nearly crazy and wild highlander enough to come and take you anyhow." Finally the telegram arrived. Isabella told Laura the surprising news that she was going to be married in two days and then burst into tears, perhaps from nerves, perhaps just from relief at the end of duplicity and strain. She immediately returned to Long Island.[16]

On July 12, President Roosevelt and his three sons rode over on horseback to the Cutcheons' place to see Bob and Isabella married in a simple ceremony beneath a towering locust tree. It was a glorious, sunny summer day. Bob gave Isabella a ring with two pearls flanking a ruby, and she wore a white serge dress that she happened to have in her closet. Dave Goodrich stood up as Bob's best man. Then the Cutcheons' hired man drove a carriage across a field of new-cut timothy hay right up to the front door, and Bob and Isabella stepped in and drove off for a week's honeymoon in Anna Cowles' cottage at Old Gate. The honeymoon was far from perfect. Isabella was ill for several days, upset by all she had been through between her mother and her lover. Bob gloated over the success of his "highland raid," insisting to Sally that any who objected to the sudden marriage—and many indeed were hurt and angry—did not have Isabella's happiness at heart. Patty, abashed, wrote her daughter to apologize for having been selfish. She added, "My only

The wedding of Isabella and Robert H. M. Ferguson, 1905

consolation is that all your trials with me may give you strength to meet your own." As an innocent young Victorian girl, Isabella had also been shocked at first to discover what was expected of her on her wedding night.[17]

Patty telegraphed Julia, who admitted the news might have been more startling if she hadn't already suspected they were planning to slip off together; she hoped there would yet be time to send her love to Isabella "before 'she's o'er the border and awa.'" Isabella apologized to her Aunt Mary Selmes, explaining to Til's sister that "Father knew [Bob] and was devoted to him when he was younger." Patty tried to pretend to others that she was happy with the turn of events but poured out her misery to Julia, who wrote sympathetically: "When a lonely woman gives up the one object of life for long and lonely years, can it be without a struggle or a pang?" She added: "I am distressed that you feel so lost . . . but you belong to me yet awhile . . . till death breaks our tie." She urged Patty to look at the situation realistically: A pretty and penniless girl without father or brother had found security with a husband. Mammy, too, missed her charge. "I do love you, Dimp, more than anyone on earth. You are the only human being whom I will surrender to. . . . You come first."[18]

At the end of July, the Fergusons sailed for Scotland, where Isabella had her own adjustments to make. She and Bob went first to his family estate at Raith, north of Edinburgh, to stay with his eldest brother, Ronald, the lord of the manor. The house was sumptuous with portraits, landscapes, books, and china; the windows looked over a great stretch of woods down on the Firth of Forth. Bob's other brother, Hector, boasted that everything was in full summer beauty, but Isabella found that Scotland, even in the summer, was freezing cold. The American girl was also indignant to discover that after dinner the men retired to the billiard room with a large, roaring fire and brandy, while the women, in evening dresses with plunging necklines, were exiled to the drawing room with a skimpy fire and glasses of cold barley water. Isabella had her own methods for coping with the cold, taking her breakfast in bed, cozy with a hot water bottle under a mound of blankets. She was also appalled by the way the servants were treated. The entire staff was made to stay up as long as any of the family and guests were awake, then expected to begin again the following morning at five.[19]

Next Bob and Isabella went to Assynt, Novar, to visit his mother at the Dower House. Novar, some sixteen thousand acres, was the Munro estate, north of Inverness, on the same latitude as Juneau, Alaska. It was colder still, but they had a warm reception. It seemed that the entire county turned out to give them a Highland welcome. The crowd cheered as bouquets were presented, and the Lovat scouts escorted them through a heather arch with "1000 welcomes" in Gaelic. The horses were taken out of the harness and the people of the estate pulled their carriage the rest of the way to the house. Isabella had received a great deal of attention as a debutante, but this was a new order of magnitude. Her equanimity in receiving the accolades would stand her in good stead in her future life in politics. To resist the cold, Isabella donned tartan stockings, flannel petticoats, and even flannel panties. Bob observed that she was so borne down with warm homespun clothing that she could hardly walk. He was taking the waters at Strathpeffer and began to look to Isabella like a new man.[20]

Meanwhile, Franklin and Eleanor Roosevelt had been honeymooning through Europe. They were very surprised to learn that the man Eleanor still referred to as Mr. Bob had carried off her young friend. At the end of August, they joined the Fergusons at Novar. "They all adore her and she looks prettier than ever," Eleanor reported to Franklin's mother. Although she found it "an incongruous marriage," still, she noted, "It is impossible to imagine how sweet she and Bob are together, for I would not know him to be the same man. He has become demonstrative, if you can believe it, and they play together like two children." Eleanor was even more

Scotland, 1905. Left to right: Eleanor Roosevelt,
Franklin Roosevelt, Isabella Ferguson

impressed by Bob's sisters, who were politically well informed and active to a degree Eleanor and Isabella had never imagined women could be. Meanwhile, the Fergusons and Roosevelts had great fun comparing housekeeping notes on the small Manhattan brownstones—"bandboxes"—both couples had acquired, sight unseen, back in New York.[21]

The Fergusons' "Bandbox" on East 69th between Lexington

and Third was a four-story building badly in need of repairs, so Bob
and Isabella moved in with the Cutcheons while their house was being renovated. The young married woman led a gay and busy life.
Her 1906 appointment book was often completely filled: luncheons
—many with Eleanor—dinners, concerts, opera, and theater, as
well as meetings of the Junior League, Three Arts Club, and Bible
class. Regulars, in addition to Eleanor, included young women Isabella had met during her debutante season, who would be her
friends for life: Corinne Robinson, Mary Harriman, and Olivia
Cutting. Characteristically, Isabella was bent on self-improvement
as well as entertainment. A list of resolutions included: "Intellect:
read: newspapers, government & history; music; French; letters every day," and "Social: calls once a week; notes every day; clothes; accounts." Isabella and Eleanor soon had another bond; both were
expecting their first babies, Eleanor in May, Isabella in August.
Edith Roosevelt wrote to Isabella in January that Eleanor was already looking "very sweet and perfectly well but the size of the
Great Pyramid." After her daughter Anna was born, Eleanor asked
Isabella to be godmother.[22]

Just before Isabella's twentieth birthday, in March 1906, she and
Bob moved into their new house. It was a modest dwelling;
Mammy, who had moved in with them, wrote Julia Dinsmore that
the backyard was not as large as Julia's small bedroom. But Ethel
and Kermit Roosevelt, Bob's godchildren, raided the White House
conservatory for plants to make it beautiful. Bob's health was still
poor, and he was forced to be away from the office a good deal. Isabella was inclined to put it down to worry, and Patty agreed that the
first year of married life could make one nervous and emotional.
She assured Isabella that he would settle down after the baby was
born, but to Julia she wrote that she noticed in Isabella "some of my
own set-teethed courage and cheerfulness." Julia was more realistic.
"What is it that ails Bob?" she demanded. "Do you think he has
weak lungs?" As summer wore on, with stifling heat, they all moved

out to Locust Valley. Isabella, vastly pregnant, was cheerful and un-complaining, walking two miles every day, Patty reported to Aunt Julia. She added that Roosevelt had told her he was glad to have his children go to Isabella's to see what happy married life should be like.[23]

The Ferguson baby arrived on September 4, an easy birth, a girl they named Martha (Patty's real name). The new grandmother noted that Bob was wild with joy, though so fussy, she was afraid the baby would be "an old batch's child." Isabella, too, was enchanted; she was hoping to have lots of babies, perhaps six. The doctor said Martha should not be picked up every time she cried, but Mammy had her own ideas of child-rearing: "I look at the father and mother over my glasses very sour so they just let me alone," she explained in a letter to Patty.[24]

Bob's health did not improve after the birth of the baby. Now, however, his complaint was bad hemorrhoids, for which he was operated on at the end of November. Their physician, Dr. Walter James, nephew of the philosopher William James, believed that this condition might account for Bob's continuing ill health. Isabella, bearing up under the double task of nursing a sick husband while literally nursing a baby, traveled back and forth between the hospital and her home on the street car. "All the winter has been made much easier by having little daughter to play with," she insisted. But Julia noted that Isabella was facing trouble at an early age. The President sternly admonished Bob to take off work for at least a year; patching himself up for two or three months would only ensure another breakdown.[25]

Isabella's twenty-first birthday fell in the midst of all these difficulties, but her Uncle Frank wanted her to celebrate it in style. He told her to order a new dress from a fashionable dressmaker and promoted her from "Goosegirl" to "Gooselady," explaining "When one is of lawful age, and the lawful mother of a family, one is entitled to be called a lady, if one's manners are fairly good. So as

Julia Dinsmore, 1908

the awful day of twenty-one is only a week away, I adopt the matronly appellation and retain the praenomen only as evidence that 'there's no hard feelings.' " Bob, meanwhile, had taken to calling her "Mitty," a Roosevelt variant of "Mommy."[26]

Bob's recovery from his operation was long and painful. In May 1907 they went back to Scotland, where they hoped the climate would again do him good. By the time they reached Assynt, Isabella realized she was pregnant again. Her family were appalled. Patty wrote, "If it's Bob's idea of taking care of you and yours of being happy, under the circumstances I have nothing to say but God help us all!" Mammy was indignant on behalf of her new charge, claiming Martha was "too little to have her nose knocked out of joint." Even Aunt Julia wrote: "I am glad you are so amiable as to be resigned to the prospect of a 'cosy family' but pray, don't become in your youth and beauty a 'cosy rabbit.' "[27]

Isabella's second pregnancy did not slow her down any more than her first had done. Aunt Julia marveled, "Isabella seems to be the most remarkable person I ever heard of in her condition to keep going into company. She must have spartan resolution as well as bodily strength." A son was born on March 13, 1908, named for his father. "I suppose we will have to 'hoop Bob's head' as we say in Boone, he will be so proud of his laddie," Julia remarked to Patty.

Bob asked Theodore Roosevelt to be his son's godfather. The Fergusons were spending the summer in Locust Valley; now that Bob was stronger, Isabella was eager to have some social life again. They were often at Sagamore Hill with the Roosevelts; the Roosevelts visited back when Franklin and Eleanor, TR's daughter Alice Roosevelt Longworth, or Dave Goodrich and his wife stayed with Bob and Isabella. Patty, who had gone to Marienbad with the Cutcheons, wrote Isabella sternly that she needed to slow down. "You seem to feel it wrong to rest, just as Eleanor does."[28]

That fall, Isabella promoted the idea of Bob taking a trip west for a bracing change with his godson Kermit Roosevelt. They visited fellow Rough Rider John Greenway, now a mining engineer in the Mesabi Range, near Coleraine, Minnesota. Bob reported to Isabella that John was still "a great old brick," in spite of his "titanic" achievements. But John lacked one essential, Bob wrote Isabella: "a 'Mitty' and 'little Red Hearts.'" Bob also admired the settlers: "One wonders how they do it—without water, without fuel, and the dreadful lone waste of it through the long cold stormy winters, and then the droughts of summer." He little thought that such a life was in his future. While Bob enjoyed himself hunting, Isabella was coping with dreary domestic tasks: tending infant Bobbie, caring for Martha who had been ill for several weeks with stomach trouble, and looking after the affairs of her mother and the Cutcheons while they were in Europe. In spite of Bob's tender reference to "Mitty and the Red Hearts," Isabella complained that his letters lacked affection: "Dearest Dada, Why don't you tell me how you want to see us the way we tell you?"[29] It was only three years since the passionate letters of his courtship.

CHAPTER THREE ∿∿∿∿∿∿∿∿∿∿∿∿∿∿

"A Heart for Any Fate"

SALLY SAYS you are a wonder of patience and cheerfulness," Aunt Julia wrote Isabella at the end of September 1908. "I am glad to hear it. A heart for any fate is what a girl needs most in this uncertain world." A hard fate befell Isabella on November 21, when Dr. James diagnosed Bob with tuberculosis of at least one lung and probably in the rectum at the site of the operation for hemorrhoids two years before. Isabella and Bob had taken it bravely, Frank Cutcheon immediately assured Bob's brother Ronald. The Fergusons planned to go at once to a sanatorium at Saranac Lake in the Adirondacks where Bob would be under the care of Dr. Edward Trudeau, the leading authority on tuberculosis in the United States. Bob's future, Frank gloomily noted to Ronald, was impossible to prophesy. Patty rose to the occasion, setting out at once for Saranac to find them a house. "I never knew Patty so fine about anything," Sally remarked. No wonder: Patty was once again central to her daughter's life. Theodore Roosevelt wrote Bob in his inimitably generous and kind manner to ask if there were any way he could be of service. He expressed gratitude not only for the Fergusons' friendship but for the good influence they had had on his children, especially Kermit.[1]

Frank Cutcheon was the person who helped most, then and always. He began by negotiating with Ronald about finances. Bob had an independent income of about $1000 a year. They could make about $2400 by renting their New York house, out of which they had to make mortgage and life insurance payments. Frank proposed that he and Ronald make up the difference needed for Bob to fight for his life under the best possible conditions. Ronald had already considered making a marriage settlement, and, since he was childless, reminded them that little Bobbie was his only heir. Eventually, a trust was created for the benefit of Isabella and the children. Ronald proposed Franklin Roosevelt as one of the trustees, but Frank wrote Ronald that "For some reason Isabella does not like the idea." He made no attempt, however, to discover the reason for her feelings. Perhaps it was because Franklin, in his youth, was considered a lightweight by many of his contemporaries. Isabella also had investments that Frank had made for her over the years, and would add to. Bob thought it proper for his wife to have her own money: "I have a preference," he later told Frank, "old-fashioned perhaps, for each of a family being somehow independently provided for." More help came from an unexpected source. John J. Astor wrote Bob offering $5000 a year as long as he needed it, in appreciation of all he had done as trustee for their estate.[2]

Isabella's New York friends came to the Bandbox to help her pack, somewhat to Sally's dismay: "They come in velvets . . . dressed for the opera, and say they have come to help." But Isabella had a genius for savoring the happiness in any situation; later she would remember that last evening in the library, "with its big fire reflected in the book case and so many friends standing round and helping. . . . We seemed off for a trip, not to be turning our backs forever on our first home." Less than two weeks after his diagnosis, Bob and Isa-

Julia Loving (Mammy) with Martha and Bobbie Ferguson, 1908

bella departed for Saranac with a trained nurse and two servants, leaving the children for the time being with Patty and Mammy at the Cutcheons'. At the sanatorium, part of the cure was sleeping out on a porch because cold dry air was thought to be especially beneficial. One night the temperature dipped to twenty below, and Isabella reported that even her eyelashes were frozen. Alone in the quiet, snowy mountains, they had to content themselves with Patty's and Mammy's reports of the children's Christmas. Ten-month-old Bobbie had received a set of wee bagpipes, and Martha, just over two, stood spellbound before her pile of presents, not knowing what to take first. The Fergusons' isolation was broken by visits from the Roosevelt tribe: Kermit, young Corinne Robinson, Franklin and Eleanor.[3]

Isabella leaned on her friends for support in this trying time, but it was hard to keep up her correspondence. She wrote Olivia Cutting in April 1909: "I've just made a list of unanswered letters—there were only 98." Olivia wrote every week, and her constancy carried Isabella over what she later called "black periods of discovery." John Greenway wrote several times, urging them to settle in Minnesota, where Bob could escape the pollution of the city and do some light work in an invigorating climate. Isabella supplied the Ferguson side of their correspondence; after one particularly newsy letter, John wrote Bob admiringly of Isabella; among the local Chippewa, he said, "there are no squaws who will match up to her."[4]

Isabella's family were naturally as concerned for her as they were for Bob. Patty cautioned: "Remember, everything depends on you keeping yourself fed up and well. . . . I know how you feel, that you can't bear to think of yourself under the circumstances. I have been through it all, but you are wrong. You must be a little selfish and rest and think of yourself or you will break down and then where will we all be?" Unc visited in the summer of 1909 and, finding her tired and thin, urged her to take some care of herself. Bob, too, was apt to treat her like a child. At forty-one and ill, he must have felt very aged. Isabella had gone back to New York off and on through the summer to get their house ready to rent and to put their belongings in storage. Bob advised her: "'tak' plenty time' as Georgie Munro, the game-keeper, used to tell me when I nearly plugged him in the leg instead of a rabbit. That was when I was learning to shoot at the age of eight, and you are not much older." She was twenty-three. Despite Isabella's determination to appear brave and strong, on a visit to New York in the fall to attend Corinne Robinson's wedding to Joseph Alsop, she broke down and wept on Unc's shoulder. However, she insisted on taking over as much of their business affairs as she could, believing that Bob would have a greater chance of recovery if he were free of monetary worries. Frank Cutcheon did his best to explain their financial situation, to outline a budget, and to get her to stick to it.[5]

Chapter Three

Bob and Isabella had a merrier Christmas their second year. The children had come to stay, and the Cutcheons joined them. After coasting and sliding, they cooked supper over a campfire by a pond in the subzero weather. Isabella rejoiced: "The still, clear, snow-covered world was as beautiful (first in the sunshine and later in the sunset) as anything I ever imagined." Frank reported to Ronald that although Bob's lung was not much improved, he looked well, ate with the family, walked to town, and had to rest only two or three hours during the daytime. The children were fat and rosy looking, although their manners, Frank said sternly, left something to be desired.[6]

Life at the turn of the century—before antibiotics—was hard for everyone. Eleanor and Franklin's third child, Franklin Jr., born in March 1909, had been poorly from the start. The child died in early November, and it was Isabella's turn to console her grieving friend. Eleanor mourned, "Sometimes I think I cannot bear the heartache which one little life has left behind but I realize . . . that it was meant for us to understand and to sympathize more deeply with all life's sorrows." She appreciated Isabella's warm understanding. "Sometimes I think it's a little help over our own sad places to know that our lives are a help to others so I wanted to tell you, dear, that your unselfish, cheerful example in all your anxiety and sorrow has helped me these past weeks more than you will ever know."[7]

Isabella went down to New York the following March to have a gynecological operation. But first she seized the opportunity to catch up with her friends, attending a small dinner Susie Parish gave for the Roosevelts' fifth wedding anniversary. The following day was the dead baby's birthday, and Eleanor, who was looking thin and nervous, broke down. Isabella planned to give her a talk on taking care of herself, but it is doubtful that Eleanor took that sort of advice any better than Isabella did. Among her other women friends, Isabella was disappointed to find no interest in politics as such; they were much more interested in the reinvigorated woman suffrage movement.[8]

Isabella had a rough time with the operation. She reduced her nurse to tears when she cried for Bob, saying the nurse couldn't understand because she didn't know him. A few days later Isabella suddenly began to hemorrhage. Frank, Patty, and the nurse quickly tilted the bed up onto chairs and summoned the doctor, who finally stanched the bleeding. By then, Patty later wrote Corinne, Isabella was looking like a beautiful piece of marble, as her mother held her hands and begged her not to let go. Aunt Julia observed succinctly that "Isabella has been through the flintmills." Once she began to recover, Isabella was impatient to go home. She begged Bob for romantic letters, promising that if she got them, she would be more likely to stay in New York and get stronger. She fantasized about him walking in on her in the library, demure in a lace cap: "There'd be a fearful mussing of the cap and dressing gown and some dozens of bear hugs as beginners!"[9]

While Isabella was recovering, Bob's sister Edith had come to stay with him at Saranac. She had been in poor health herself and hoped the change of climate would do her good. Isabella went home at the end of April and found Edie and Bob happily planting flowers and vegetables. But the Fergusons could not put down roots in Saranac. His doctors warned Bob that if he remained in the East, the tuberculosis might kill him within a few months. His only chance of recovery was to go west, to a drier climate. Isabella was brave about having to leave not only their dear little Bandbox, and treasures like their beloved four-poster brass bed but also the city and region that had been her home for nearly half her life. She wrote her mother that the struggle for life had gotten them down to bedrock. Although she loved the idea of a home with its many associations, she said, people who would be happy should always "build theirs in their hearts or the hearts of others. Here's to Life in a

Pueblo sitting on Navajo blankets." Bronson Cutting, the brother of Isabella's friend Olivia, had moved to Santa Fe after he, too, developed tuberculosis, so the Fergusons began to investigate New Mexico. Meanwhile, John Greenway had moved to Bisbee, Arizona, where he was now general manager of the Calumet and Arizona Copper Company. He hoped they would locate near him, so that when Bob recovered, John could give him some light work at the mines.[10]

Bob and Isabella chose to settle near Silver City, New Mexico, in the southwest corner of the state, in the foothills of the Mogollon Mountains. Silver City enjoyed a fine reputation as a health resort, boasting four hospitals, as well as rest homes and sanatoriums. The most notable of these was the Cottage Sanatorium, run by Dr. E. S. Bullock, who claimed a cure rate significantly higher than in New York state. In the Southwest, patients could spend more time out of doors, the dry climate was considered beneficial, and sunshine was thought to kill the TB bacteria. A physical examination before they set out showed that Bob's condition was even worse than the doctors had feared: The infection had spread, and he now had tuberculosis in both lungs. Isabella, though she was not told the full extent of the bad news, was very depressed. Before they left, Dr. Trudeau gave Isabella two pieces of advice that she evidently took very much to heart. "Never admit the word 'nerves,' into your vocabulary," he said, "and don't live out of a suitcase. Unpack as if you were going to stay."[11]

CHAPTER FOUR

Cat Canyon

Bob and Isabella arrived in New Mexico on November 17, 1910. They had rented a cottage in Cat Canyon, three miles northwest of Silver City. Two small houses served as the main dining and sitting rooms, flanked by Adirondack tents. Bob had one tent to himself, to avoid contagion. His dishes and silverware had to be sterilized. He could not be kissed on the mouth. Patty and Mammy had come, too, to help Isabella adjust to her demanding new life. Patty had other obligations, especially to Aunt Julia, but she would spend at least part of every year helping her daughter until the end of her life.[1]

Within days, Isabella was writing her first impressions to Eleanor: "How you would laugh, Eleanor dearest, were you to drive up Cat's Canyon to find us wild Mexicans basking in the sun.... Mother, Buzz [Bobbie] and Martha rattle down the cañon in the wagon after the dinner and the family milk, to be found on a neighbor's fence post half way to town. Bob on the porch of the living room looks far off over hills—pink and blue far hills and sandy near

Cat Canyon, 1911

ones with scrubby dwarf evergreens that break the desert sweep. . . .
I wish you could look in on our 6:00 evening meal, off an oil cloth
table cover, a kerosene lamp for a centerpiece." It was Isabella's genius always to revel in adventure. Mammy was not so sanguine: "I
like living under a roof with other people, not in a tent. When the
winds blow (which is quite often) one is frightened to death for fear
of being carried away," she confided to Aunt Julia.[2]

Camp life was primitive. There were outhouses and no running
water; water was caught in tubs as it ran off the roofs of the tents. At
night their water basins froze. They gathered wood for fuel. If Patty
had feared five years earlier that she would have no future role in
her daughter's life, that certainly was not the case now; she was serving, as Mammy put it to Aunt Julia, as "scavenger, wood chopper,
market woman, painter, yard cleaner and general servant." To some
extent, she was reliving her own early days on the frontier. Isabella
was quickly discovering pioneer life herself, learning to drive a

horse and carriage as well as a motor car. When a neighbor woman twenty-five miles away invited her for lunch, she set out on horseback but dramatically miscalculated and arrived more than an hour late.[3]

Life in Cat Canyon was hard for people who had always lived at least at the fringes of elite society, but compared to many homesteaders of the period, the Fergusons' life may have seemed practically opulent. Isabella found a surprising lack of sympathy among her new neighbors. "They evidently think we live a life of . . . *idle* luxury, and utter selfishness . . . because we have a cook," she told her grandmother Selmes. But she had made two wonderful new friends: Belle Eckles, the state's first female school superintendent, and her sister Mary. Isabella wrote Olivia that they were "as fine as any you'd stumble on in any part of the world."[4]

Two hundred miles away in Bisbee, John Greenway considered himself a neighbor, too. Early in the new year 1911, he dropped in on the Cat Canyon family. He found Bob plunged in depression and urged him not to brood. A month later John was back again to see his fellow Rough Rider Dave Goodrich, who had come to visit the Fergusons for two days and wound up staying six weeks. The house party swelled when Olivia Cutting came down from Albuquerque where she was visiting her brother Bronson. Sally arrived with Aunt Julia, who celebrated her seventy-eighth birthday surrounded by her "great-greats." Edith Roosevelt dropped by with her daughter Ethel, making fourteen altogether. A few months later, Kermit Roosevelt came, too. TR followed up with one of his characteristically thoughtful letters, giving the unemployed man a shred of solace: "My dear Bob, you have been to Kermit, as to me, the kind of friend for whom no man can ever be sufficiently grateful." Isabella must have been touched that even in what seemed an isolated spot, they had not been forgotten.[5]

Still, she longed for Eleanor. Just before Isabella and Bob had set out west, Franklin was elected to the New York state legislature, and the Roosevelts moved to Albany, where Eleanor had to make her own adjustments. She was intimidated by the elaborate entertaining: "I am sure I can never live up to their standards." Isabella's example gave her courage: "I wonder if you realize what a wonderful influence your sweet and cheerful spirit always is to me?" she wrote. Isabella answered: "I wish very often we weren't at the ends of the earth from each other. . . . We've had the pleasure of following Franklin's work this winter . . . and like to think of the big share that's been yours."[6]

In spite of all the company, or because of the work it had entailed, by the end of June, six months after their arrival, Bob thought that his young wife deserved a break and urged her to accept John Greenway's invitation to visit him in Arizona. John's aunt and uncle were staying with him, making such a plan perfectly respectable. The journey west put Isabella in an exalted frame of mind. The countryside was beautiful, she wrote Bob: "There's a tender new green over all the plains that creeps a little up the foot-hills. . . . The whole heavens were masses of golden and blue-grey castles like Maxfield P[arish], except here and there where it show-ered hard in the shining sunlight, making almost next to it lovely rainbows." John met her in Bisbee. Much later he would confess to her that he had been overcome by the sight of her on the platform. Isabella was dazzled by his house in Bisbee, large and full of com-forts. John had insisted she take his room, where she enjoyed cool breezes blowing across her bed and a cool tub in the morning. After a dry camp in tents, it must have seemed luxurious indeed.[7]

She was as impressed by John's success in Arizona as Bob had been in Minnesota. In the evenings they went for starlight rides and picnic suppers in the mountains. She wrote artlessly of these charms to her husband, and of her host as well: "It's quite pathetic to see him smiling in complete satisfaction over his guest. . . . He's inclined to look ten years younger, sitting cross legged and sucking an orange at bedtime. [His aunt] declares he's cheered up enor-mously!" John wrote Bob too: "I have always been her warm ad-mirer and seeing her each day here only makes me appreciate the more what she really is." Bob endorsed John's request that Isabella stay for their Fourth of July celebrations. "Wear [your best clothes] to a frazzle," Bob wrote his wife. "Have a good time and give it to everybody else and then come home and tell us all about it." She agreed only because she thought the holiday would help her return strong enough to resume the task of nursing an invalid: "I hope your reply is sincere about my staying on here, for it's the only rea-son I do. I am trying to be perfectly sensible and make the most of the change. . . . When I do come back, it will be less of a hen pecker and a more generally useful Mittie."[8]

Perhaps because another man's appreciation kindled his own, Bob wrote her a rare tender missive: "The stars came out again and a tiny wisp of a new moon. . . . What do you think the little family's wish under the new moon could have been? They had been thinking about Mittie." But Isabella was thinking of John: "We talk until all hours of the night and I think shock Miss W. and Mr. W. awfully. They retire shortly before nine!!! and John claims he's never talked so much before." Bob professed alarm: "How about John's character? Tell him I'm getting anxious about it, with a belle of New York." She reassured him: "You needn't worry as to his character. He has plenty of that and some to spare." But Isabella picked up on Bob's anxiety and quickly wrote that she was not going to allow any more sitting up late, as John needed to be rested for his work. She promised to "show discretion enough for two. He has none. He's far too hungry for 'play' after such a constant diet of work and responsibility and the lines of his face are very careworn at times, too much so for a man of his youth and vigor." John, at 39, was not exactly young. Nevertheless, she thought he should "marry deliberately when he's well bowled over, but not in a panic of approaching 40." John, however, had already been bowled over.[9]

After she returned, Unc twitted her about her "elopement to or with Mr. Greenway." Isabella assured her family that Bob had gained confidence by being in charge at the Canyon. Ferguson and Greenway remained companionable. Later that summer, John took a trip to Great Britain and visited Bob's family in Scotland; in the fall, he and the Fergusons took a two-day road trip. John reported to Theodore Roosevelt with some concern that Bob seemed to lack all confidence, did not care to see people or talk to them, and never went out. John and Isabella both thought the excursion had done Bob's spirits good. Politics also presented another stimulus for the sick man. Isabella found the local variety astonishing, she wrote Eleanor. From Bronson Cutting, who was publishing a newspaper in Albuquerque, she had learned that "no one is a proved politician till he's been shot at a certain number of times in the public plaza!" But there was "a young crude life and enthusiasm about most of it that is invigorating," she explained. In December 1911, John Greenway met with Theodore Roosevelt in Albuquerque and informed Bob that TR was planning to run for president if he was convinced the people wanted him. Roosevelt told Bob to start lining up New Mexico delegates for the Republican convention in June.[10]

Isabella wrote Eleanor that they had "jogged through" their first year well enough. She thought Bob was getting better, though it was "a tedious business . . . at best. Slow and with setbacks." She confided to Olivia that "We slump so appallingly without the fellow humans we love." In particular, she longed for some stimulating women friends, either in real life or literature, and asked Olivia if she knew of any. "I'm tired of men—Disraeli, Professor Blackie, Voltaire, etc.—Tis a queer thing that it takes women to make men's lives interesting and yet few of them stand interesting in lives of their own." Isabella had made the surprising discovery that she "had the makings of a man within and the glory of a woman concealing it. . . . One must have some men's common sense to know when to be the woman. . . . It takes some tact to judge. . . . I've made up my mind to be a man for at least 5 years, possibly longer." Being a man would have made life easier, not only to accomplish everything she had to do but to avoid the complications of a budding relationship with John Greenway.[11]

The start of 1912, however, showed that the previous year had taken its toll. Patty arrived to find Isabella thin and, she thought, on the verge of a breakdown. Isabella and the children had been sick since Christmas, Bob seldom got out of bed, and Mammy, overworked, was in such a state that she "wept if you gave her a kind word." Patty realized that her help was critical if Isabella was going to be able to cope with her arduous life. At first the work almost overwhelmed Patty, now fifty, but she "set my teeth and my old heart got readjusted."[12]

Isabella admitted only in occasional letters to intimate friends that she was having a hard time. That spring, she wrote Olivia poignantly of seeing a small bird dash itself against the window, while its little grey mate flapped around over his body. She noted, "Some stand beautifully happy through life knowing theirs has been the supreme bliss—that of one moment of normal life . . . but few of us are big enough—and are too selfishly hungry." She tried to hold fast to those sweet moments of normal life, explaining that "while tomorrow may hold a depressing slump again! we try to make the most of today." Typical was the time she returned from a horseback ride, hot, dusty, and tired, and dove directly into a neighbor's pool, boots and all. Out of a life that might have been seen as full of hardship and even tragedy, she created adventures, humor, and enjoyment for her family.[13]

Isabella and Bob also depended on visitors to cheer them up. They had been hoping for a visit from Bob's sister Edie, but his eldest sister, Alice, had contracted tuberculosis, and Edie stayed in Scotland to nurse her. In mid-May 1912, John Greenway stopped by on his way to Chicago for the Republican Convention. He had a good effect on Bob, talking with him far into the night about politics, on which they mostly agreed. John was supporting Theodore Roosevelt, who was challenging his successor, William Howard Taft, to the presidency; Taft's conservative policies had sadly disappointed TR.[14]

Roosevelt was a reluctant candidate, he confessed to Bob: "I am having a horrid time. . . . Between ourselves, I think the chances are small that I shall be nominated." He thought the Democratic Party incapable of solving the nation's problems, but the Republicans were split into two factions, the "stupid and sometimes sinister reactionaries" under Taft and the "foolish and violent extremists under the . . . somewhat demagogic leadership of La Follette." Roosevelt believed that he was the only man who could unite and lead the two factions.[15]

Since the beginning of the year, Eleanor Roosevelt, though a Democrat, had been discussing her uncle's candidacy with Isabella, asking, "How do they feel out your way about Uncle Ted and do you think any other Republican could carry the state?" In early May she and Franklin detoured through New Mexico to see the Fergusons on their way home from an official trip to Panama. For Eleanor, who had never been west of Albany, it was an eye-opening experience. The Roosevelts missed their train connection in Deming, and tried to continue in a hired car. On the rough road, the car suffered multiple tire punctures, and a wind storm sprang up, chilling them in their light spring clothes. By the time a rescue car sent by the Fergusons with hot coffee and warm coats arrived, they had a taste of the life Isabella was learning to endure.[16]

Eleanor also appreciated the beauties of the new landscape, Isabella noted, "marvelling over every cactus and yucca." Eleanor was also touched by a visit to the sanatorium, which, she later wrote, opened a whole new vista to her. The Roosevelts were, Isabella thought, "much stronger and keener in their interests since the Albany experience." Isabella rejoiced that Eleanor also seemed to exhibit a new sense of fun. They talked far into the night catching up. Afterwards Eleanor wrote, "It makes me realize even more how much I miss you dear people out of my daily life."[17]

Eleanor and Isabella continued to correspond briskly as the political situation heated up. Roosevelt lost the Republican nomination to Taft and formed a third party, the Progressive or Bull Moose party. John Greenway visited New Mexico, to help them organize there as he had in Arizona. New Mexico and Arizona had just become states, but only Arizona had granted women as well as men the right to vote. Bob was recovering from a relapse but was so interested in the extraordinary political conflict that be began to push Isabella "in the most shameless manner," she told Eleanor, to get involved. Although the 1912 campaign was the first time all major political parties had women's divisions, it was still unusual for women to be active in partisan politics, and Isabella seemed to feel it necessary to cite Bob's insistence for her participation. But a month later, after attending a rally in Albuquerque and touring for two hours with Roosevelt, she was captivated. She explained to

Olivia that "To be a western progressive, one must wear a black felt hat heavily laden with railroad dust. Always be too busy to tie your tie and always be on the verge of washing."[18]

Isabella was assigned to poll the local citizenry, in hopes of signing up voters before November. Many of the Rough Riders had come from New Mexico and their Colonel was immensely popular. Typical was the man who told Isabella, "Well, I ain't never heard of this Progressive business but I vote for Roosevelt." Isabella also began to understand, she told Eleanor, that "Our Spanish race has never been fairly handled and remains a heavy complication." Altogether she found it fascinating, especially because statehood had just come and what they were doing would influence politics in years to come. By August, Greenway reported proudly to Dave Goodrich, Isabella had signed up forty-five men for a Progressive pledge in the "reactionary" town of Silver City. By election day, he had come to believe that she was doing most of the work for the party in Grant County. He added tellingly, "No man seems able to resist her."[19]

Unc addressed her as "Lady Boss," but, as usual, struck at the heart of the matter by inquiring, "Seriously, if you are going to lead the party, wouldn't it be just as well to have the ballot?"[20]

The Republican vote split between Theodore Roosevelt and William Howard Taft; Woodrow Wilson, the Democratic nominee, was elected. Although Theodore lost his second bid for the presidency, his fifth cousin Franklin Roosevelt, a Democrat, was reelected to the New York state legislature. Eleanor had become a political participant, too, complaining to Isabella: "Can't you see . . . how many Mrs. Snooks and Mrs. Jones I will have to pretend to know when I really never remember seeing them before." However, Franklin soon received an appointment in the Wilson administration as assistant secretary of the Navy (the same position Theodore Roosevelt had held in 1898) and the FDRs moved to Washington,

Theodore Roosevelt (center) and John C. Greenway (right), 1912.
The man at left is unidentified.

D.C., in the spring of 1913. Eleanor confided to Isabella that she was afraid she would not be able to meet her responsibilities in this wider sphere.[21]

The campaign had thrown Isabella together with John Greenway even more than before. She still wrote artlessly to Olivia: "John G was here for 3 days. He is so gloriously above anything mean or little in any line and accomplishes so much every day." John wrote Dave Goodrich about Isabella, too, with undisguised concern: "It makes me almost cry when I look at Isabella. At the first look she appears all right, but it soon becomes apparent that she is deadly tired, very thin, ... and is just in condition to contract the deadly disease which Bob has. You or some of her kinspeople ought to come and take her away at once for a good rest." Soon Isabella began to sense, as she noted in her diary, "a queer subconsciousness of local gossip of a vicious nature. Too small to contemplate. And yet some have capsized in such a whiff?" She advised herself: "Steady now: keep the boat quiet; the anchor is not lost.... My boat is my soul. My anchor is my self-control. Love is the depth untold below."[22]

What is not clear in this analogy is whom she loved. Her early years with Bob Ferguson had been happy ones and they shared care and concern for their children. She admired his courage in the face of his devastating illness, but his depression, a common symptom of tuberculosis, must have eroded some of her affection over the four years he had been sick. And it is likely that they no longer could have sexual relations more intense than mere hugs. But he was her husband and the father of her children and she felt a duty to him. In those days, couples took seriously their marriage vows "for better or worse." Other women of her generation also stood by invalid husbands, among them Eleanor Roosevelt and Frances Perkins, who would be FDR's secretary of labor. However, Isabella may have been able to stay happy in her difficult marriage by knowing another man appreciated her at those times when Bob, preoccupied with his mortal illness, did not seem to.

Greenway was not the only one concerned about Isabella. Even before the end of the campaign, TR took the trouble to write Bob: "Some time I want you to make Isabella go off for two or three weeks. . . . Like myself, you have a wife who will persist in refusing to think of herself—and therefore you and I must think of them. I have always insisted that Mrs. Roosevelt benefitted in no way as much as by a complete holiday from me and the children, in entirely different surroundings."[23]

Isabella did get away, but hardly in the way Greenway and his Colonel might have hoped. Bob's sister Alice had died in July and his surviving sister, Edie, had come to the States with the Cutcheons in late September, planning to travel on to New Mexico where she could rest and recover from the strain of nursing Alice. But Frank wrote Isabella that by the time Edie arrived in New York, she was looking jaundiced and was too fatigued to continue the journey. Dr. James examined her and wired Isabella to come at once. On December 4, Isabella took a train east, crossing paths with Patty, who was heading west to manage the Cat Canyon household in Isabella's absence. Dave Goodrich also went to New Mexico to keep Bob company, since Patty was becoming increasingly impatient with her former friend's moodiness and demands on her daughter.[24]

Isabella arrived in New York to find Edie "bright yellow," and Dr. James baffled. He called in another doctor, and they decided to operate on her bile duct. Bob was anguished that he could not be with his sister; he told Isabella he had always hoped Martha and Bobbie would be playmates as he and Edie had been when they romped "in the heather round Novar." He was sorry, too, that Isabella should "have such a thing come on your willing shoulders after so much. And yet I would not have it quite pass from you. . . .

You will take the pride and joy in it that I do and treasure it for our bairns." The operation disclosed a tumor on the ovary, which had metastasized to the liver. Isabella reported to Bob that Edie seemed "as ready to go on to Alice as to come back to us." Edie died three days later, and Isabella laid her out in a plaid with white heather on her breast. Bob wrote to praise "our own little Mits, our own Redheart, you have been to brave Edie something untold, for we all need something besides our own courage at such times, and that other you have given her in overflowing measure." Perhaps he was imagining his own future.[25]

John Greenway had been following the situation closely and wired his sympathy, along with soothing assurances from Dave Goodrich that Bob was doing well. Eleanor, too, had been a solid comfort, and afterwards Isabella wrote, "You were everything to me in those weeks, and if I can love you more than before, I do now. . . . May Anna know one friend like you." Isabella, exhausted, stayed on in New York through Christmas, while Patty, with Dave Goodrich and the Eckles sisters, contrived a celebration for the children. Isabella sent an orchid to Belle Eckles, who wrote back, "I just sat down and cried. . . . To think that you thought of me, in it all, was too much."[26]

Early in the new year 1913, Isabella returned to New Mexico. She admitted to her Grandmother Selmes that the whole affair had "wrenched me deeper than I knew." She tried to distract herself with company, up to ten guests at a time. She had also begun to home-school Martha and Bobbie, now seven and five years old. "The nursery university is in full morning swing," she wrote Eleanor one snowy February morning. "Buzz [Bobbie] writes and illustrates original composition!! Martha and Hazel [one of the help] take turns at the blackboard. Mother writes for the post and Bob takes a day in bed for complete coziness." But Isabella had been going full tilt for many months, and Bob sent her off for another rest-cure at John Greenway's, accompanied by two women friends.

Isabella with Martha and Bobbie, 1913

Once again, though, she found no relief. Isabella arrived to discover that John had been laid low by a stab from a poisonous cactus; his sister-in-law, who was keeping house for him, had broken her ankle; and nearby on the border, the Fifth Cavalry had just had a skirmish with the Mexicans.[27]

As before, Isabella rationalized her trip, writing Olivia that it would be "no bad thing for Bob to be rid of the eternal petticoat—a return of independence being now a vital part of the cure." But Bob missed her: "To say that I long to be with Mits is saying little. I long to hold her by the hand and, in spite of the danger of spoiling her journey, hold it as firmly and constantly as my weak grasp may, for I am uneasy about our Mittie at times, and somehow especially at this time, and feel she needs all the care possible that she might not give thought to take for herself and that I am so unable to give." Was he worried about her physical well-being only? Well might he have worried. When John had recovered enough to be able to see to the care of his horses, Isabella strolled out with him one evening to the stable behind the house. Out of earshot of their chaperones, John broke down and confessed that he was wildly in love with her. By then she had come to love him, too.[28]

Unremitting work and worry and grief—and possibly the tumult of her feelings for John—plunged Isabella into a "nightmarish . . . weariness I never before had," she confessed to Eleanor. She escaped with the children and Mammy to the California coast, where they rented a cottage in Santa Barbara, two hundred yards from the sea. At first she was so worn out that she collapsed and simply cried for two days, then rested calmly in bed until she felt able to face the world again. She stayed on for seven weeks, eating and sleeping, swimming and gardening and painting, until she could return home strong enough to work again.[29]

During those seven weeks Bob wrote her extraordinary letters. Perhaps he had some sense of what had happened in Arizona. She was, after all, a vivacious twenty-seven and he a faltering forty-five. He reminded her of their courtship and honeymoon: "I kiss her and hold her softly and close on those old rocks on Cherry Hill [in Central Park], among the Kentucky beeches, in the old graveyard, when she really was mine; under the locust and the elm, even the heather arch and mother's room at Raith; in 75th street and our own little home and fourposter . . . and ever, ever since, Mits. Do you ever doubt it?" He had heard from Anna Cowles that Isabella was very popular in California: "I'm so proud of our own little family Mits, who always puts such good heart and fun into everybody, babies or old, grouchy grey Scotch folk. It's all the same and we all adore her. And of course everybody longs to hug and kiss and caress her as I would, and so many would make her so much more happy than I can do. But she's dear and patient and loving and loyal, whatever comes. And we'll have happiness of all kinds, unexpected, some perhaps undeserved. And as the Colonel said under the old Locust, 'Be lovers to the end.' "[30]

He looked forward to the time when she would "put her beloved dimpled rosy face up to his and give such a soft, gentle true-love kiss, making him love her more and more." Bob used the names Jenny and Peter as a private code for their sex life. "This kind of thing isn't the whole show, Jenny, by a long shot, but it's a pretty big part at times, even with peaceful, respectable, homey folk like you and me. I do just love to be *fondled truly*. Your passionate Peter." TB patients were usually restricted from physical contact; as an adult, Martha believed her parents had no sexual relations after he was diagnosed. Isabella would have liked to have more children; that they didn't suggests that Martha may have been right. These letters, then, are doubly poignant.[31]

Shortly after Isabella's return in July, Bob was buoyed by a visit from his old Colonel. Theodore Roosevelt stopped over for a day and a night with his teenaged sons Archie and Quentin on their way to the Grand Canyon. John Greenway met them off the train in Deming, and a number of Rough Riders rode in to greet him. But Roosevelt also made time for private talks with Bob. Patty, concerned about the Fergusons' relationship, had asked her old friend to let her know how he assessed the situation. He must have found them getting on well, for he wrote Bob that he had wanted his boys to "get the atmosphere of your family life."[32]

However, at some point, possibly that summer, John made a clean breast to Bob of his feelings for Isabella. In those days, it would have been considered the honorable thing to do. He offered to go off to Africa, where he could find plenty of mining work, but Bob merely asked John to promise he and Isabella would never be alone together again. Martha later summed up the situation: "Ma wasn't about to abandon a sick man like my father, whom she respected enormously," even though she was in love with John Greenway.[33] But the confession changed the Fergusons' relationship. Bob's letters to Isabella became more businesslike, never again the passionate and erotic ones of her 1913 Santa Barbara sojourn. Her references to John in her letters to friends dwindled away. John's visits to Silver City all but stopped, although the occasional letter from this period suggests they did keep in touch. Isabella would take care of Bob until he died, making allowances for his behavior because of his illness and celebrating his virtues—his care for their children, his stoicism, his heroic attempts to live a normal life. While she loyally adhered to the letter of her promise, no doubt the knowledge that John intended to wait for her must have been like hot bricks at her feet on a long, cold sleigh ride.

Isabella had returned from California "new made over and ready for anything," she boasted to Eleanor. Almost at once, however, she was challenged by Martha's falling ill with an intestinal disorder as the rainy season began and the temperature in their mountains plummeted fifty degrees. Isabella nursed her little daughter night and day. Martha was ill for more than two months, and everything from "subacute appendicitis" to typhoid was suspected. Isabella naturally dreaded tuberculosis. Finally, a doctor from El Paso examined Martha and pronounced her lungs sound; if anything, he said, she was suffering from too much nursing. "Ye Gods be praised!" Isabella rejoiced to Eleanor. A long-hoped-for visit from her beloved Uncle Frank and Aunt Sally also sent her spirits soaring.[34]

The next health crisis involved Mammy, by then in her mid-fifties. She had been sick for some time but refused to leave, insisting she would stay at Cat Canyon until "the Maker called her." In early December 1913 she became critically ill and was immediately sent off to Patty in New York, where she underwent a combination appendectomy and hysterectomy. Isabella, shorthanded, became nurse, tutor, and housekeeper. When it snowed, she wrote Olivia, she faced "all the usual complications: feed run out, M & B soaking every other moment; chickens dying; Mexicans growing cold and surly." She wrote her mother: "Can't you see it? And don't you thank heaven for a sense of humor?" All was not grim however; she attended a wedding dance at the Burro Mountain mines that attracted two hundred people within a fifty-mile radius. "We ragged . . . and tangoed and one-stepped and I've ached ever since, but feel 10 years younger!" she boasted to Olivia.[35]

While Frank Cutcheon was visiting in New Mexico, he had encouraged the Fergusons to build a house, as an investment and to provide a permanent home for the children. After three years in tents, the Fergusons were longing to gather again under one roof. At the end of 1913 they filed a claim to homestead fifty acres on Burro Mountain, a picturesque site at an elevation of 6,660 feet, in a wide valley near a creek, surrounded by western pine forest. Homesteaders could get free land from the government by improving it and living on it for three years. Isabella saw an extra benefit to the new project, she told Olivia: "Bob is *keen* as not in years." Regarding Dr. Trudeau's advice to Isabella not to live out of a suitcase but to settle down, Isabella "got a little carried away," Martha later concluded: "She built a house wherever she went." To supervise the construction, the family camped out on Burro Mountain. Life in the new encampment kept Isabella busy. Bob detailed her activities to Frank: "She's Chinese gardener, cook, housemaid, chicken-woman, irrigator, pump-man, chauffeur, and store-keeper."[36]

As the warm weather approached, Martha again suffered from stomach complaint. Isabella decided to take the children to New England for the summer of 1914 in hopes that the cool air would relieve her. Uncle Frank rented a summer house in York Harbor, Maine, so he and Sally could help with the children while Patty escaped to Marienbad with Susie and Henry Parish. Isabella left Bob reluctantly, but she was even more anxious about Martha. Once in Maine, however, she took full advantage of the change of scene to amuse herself with sketching and dancing lessons with her cousin Belle Breckinridge. They would dance themselves giddy, she wrote Bob, and then fall into a swimming pool.[37]

By early August, however, Isabella was getting reports that Bob was thin and tired, and she began to feel she should go home: "Your letter last night made me too blue," she wrote him. "Saying we might pay you a visit!! Well, upon my word. Never mind, Dearie, what you need is a sound hugging! And that you'll get and ere long." She promised they would be home as soon as Martha was well and the furniture from the Bandbox was packed up for their new house. Their personal problems were suddenly submerged in a new worry, when, on August 8, Great Britain declared war on Germany. Bob was afraid that Hector would be sent straight to Belgium and tele-graphed Frank for news, but there was none. In addition to anxiety, Bob also felt frustration: "I only wish I might go with him, instead of idling here among the flowers. The time and opportunity that all men look for is here and I cannot meet the chance of a life-time." He must have forgotten his glorious moment on the heights of San Juan Hill. Isabella tried for a light note when she wrote him: "We all picture Mother and Susie [Parish] returning on a warship, but prob-ably thoroughly enjoying themselves meantime." It would take Patty a month to reach England, where she found Hector still stationed.[38]

In spite of all the uncertainty, Isabella made a long-hoped-for pilgrimage to Franklin and Eleanor's summer home in Campo-bello, just over the Canadian border with Maine. Eleanor was ex-pecting another baby within a week's time, but the two women were still able to enjoy a tranquil time basking in each other's under-standing company. Both appreciated their precious time together, snatched from other obligations. Eleanor wrote: "I know it must have been an effort to come so far and leave the children," and Isabella responded, "I feel very guilty when I think that it was too near the [baby's] arrival and you oughtn't to have bothered."[39]

Bob's letters to Isabella were noticeably less amorous than those of the year before and ran to accounts of house building: Does she realize there are fifty-five windows in the house, all of which will have to be curtained? He asks for lamps: "Won't it be queer going from room to room without a lantern?" He tells amusing stories about the antics of mice on the roof. Isabella, twenty-eight, complained that her youth was passing: "I'm growing old, Dads!! and drying up!! And it comes to me grimly when I see the lines around my eyes increasing rather than smoothing out under this luxury." Unc reported to Bob that she still was very thin and had black circles under her eyes and lines around her mouth. He warned: "You need to be a bit careful, Bob, that all the spirit is not squeezed out of her by a life that at best is bound to be hard and uninteresting, relatively, to one whose vital, instinctive interests are in people, rather than places, things, or books." It's unclear what he thought Bob could do. By the end of August Martha had improved, and they adjourned to New York for Isabella to pack up the furniture from the Bandbox for their new dwelling. Bob also commissioned her to buy supplies from a wholesale grocery: dried fruits, sardines, cheeses, canned delicacies like asparagus tips, nuts, seasonings and pickles, a few tins of pâté de foie gras. Isabella joyfully reconnected with friends she had not seen for four long years.[40]

Worried that Martha might have another relapse, Isabella persuaded Miss Thorpe, the baby nurse she'd had when the children were born, to go back with them to New Mexico. Isabella also needed Miss Thorpe to help with the children's education, as she had too many other responsibilities to teach without interruption. It had been hard to find someone suitable: "Our life out here is rough at times, grim in its loneliness, and then again filled with amusement of a unique kind to any one with humor." Mammy, who had been recuperating that summer with Julia Dinsmore at Boone,

The Burro Mountain Homestead

was loathe to return to "God-forsaken" New Mexico. After she recovered, she took a job in New York City. Although Isabella continued to send her monthly checks, she did not rejoin the family until they left New Mexico.[41]

Isabella arrived home October 19, entranced to find the house all finished, looking in its isolated spot like a house in a fairy tale. The Burro Mountain Homestead was a large squared-off U-shaped building, with two wings of bedrooms extending from a living-dining-kitchen area. The house had a Spanish flavor, constructed of adobe bricks, soft orange-pink with contrasting blue-green trim. Over the fireplaces, their initials were picked out in rough nuggets of local turquoise. Bob, though not affluent, was the scion of a noble family, and the interior looked a little like a baronial hall: hand-hewn rafters, built-in bookcases, oriental rugs, Adams and Chippendale furniture. Large bay windows opened onto the beautifully rugged landscape. At the end of the south wing was a room for Bob with a screened-in sleeping porch. And for Isabella, indoor plumbing. Bob had taken great delight in planning the house and land-scaping the terraced gardens. Honeysuckle, wisteria, and roses grew along the walls on trellises. He grew raspberries, gooseberries, and asparagus. The orchard boasted several varieties of apples, as well as peaches, cherries, damson plums, pears, grapes, and currants. "They all had to be watered," Martha later recalled. "You couldn't afford to let the water run through ditches because you didn't have enough. You carried water in buckets."[42]

Servants were needed just to maintain a minimum of middle-class comfort. Light was provided by eighteen kerosene lamps that had to be tended every day. "You had to fill them, trim the wicks, and clean the chimneys," said Martha. Cows had to be milked. Drinking water had to be boiled. In times of drought, water was hauled by wagon from a spring. Ice was fetched from town for the icebox. Rooms were heated with wood-burning Franklin stoves, and the cookstove was wood-fired as well. The children did their part, milking the cows and carrying firewood, for which they were paid a penny a basket. The Fergusons usually ate in the kitchen with the Chinese cook unless there were guests. But they dressed much as they would have done in New York: Isabella, with her hair in a pompadour, wore lace-trimmed gowns for tea; Bob wore white suits.[43]

Even in her beautiful new house, Isabella felt isolated after her sociable summer. She thought back on her happy time with Elea-nor: "one goes over and over the times that count away off here in our bit of the moon." They longed for war news, impatient with mail that came only every two or three days. Still, Isabella professed herself strong and ready for a one-year lap. Miss Thorpe proved to be a cheerful companion, and work kept Isabella from brooding: "unmade curtains, stoves to be erected, frozen plumbing, unpaid bills, uneducated children, Xmas upon us!" Christmas was a bright spot, even though a blizzard descended. Horses fetched local fami-lies, including twenty-five children. "A real Santa Claus just paralyzed them with joy and when, out of his sack after all the presents, jumped two New Zealand hares, our cup was full to overflowing!" Isabella reported to Eleanor, adding: "May the New Year bring all that's real living—for what else can we be here for?" Even under difficult conditions, Isabella could celebrate life with gusto.[44]

It was a testament to the Fergusons' capacity for friendship that so many people made their way—often in wagons through snow-drifts—to the remote mountaintop on which they lived. During 1915 they entertained nearly fifty houseguests, including Joe and Corinne Robinson Alsop, and Margaret Douglas, the wife of Walter Douglas, manager of the nearby Phelps Dodge mining company. Isabella was amused by the idiosyncrasies of her houseguests, commenting to Eleanor: "Some use 6 towels a day. Others none—and one arose at 6:30 and washed in the kitchen sink, having slept in his coat for fear of mussing the pillow! And one room was occupied by two successive guests & the wrapper of the soap never opened!!"[45]

Best of all was another visit from Eleanor and Franklin, who stopped off on their way back from the San Francisco Exposition. Eleanor was struck anew by Isabella's effort to make a home in the mountains. But she noted that "Bob was no longer his old self, and in spite of the charm which was always his, his illness was taking its toll; and these were sad days for those who loved him and could realize what a burden Isabella was carrying." The two women took courage from each other. Isabella wrote gratefully, "The privilege of seeing . . . into your life has always been the most invigorating inspiration to mine." And Eleanor replied that "to . . . see all you do and how you meet life's problems is always a help."[46]

Miss Thorpe advised Isabella on structuring the children's schooling, but the whole family participated. Isabella taught mathematics and geography, although she felt herself woefully unequal to the task. Bob taught Bible studies, with mixed results: After a dramatic rendition by their father of the story of the serpent and the apple, Bobbie's only reaction was, "Well, Daddy, was it a rattlesnake?" At night, they sat in front of the fireplace while Bob read poetry out loud. Martha recalled: "It was very cold in the wintertime, in that sixty-foot room. We would wear overcoats and [hats] and laprobes around us. Granny and Ma would sew and Bobbie and I would listen. We had to learn the poems by heart." But it was a sketchy education at best. From time to time Isabella would take the children to the school at Silver City for a day or two, to satisfy herself that they were keeping up with their peers.[47]

Even this minimal arrangement fell apart when, in June 1915, Miss Thorpe became seriously ill and was sent back to New York, where she was diagnosed with tubercular meningitis. Facing death, Miss Thorpe wrote Isabella an unabashed love letter: "I have thought for many years my capacity for loving *intensely* (man or woman) was gone completely, but you have revived it, and I love you so much it frightens me." Her death devastated Isabella, who described their relationship to Eleanor as a "sacred . . . mutual dependence." In isolation, friendships develop quickly and intensely. As Bob became more depressed and withdrawn, Miss Thorpe must have seemed a safe soul on whom Isabella could lavish her love. She also frankly missed the help. "The chores of life have run away with the days," she apologized to her grandmother. She was anxious at facing a summer without a trained nurse to help her cope with Martha's recurrent digestive upsets but philosophically wrote "as so often happens, we find ourselves obliged to mount the thing, of all others, that looked insurmountable."[48]

During the long hot summer, Bob suffered a relapse. Yet he yearned to go to England, to such an extent that Theodore Roosevelt rebuked him: "You cannot think of going abroad. . . . They would never let you go to the front or do anything else. . . . You would merely die after having been rather a nuisance and not having accomplished anything! You must not think of it, Bob." Isabella tried to divert her husband by discussing national affairs: "the one bright spot in our troubled horizon seems Mr. Bryan's elimination," she wrote her grandmother after the secretary of state's resignation.[49]

Isabella, worn out from caring for Bob and Martha, was subject to fainting spells, which she described to Eleanor in a defiantly lighthearted way: "I left a portion of my face on a chair." Patty was her mainstay. The older woman looked after the children, twelve dozen chickens, the mending, and the housework. They finally had reliable domestic help—the Chinese cook, a Mexican houseboy (although he was apt to serve the soup as if he were handling dynamite), and a maid—so that Isabella could concentrate on the children's education. Patty loved being with, and needed by, her daughter; when she left in October to take a turn with the aged Aunt Julia, she assured Isabella "you are the only *real* companionship I have, the only person on earth I talk true to." She hated to leave, lamenting to Corinne Robinson, whom she sorely missed: "I often wonder how long I shall hold together being thus torn in two, and three?"[50]

By the autumn of 1915, Isabella had been in the canyon for more than a year and was beginning to go a little stir-crazy. "Seldom an outside thought . . . an 'idea' would swoon at the far end of the canyon . . . if it tried to get in edgewise," she told Eleanor. She added, with perhaps unconscious candor, "If I weren't thirty—married many moons & waiting for my grandchildren, I'd feel a veritable princess in her hundred year sleep—waiting for her knight." She was wistful on learning that Eleanor was expecting another baby: "the strange part of it is, I believe I was built for such a career! And I envy you your right possibly more than you can think."[51]

Each New Year Isabella made a financial accounting to Unc, hoping to spare Bob the tedium and worry of accounts. In January 1916 she wrote Frank appreciatively: "You have made my life possible. . . . It is given to few to do this for another." She told him she wanted to spend her own money for small luxuries for Bob, because they made a big difference in his monotonous life. He was more de-

Isabella in the main room of Burro Mountain Homestead

pressed than ever now, because of the war. Isabella herself was beginning to feel very stale, she confessed to Frank. But she took comfort where she could. Martha, nearly ten, was becoming a real companion to her mother. John Greenway, still Isabella's admirer, turned up in nearby Tyrone on business and came out to the Homestead for dinner. Isabella also found solace in the beauty of her natural surroundings, marveling at a snowy landscape shimmering in a rose-blue sunset.[52]

Even though the United States had not yet entered the war, it seemed only a matter of time before they would be drawn in. Early in 1916, Isabella asked Eleanor about plans for a woman's defense project. She thought that a grassroots organization under a national umbrella would have real potential.[53]

Meanwhile, Isabella had her own private battle as Bob's health continued to deteriorate. He had been in bed for weeks, weak and coughing. When Dr. Bullock examined him, he found the disease slowly and relentlessly progressing. Patty bluntly reported the doctor's prognosis to Frank: "The right lung is all right, the left, rotten through and through. He's got about ten years if nothing happens. Of course, a bad go of grippe or pneumonia would take him off in a flash." Not surprisingly, Bob was overwhelmingly depressed. For the first time, Bullock became aware of Bob's mental condition. Isabella reported to Unc: "He [Dr. Bullock] came and sat down in my room with: 'Well! you haven't a G—d d—m grain of sense. Your mother hasn't a G—d d—m grain of sense, and I haven't a G—d d—m grain of sense, and what in h—l are we to do?' "[54]

Bullock consulted with Walter James, by then president of the Academy of Medicine. They agreed to try "compression," injecting gas into the infected lung. James believed that the "chronic toxemia" of TB accounted for the depressed mental state of many patients. He thought Bob might improve, physically and mentally, if he could go to the coast for a while. However, Bob refused to consider such a trip, Patty told Frank, saying "he couldn't leave this place for a moment because neither Isabella or I had one grain of sense, that we didn't know enough to take care of the plumbing let alone the children, that everything that required any mind was on him." Dr. Bullock, who admired Patty's judgment, thought Bob was "decidedly off in some directions." Patty's early admiration and friendship for Bob had badly eroded over the years. She bitterly noted that the day after the doctor had visited, four neighbors came to call, and Bob, who kept sullenly to his bed when alone with his family, rose up and conversed and was much cheered by their visit.[55]

Bob refused to move, but Isabella was longing to take the children to visit the old family farm in Kentucky. Julia Dinsmore wrote invitingly that the hillsides were pretty and green. Now eighty-three, she longed to see Martha and Bobbie romp on the grass where she and their great-grandmother, her sister Belle, used to play "in the days that are no more." Isabella had another reason for wanting to leave: She was concerned about trouble on the Mexican border. Germany was hoping to foment a Mexican uprising against the United States, to divert her from the European action. On March 9, 1916, Pancho Villa raided the border town of Columbus, New Mexico, seventy-five miles southwest of Tyrone, killing seventeen Americans. This provided Isabella with a good excuse to take her children, now eight and ten, back to her childhood home. It was Isabella's first visit in eleven difficult years. She reported to Bob: "The old place . . . seemed to beam on the fifth generation—I saw it through a flood of foolish tears—Owny's dear old bent figure in black and white calico—made by herself—hugging and kissing M. and B." The children loved exploring Dinsmore Farm, fishing in the creek and swinging from the wild grape vines, while Isabella stretched out on a blanket under a snowball bush in full bloom, comforted and cosseted by her family.[56]

Isabella had plenty of visitors, too, including TR's eldest daughter, Alice Roosevelt Longworth, now living in Cincinnati. Alice, though married to Ohio congressman Nicholas Longworth, remained as lively as ever, Isabella reported to Eleanor. Although Alice often teased her more serious cousin, Eleanor, Alice did appreciate, Isabella wrote, that Eleanor did her job in Washington better than anyone else. Pleased with having made the pilgrimage to Boone with her children at last, Isabella returned home ready to take on new challenges after her six-week holiday.[57]

CHAPTER FIVE ∞∞∞∞∞∞∞∞∞∞∞∞∞∞∞∞∞

"Potato Patriotism"

BOB HAD RALLIED during the tense border situation, sending away for Springfield rifles and investing in road repair; patrolling the border gave him a sense of contributing to the war effort. The men of the community made an emergency plan to use the large, well-built Burro Mountain Homestead as a defensive position in case of attack. Eventually, the Army was sent to chase Villa back to Mexico, and the Arizona and New Mexico National Guards were stationed along the Mexican border to keep the peace. As summer wore on, though, Bob relapsed. Weak and miserable, he lay on the couch all day, except, as Isabella told Patty, "when I go to town, as yesterday, when he spends all his time calling everyone in the county to locate me. Literally, he called twelve different times in three hours." Isabella hoped he would be diverted once again by the political situation, as 1916 was a presidential election year. John Greenway had attended the Progressive Convention in Chicago, which had nominated Theodore Roosevelt, but Roosevelt declined, throwing his support to the Republican nominee, Charles Evans

∞∞∞∞∞∞∞∞∞∞∞∞∞∞∞∞∞∞∞∞∞∞∞

Hughes. With the cool weather, Bob revived remarkably. In October he went by himself to Albuquerque to hear Roosevelt give a speech. Once home, he continued to take a lively interest in national and international affairs, devoting "considerable time daily to bury Wilson and kill Germans," Isabella reported to Eleanor.[1]

Isabella's six years in New Mexico had oscillated between the debilitating summers and winter rounds of colds and flu. At the end of 1916, she faced an unusually severe six-week siege, with the governess, the cook, and the houseboy all ill. She began to feel as though she were running a hospital, she told Olivia. "I shut my eyes & see *trays* & hot water bottles and pills as far as the eye can reach." Patty arrived to help, but Isabella was worried about her, too; her mother seemed tired. Patty confessed privately to Corinne Robinson, "I want to come and play with you . . . to motor with you, and be frivolous and forgetful—and happy. It has been so long since I was frivolous or even pretended I was young. . . . I am busy all the time." But she thought that Isabella needed a break even more. Patty reported to Frank that "Bob never thinks of or considers her in any way and nothing makes him as furious as to have anyone else do it." Bob did resent her friends and family thinking she was overworked, remarking to Isabella that if her friends had a fraction of her health, they would be doing well. He told Frank that any threat to her well-being came from going off to dances and dinners and coming home late in all kinds of weather.[2]

In spite of a few bouts of merriment, Isabella admitted to Unc in early January 1917 that she felt horribly stale and reasoned she was not much good to anyone in that state. Patty's arrival, together with another nurse-governess, gave Isabella the chance to get away. She planned a trip East with Walter and Margaret Douglas in their private railroad car. Bob endorsed the plan, telling Frank he thought such trips should be frequent and normal. But he was not at all pleased with the Douglases' plan to leave via Bisbee, where Isabella would see John Greenway. In fact, as the Douglases lingered in Arizona for more than two weeks, Bob became quite upset, complaining to Isabella of "a certain lack of sincerity and openness between ourselves, an apparent unwillingness . . . to have everything ready to lay on the table. The 'backstairs' will quickly creep in . . . and life become common and unclean for the family and all of us." He urged her to "say what you want to do and do it, openly. I have never tried to stop your doing anything that looks reasonable," even though she was "a young woman of fatal attractions."[3]

Once back East, Isabella embarked on a lively time; Aunt Julia, visiting the Cutcheons, reported to Patty that Isabella was continuously on the move but warned Patty not to tell Bob. Bob, though, had recovered his composure, now that she was no longer in John Greenway territory. He wrote Frank, "They tell me you can't see [Isabella] for dust, but that it all means she is having a good time. If you could tame her and rub her down a little and see she cools off . . . before starting home, we'd all feel easier." He must have been pleased, too, when she wrote "Dads, what a true happiness it would be to be going with you to all these parties."[4]

Isabella spent a week in Washington, where she and Eleanor attended the final session of Congress until nearly two in the morning. "The Senators were all saying loving farewells to each other," she wrote Bob. "I never knew that men could be so silly, tendering each other gentle and loving eloquence by the yard." People were depressed by the government's inaction in the war, especially after Germany had resumed unrestricted submarine warfare on February 1. Isabella herself despaired of anything happening unless a provocation occurred, most likely, she thought, on the Mexican border. Her fears intensified when, on March 1, Wilson announced that the United States had intercepted a German message to Mexico, promising the return of Arizona, New Mexico, and Texas in exchange for support. Eastern reporting on the West was very poor, she complained to Bob; periodicals like *The New Republic* were simply writing about the West from hearsay.[5]

On April 6, 1917, soon after Isabella's return home, the United States declared war on Germany. Theodore Roosevelt at once offered to raise a volunteer regiment like the Rough Riders. John Greenway began recruiting volunteers for him in Arizona, and Bob Ferguson was doing what he could in New Mexico, although any exertion still put him back in bed. Both houses of Congress approved the Roosevelt regiment, but President Wilson refused to authorize it. Bob, meanwhile, kept harping on preparedness, alarming Isabella, who feared that the many Germans living in Mexico might join forces with Pancho Villa in another attack. Unc tried to reassure her, explaining that Bob just wanted "to excite people to take protective measures . . . he doesn't understand how it acts on your nerves, nor how much less good your nerves are than they used to be."[6]

Isabella had the opportunity to channel her nervous energy into war work when the governor's wife, Maude Lindsay, tapped her to organize the Woman's Auxiliary of the Council of Defense for New Mexico in Grant and Luna Counties. Isabella was to instruct women in economizing, planting, and canning. "Everyone is concentrating on 'potato patriotism,'" Isabella noted to her Aunt Mary Selmes. She was also active in the Red Cross, helping to start a chapter in Tyrone. She enrolled in first aid classes there with ten-year-old Martha. Their trips to town became an adventure when they returned late at night over eight miles of treacherous roads, Martha holding a cocked pistol while her mother drove. Isabella covered some 3,500 miles in their new car, a Hupmobile.[7]

Isabella organized the Defense Council through local precincts, nine in Luna County and thirty-one in Grant, with offices in all the big towns. In one precinct, she used fifteen secretaries for two days to write letters to 250 women, all of whom signed the Hoover Pledge to observe "wheatless and meatless" days. She wryly remarked that most of them were already eating less than the Hoover Pledge required. She also observed that those who had a maid volunteered less time than those who were already doing everything for good-sized families. Isabella visited each precinct with the state canner to give demonstrations and was stunned to learn one woman had walked ten miles to see them. That summer, the Fergusons held a fund-raising fair for 450 people, carting a piano up the mountain road to provide music for dancing until nearly midnight. They had a bar, a roulette manned by three sheriffs, a millinery booth, hot dogs, ice cream cones, lemonade, and cake, netting several hundred dollars for the Red Cross Auxiliary. By late August, Isabella proudly reported that Grant County was leading the state in ground planted, conservation started, and wool given out for knitting. It was the best possible training for political work. She was even getting fan mail, including a letter from one woman who wondered if it would be "too intimate" to ask for a photograph.[8]

While Isabella was making a good name for herself among the citizenry, John Greenway had become involved in what was later called "one of the bitterest episodes in the history of labor relations in the United States," the Bisbee Deportation. On June 27, 1917, members of the Industrial Workers of the World (IWW or "Wobblies"), led a strike against Phelps Dodge and the Calumet and Arizona Copper Company in Bisbee. Although the IWW members numbered only around four hundred, nearly two thousand other workers, about half of the Bisbee miners, joined in, hoping for an increase in wages commensurate with the wartime rise in copper prices. Although no striker violence was reported in the newspaper, Greenway claimed that the strikers threatened public safety. He also regarded a strike in wartime as treasonous. He convinced Cochise County sheriff Harry Wheeler, a fellow Rough Rider, that the strikers should be deported. Although Wheeler later took responsibility for the action, Greenway organized it. On July 17, a posse of around two thousand men arrested slightly more than two thousand strikers. Greenway begged the men one last time to return to work; about half did so. The remaining 1,186 were herded into twenty-three waiting boxcars of the El Paso and Southwestern Railroad, a subsidiary of Phelps Dodge, and deported to Columbus, New Mexico, almost two hundred miles away. A year later, in May 1918, Greenway, along with a number of other mining company officials, was indicted for conspiracy to violate the rights of citizens to peaceably reside in the state of Arizona. By then, Greenway was serving in France. When he returned home, he faced the possibility of a jail term, but eventually charges against the defendants were dismissed. Nevertheless, this vigilante action was widely condemned and would come back to haunt Greenway when he began to consider a role for himself in politics.[9]

John and Isabella had a chance to meet in New York that autumn. Frank Cutcheon had been offered a staff job with General John Pershing, commander of the American Expeditionary Force (AEF), and was preparing to go overseas. Before he sailed, Isabella went East with the children to confer with him about her financial affairs and to say farewell. John Greenway was in New York preparing to leave for France as a major in the Engineer Officers Reserve Corps. He later told Isabella she had inspired him to ask for assignment overseas. His enlistment form depicts a man in the prime of life: "Height—6′1″; weight—194; hair—brown; eyes—blue-gray; complexion—tanned; physical condition—good; experience in handling men, riding, swimming, shooting, explosives, automobile driving, locomotive engineer, can operate a machine gun." John, scheduled to depart at the end of October, spent most of his last remaining days with Isabella, most properly in the company of his sister Sadie and sister-in-law Harriet. John and Isabella attended a final, unforgettable dinner at Walter and Margaret Douglas's New York house; for the next twelve months he would cherish the memory of Isabella in a white dress with a spray of roses and forget-me-nots on the bodice. Before they parted, John kissed the flowers and whispered one tender question.[10]

Isabella mentioned casually in a letter to Bob that she had seen

John C. Greenway in World War I

Greenway, among others. Bob, however, may have had some inkling of the situation, or some fear. He had written only once in two weeks, prompting Isabella to ask if she should return home. A week later, she received a huge envelope from him but was disappointed to find it contained nothing but accounts. Perhaps his neglect may have made her feel freer to bestow her love elsewhere. John and Isabella, who had faithfully honored their promise to Bob never to be alone together, were permitted one small lapse before John left for battle. Margaret Douglas, who knew their secret, was supposed to be chaperoning them. But she allowed Isabella a half-hour ride in a hansom cab through Central Park alone with John just before he sailed. John arrived in France on November 17, after a rough and sometimes anxious crossing beset with U-boats, and promptly cabled Cutcheon's office: "Ferguson. Arrived Safely. Greenway." Unc, too, was aware of the situation.[11]

John began to write Isabella, at first very circumspectly. In an early letter, he recalled that as his ship had plowed through darkness, wind and rain, he thought of the past and the future rather than the grim present. In another letter, he referred to their time at the Douglases', "and the beautiful things we talked of." At the end of four weeks, he had sent her two cables and five letters but had yet to hear anything back. Finally, after forty-five anxious days, five letters from Isabella arrived at once. Bob permitted the wartime correspondence between John and Isabella because he knew firsthand the solace letters could bring to a soldier.[12]

Isabella and the children returned to their New Mexico home on December 4, and Bob, looking wan, met their train in Silver City. Isabella, somewhat stricken by his appearance, vowed to limit her outside activities, to concentrate on taking care of Bob and schooling the children five days a week. They had a quiet winter, snowed in, with few visitors. Isabella mused to her Aunt Mary, "All who used to come are in France or working for those there, and our circle is narrowed to a handful. . . . We live quite primitively. . . . We feel it is our 'bit.' " A letter from Eleanor prompted her to exclaim: "Anything you send means such a pleasant touch from the outside." Eleanor had been working for the Red Cross in Washington, where, she said, "we all try . . . to be more people than we've ever been before," and where she was receiving "a liberal education in the American soldier." A mutual friend informed Isabella: "Eleanor works all day and half the night. . . . I used to make mild suggestions that she might sometimes take one hour out of the 24 to come and sit with me in the garden, but she merely looked at me as though I were wildly insane and said it was impossible." Eleanor thought Isabella was also working too hard. "Bob's letter . . . sounded as though you must have had a lot on your shoulders but of course you wouldn't say so if you were nearly dead." She added wistfully, "How I wish often and often that only happiness ought to lie along your path but that never is the lot of really fine people."[13]

Letters from John Greenway must have provided yet another pleasant touch. In one he thanked her for socks made "by your dear hands" and forwarded via Belle Eckles. A letter two weeks later was more explicit: "I think of the Burros, the pines, a gentle voice and the week of parting." She received many letters from Greenway during his year of service. Mostly, they opened with only her name, no other salutation, and closed "Aff'ly Jno." Were they purposely cool in case anyone saw them? For Isabella saved them. A line, "Time passes like a flash," perhaps code for a love message, appears in almost every note. John had applied to the artillery, hoping to "get on the line." In March, he got his wish, traveling to the front with the 1st Engineer Battalion, 1st Infantry Division. "My thoughts are of you," he assured Isabella. "I have no regrets." A battle on the western front had been raging for a week—"the Gettysburg of this war," as John saw it; he was among the first Americans to see action. In mid-April John and his unit marched into what became known as the Picardy offensive. He was working on the front-line trenches, "with which only I am familiar." He had come under shell fire and was relieved to find he was not afraid. "One can't help thinking of the disgrace if the nerves won't stand the racket," he confessed. Though he had been under fire in Cuba, the intensity of this new warfare and perhaps his age—forty-six—must have made him wonder if he was still up to fighting.[14]

Danger made John less constrained in his letters to Isabella. On his way into battle he wrote: "Cold and damp but in spite of this violets show shyly along the roadside . . . 3 oh joyful letters from you today." Some of his letters must have left her desperately frightened,

like his account of inspecting the line with an officer he was reliev-
ing. Greenway headed down the line; when he returned, he found
the officer had been killed by a shell. Accounts of his doings alternated with veiled promises: "Have had no leave yet and see none in
sight. But refresh myself with thoughts of the homeland and the
deep enjoyment that must come when I return there." At times he
could not contain himself. In a letter written at midnight, he cried
out: "Oh for a touch of your hand!"[15]

Life in New Mexico was mundane by comparison. Isabella was
struggling to raise hundreds of chickens. Bob and the children,
then ten and twelve, had put in a vegetable garden and took their
produce to Tyrone in a horse-drawn wagon to sell at the company
store. Martha looked forward to these trips for the novelty of buying ginger ale and pimento-stuffed olives, but Bob, though his vegetables fetched a very respectable $900, grumbled that their efforts
were mere "futilities."[16]

Isabella was soon drafted herself. At the start of June, Governor
W. E. Lindsey named her to head the Women's Land Army for the
State of New Mexico, to build on her earlier work for the Women's
Council of State Defense. In England, France and Canada, much of
the farm work was being done by women, as men were called out
into the battlefields, and in the United States, Women's Land Ar-
mies had already been established in several states. The governor's
wife, Maude Lindsey, serving as chairman, wrote Isabella that
women needed to be shown that more could be done than knitting
socks and making surgical dressings. In the East, she said, many educated women of social position were taking up manual labor. Isabella was responsible for organization, publicity, financing, and
housing. She wrote big producers asking them to estimate what labor they might need but quickly learned that farmers were far from
eager to have women work in the fields; they believed women
should work indoors, while men who were working indoors should
do farm work. But they conceded that they would use the women if

they needed to. Isabella's Las Cruces chairwoman wrote plausibly that "the best way to convince them is to show them. One successful unit would be more convincing than any amount of reasoning."[17]

Isabella and her team set out to convince skeptics by harvesting thirty acres of hay. Housing and utensils were supplied, but the women brought their bedding and did their own cooking, so as not to burden the farmers' wives. Patty joined Isabella on the hay harvest, where the women put up sixteen tons of alfalfa. The older woman entered into the work enthusiastically, writing Corinne: "I have had a feeling of youth returned as I slept under cottonwood and heard the field larks yodel. . . . I feel I am doing more good here than I could anywhere else. . . . At least Isabella doesn't have to do it if I do it first." Isabella took a less romantic view: They were sleeping "on the floor of squalid farm houses, with all our worldly possessions in a suitcase. . . . Off before the sun was up and back after dark, for $2.50 a day."[18]

They also struggled with illness. Patty suffered from gout and rheumatism, as well as a spell of what was thought to be malaria. More alarmingly, an epidemic of influenza swept through the country in the fall of 1918, resulting in five hundred thousand deaths; Land Army workers in other parts of New Mexico had already died. In October, Isabella was up in the mountains with a crew of fifty women picking, grading, and packing a bumper crop of apples. She knew that influenza was quite extensive in the area; she had had to nurse several of her women until they could be taken to the nearest hospital twenty miles away. They were touchingly grateful. One said: "I really don't know what we would have done without so great a woman as you are." Another gushed: "[Y]ou was like a fairy Godmother to all of us." Isabella made light of the danger of influenza, noting that the cold and starvation rations seemed to be proof against infection. One afternoon, though, she felt feverish and feared she might be coming down with flu. She took her bedding

The Women's Land Army, 1918. Isabella, top left; Bobbie, top, fourth from left; Patty, center, holding pole; Martha in haystack, right

and lay down under a tree, where she consumed vast amounts of quinine, then considered a cure-all. The next day she felt fine again. Worldwide, the influenza epidemic of 1918–1919 killed more than twenty million people, many more than died in the war. In a very real sense, Isabella was at the front lines in her war work.[19]

Bob was anxious about Isabella. He claimed the fruit growers were so greedy to harvest their crops they had hired sick men and women from Alamogordo where there had been five hundred cases of influenza, and four or five deaths a day. Isabella tried to reassure Bob, but when she asked him to be sure the Hupmobile was in running order—"It may get to a point where some one might have to fetch me out of here"—Bob, who had been in bed, got up and drove to Mountain Park, nearly 150 miles from Tyrone, to bring her

Isabella Ferguson in the Women's Land Army

home. Isabella was proud of her summer's work: cutting hay, harvesting corn, putting up silage. They had filled over a hundred carloads of apples, six hundred boxes in each car. Other groups picked beans, picked and canned tomatoes, and picked and packed other produce. Isabella told her Aunt Mary that it had been an amazing experience—"all ages, kinds and classes living together"—but a successful one. Once again, she was gaining valuable expertise for public life. Isabella's organizational work was recognized when, after the Armistice, she was asked to chair the Land Service Committee for New Mexico, to increase food production. She was also named as women's representative to the State Labor and Reconstruction Board.[20]

Her work in the field had put a temporary halt to her letters to John Greenway. By the end of August, he had not heard from her for more than eight weeks. He wrote as always, "Time passes like a flash," but this time he added wistfully, "it seems like ten years since I left Arizona." The next day he wrote more explicitly, "Only peace and friends' kindness and home seems of importance at this moment. . . . Time passes like a flash in thinking of 'blessed associations.'" He had seen action in many of the major battles. In May he dug trenches for the attack at Cantigny. In June he took part in the decisive second battle of the Marne, when Marines stopped the German drive on Paris at Belleau Wood. They endured eight sleepless days and nights but finally drove the Germans back twenty kilometers, albeit with heavy losses. Belleau Wood was the scene of savage fighting, and Greenway hardly expected to come out alive. "We went in with 42 officers and came out with six," he later told Isabella. "I have really drunk deeply . . . of the duty I owe my country." More prosaically he noted, "I need socks, will you send me a pair?" Despite his own victories, he commended her for making a double contribution. One was her direct effort: He admired her leadership of the "lady laborer movement." Another was convincing him that his duty lay on the firing line, for which he thanked her.[21]

Greenway had survived thus far, but Quentin Roosevelt, TR's youngest, had been shot down over France. The father was devastated, though proud his son had died like a war hawk fighting to the last. Theodore wrote his old companion-in-arms, Bob Ferguson: "When you and I had the chance we did our duty, although it was on such an infinitely smaller scale; indeed if I had not myself gone to war in my day I don't think I could have borne to send my sons to face death now." He concluded, though, that "there are things worse than death and for nothing under Heaven would I have had my sons act otherwise than as they have acted." He listed the wounds and honors garnered by his other sons but admitted, "Ugh! It isn't pleasant for the old man to be reduced to doing nothing but tally-tally." Bob doubtless felt the same, and it must have been galling to him to hear of Greenway's impressive war record.[22]

In mid-August John Greenway, by then transferred to the 26th "Yankee" Division in the 101st Infantry Regiment, and promoted to lieutenant colonel, took part in the St. Mihiel salient just south of Verdun. Before the battle, he wrote Isabella from his position "tucked away in a little dugout on a bleak hillside at 12 pm with a sputtering candle along side." Two weeks of incessant rain had left the battle fields afloat with mud. The guns of Verdun were booming in the distance. "We go in an attack within a few hours. But I feel I have gone unscathed so far [and] I will . . . come back to hear you say well done." Later, he fought in the Meuse-Argonne offensive; the splendid emotions of battle were worth the risk, he wrote Isabella. Meanwhile, knowing he was in danger, Isabella endured long nights of anguish and hope, praying under the stars. Promoted again to a full colonel, John Greenway was later awarded a Distinguished Service Cross for bravery under fire, and the French Croix de Guerre. Eventually he would receive a brevet promotion to brigadier general.[23]

The Armistice on November 11, 1918, came exactly one year after Greenway landed in France. He could hardly grasp that the war was over, he told Isabella. He felt grateful for having had the opportunity to serve, and for having survived. After the cease-fire, he had wound up in a hospital with "trench fever," as well as "cooties, the itch, and every conceivable unpleasant thing that goes with the army," he reported. He had also suffered from inhaling mustard gas. But he revived quickly on being told he could leave on the next hospital train and would arrive in New York by the end of the year. Isabella could not restrain her joy: "John! That you are *coming home* and *getting well* is my only thought. . . . I am so utterly happy it leaves little or no room for the selfish desire to greet you." She urged him to rest. "It must take time to feel your old self. But the wonderful part is you can never feel your old self again—nor can any of us—we must always walk in the new radiance of the peace you have earned for us." Their passion for each other was fueled by their shared ideals, hers in insisting he go and his in wanting to.[24]

She could not come to greet him in person but hoped that he would go to see Margaret Douglas and reminisce in her living room. John's safe homecoming eroded his caution, too. He wrote Isabella: "I got the *wonderful letter* through Mrs. Selmes. The dearest, delightfulest letter ever written." Patty, too, must have known of and approved their relationship. At Isabella's request John had destroyed all her letters to him, but now he begged for a reprieve: "One letter you must let me keep?" She did. In his reply, John enclosed an official letter from Pershing's assistant chief of staff, detailing his impressive record. "This I hand to you because it was you who sent me and it was for you I went. I gave the best that was in me and am content in the feeling that I did my utmost. . . . I send it laden with my love."[25]

Next to Isabella, John said, Theodore Roosevelt had been his greatest inspiration. Soon after Greenway's homecoming, on January 4, he paid a visit to his old Colonel. Roosevelt was close to death, pale, with swollen hands, but he sat erect and asked, in a husky voice, for the news. They talked for an hour of many things. Two days later Roosevelt was dead. John attended Roosevelt's simple and moving funeral: "We have both lost a great friend," he told Isabella sadly.[26]

With John safely home, Isabella could not grieve for long. Her birthday in March found her in a mood of elation, writing Patty to thank her for the gift of life: "I love living and wouldn't have missed it for worlds!" Patty, on the other hand, was overwhelmingly depressed. She had, after all, been closer to Roosevelt than Isabella had. And back in Boone, she was going through terrible times, as she wrote her sister-in-law Mary Selmes: "I didn't . . . think Fate had anything in store so bad—even for me." She had accidentally run over Aunt Julia, her "own Mommy," with her car. Luckily, the ground was soft with rain and Julia escaped with no broken bones. But she was eighty-six and had to stay in bed for a month. The effect was almost worse on Patty: "To think I was the instrument selected to knock her out in her brave struggle against old age and its horrors has left me grim. . . . When my time comes to go, I want you to know how glad I shall be, how I have hated life, with all its agonies, pretenses, hypocrisies, injustice and cruelty." But she added, "my greatest comfort is that the one human being for whom I am responsible, Isabella, loves life and feels differently about it all."[27]

Isabella, who had not left the Homestead for eighteen months, now rented a cottage in Santa Barbara for April, May, and June. She reveled in the bracing sea breezes and warm water, swimming naked under the moonlight, playing baseball with the children on the beach, and skipping rope with seaweed. Bobbie and Martha were less enthralled; they were homesick for the Burro Mountains. John Greenway was nearby, relaxing with his brother. Bob may have found this out; he complained that Isabella was not being candid. She answered that she appreciated his attempt to save her "from the rocks," but did not think she had ever done anything that would reflect harmfully on him or their family. She added, "A very long time ago I decided not to bring up quite a number of subjects with you, believing from your attitude on repeated such attempts that you either did not wish to discuss them or . . . had nothing to say on the subject . . . often I wish you would talk to me . . . believing it helps to lift unjustified worry." She concluded, "I cannot believe that you meant certain things in your letter, so I will neither refer to them or worry about them."[28]

Bob was on edge for another reason, too. His brother Ronald, who was childless, wanted Bobbie to be his heir but insisted that the boy be educated in Britain. Bob apologized to Isabella for having "written shortly." He explained that he had received two letters on one day, Ronald's "demanding the total surrender of my entire family (for that is what it meant)" and a "casual note in the same mail from you saying the children would have to spend at least six months in every year away from here [for their schooling]. . . . I was naturally bound to think that my relatives had all ceased to think . . . with any regard for my existence." Nevertheless, Bob thought he and Isabella needed to consider both propositions dispassionately, for the best interests of the children. Isabella, for her part, was dismayed to learn from Frank Cutcheon that she had no legal rights if she disagreed with any plans made by the men. "The only voice I might have in the whole is what Bob, Ronald and you may choose, out of courtesy, to offer me," she protested.[29]

Bob also rebuked Isabella for having a good time while he languished at home. She bristled: "I do not get the pleasure out of my sojourns that you evidently imagine, though I write as cheerfully as possible, while picturing your isolation and ill health." At the end of May, she took Bobbie to Los Angeles to have his tonsils out. Isabella and the two children spent a week in a hotel while he recuperated; she told Eleanor it was "the best week I've had in years," a testimony to Isabella's remarkable ability to enjoy life, even under trying circumstances.[30]

Chapter Five

Her one regret was not having seen Eleanor Roosevelt over the summer—"The best I have is always yours," Isabella wrote Eleanor that fall, "and I depend on you as on no one." Eleanor had been through a difficult year herself. After discovering Franklin's affair with her social secretary, Lucy Mercer, Eleanor had not had the heart to write Isabella for many months. When she finally wrote on July 11, she alluded indirectly to her heartbreak: "This past year has rather got the better of me. It has been so full of all kinds of things that I still have a breathless, hunted feeling about it." She assured Isabella that "though I don't write, my feelings never change." She wrote again a few weeks later, "You mean more to me every year and your life and the way you have faced it . . . has meant so much to me in example and inspiration."[31]

Isabella, back in New Mexico, had not been a good correspondent, either. "Dear soul, there's nothing from cooking to house painting that hasn't taken me from my desk," she confessed, but "somehow I know you will understand." Isabella had been even busier than usual: "I sometimes lie down, I never sit down," she told her Aunt Mary. Housework began at 6:30 or 7, and she was on the run until she tumbled into bed. In addition to housekeeping, she still had to oversee the children's education. She wanted to keep the children at home a little while longer, explaining to Eleanor, "Were we to leave Bob until it is an absolute necessity, I always feel that the children would have failed their first duty. For, after all, Bob is their first problem and they must help make his years possible while they can." Eleanor admired her friend's steadfastness and courage: "I need your help and advice in so many ways for I never want anyone as I want you. . . . I know no one, least of all myself, who could have done what you've done with your life so far." After the Lucy Mercer affair, Eleanor and Franklin's marriage continued as a political partnership. Eleanor had sent Isabella a family photograph at Christmas, about which Isabella had only one regret: "It looks alarmingly like the ones of families that end up in the White House, and that

I'm not sure I would wish for anyone I loved." Isabella herself had made a foray into politics, serving on the five-member Grant County Board of Education, of which Belle Eckles was president.[32]

In January 1920, Isabella wrote Eleanor some surprising news, warning her to "take hold of something *very tight*." Bob had rallied to an amazing extent and had gone to California with his brother Hector, "after ten years without budging," Isabella said. "It's like suddenly finding yourself adrift in the South Seas after picking your way through icebergs for years." Letters at this time between Bob and Isabella showed they retained their affection for each other. She wrote to send "a kiss so rapid you don't know what's happened and can't possibly catch me." Bob had gone to Santa Barbara to look into schools for the children. Hard as it was to face up to their going away, he realized they would need some proper schooling by the following year if they wanted to go to Eastern colleges. He had also proved to himself that he could go to the coast to visit them. He was looking to buy a cottage, but Isabella suggested they might build a little house that they could later rent out. In mid-March, Bob and Isabella went to Santa Barbara together and bought a lot. "Bob pretends it's wholly my doing," Isabella reported to Unc, "but is really keen as mustard and interested as I haven't seen him in years." Unc replied dryly that "your enthusiasm seems to be a guaranty that there is a good deal of desirability, whether or not a good deal of wisdom, in what you are doing."[33]

Bob was well, but Patty, who had been staying in New Mexico with the children, suddenly fell ill with what seemed to be jaundice. Isabella rushed back to New Mexico. She and her mother took the next train east, through shrieking sandstorms, to New York. Distraught, Isabella wired John, "Mother making splendid fight for life. There is hope. Help us with your thoughts." Patty was diagnosed with "soft gallstones," and improved slowly but steadily over the next three weeks. Isabella returned to New Mexico in late May but immediately set off again for Santa Barbara to start "the small-

est of little shelters" for herself and Martha, who would be attending a day school in the fall, while Bobbie went to boarding
school nearby. The children were growing up fast. Bobbie had invested his savings in calves; that summer, at twelve, he had branded
and inoculated them with the help of a cowboy, who informed Isabella, "This baby of yours is a man!" Martha, thirteen, was now the
same height as her mother, but, as Isabella observed to Aunt Mary,
"the shocking part of it all is I don't feel a day older than Martha."[34]
She was thirty-four.

For a while, politics had receded into the background, but, with
a presidential election looming, the Progressives were girding
themselves once again for battle. The death of their old leader, Theodore Roosevelt, had changed the political landscape entirely. Isabella was appalled by the outcome of the 1920 Republican Convention, where Ohio senator Warren G. Harding was nominated in an
old-fashioned back-room political deal. "What will we come to in
this country with the high-handed methods of the old machine Republicans?" she wondered. John Greenway, who had become popular throughout the state, was being urged by Arizona Republicans
to run for the Senate. He declined when the GOP nominated Harding, who had offended Greenway by calling Theodore Roosevelt
the "Benedict Arnold" of his party, for his third-party bid in 1912.
Greenway liked the Democrats' proposal for a League of Nations;
he had twice been to war and mourned the loss of courageous
youth on the battlefield. Many Progressive Republicans were re-
thinking their allegiance.[35]

The Democrats nominated Ohio governor James Cox and, for
vice president, picked none other than Franklin D. Roosevelt. Now,
instead of apologizing for not writing Eleanor, Isabella feared it was
an imposition to write to her friend when she was busy with the
campaign and assured her, "if I don't hear a word from you I'll understand *absolutely* & it would be a great comfort to me to think that
if you had an inspiration to write me a line you will, instead, stretch

A portrait of Robert Munro Ferguson by Bay Emmett Rand

out with a good book." She sent Eleanor a copy of Ralph Waldo Emerson's essays, noting, "They have meant more to me than any influence almost in the world, and I attribute most that has spelt happiness to their interpretation of life." Isabella was as usual going flat out herself. Men who had come for the cattle roundup filled the house, and they had to take turns at the dinner table. She was also coaching the children for school and continuing her work on the school board, as well as helping all the neighbors.[36]

In the fall of 1920, Isabella and Patty took the children to Santa Barbara and enrolled them in school for the first time in their lives. Martha was just fourteen and Bobbie twelve. Isabella ruefully admitted, "I don't see how Bobbie will stand it," and Unc chipped in to buy him a horse for consolation. Now that the Fergusons were back in civilization, Mammy returned. Bob tried to resign himself to staying alone at the Homestead. "I firmly believe it's the only place I can hang on for a period," he wrote Frank. But Isabella found the prospect of living apart for a prolonged period very unsatisfactory. "I'll do my part for this school year," she told Bob, "but will not undertake it again, it is too much of a strain mentally and financially." The strain came through in their letters. Bob, as usual, was finding fault with her behavior, complaining that she was not finding time for her family. Isabella, in a twelve-page letter, patiently accounted for all her activities, concluding: "my time has not been distracted, but absolutely concentrated steadily and quietly and successfully, and I am very pleased with the result of two well children doing good work." His criticism may have resulted from feeling isolated and useless. He confessed to Frank: "I realize Isabella has had a hectic time, and I have been able to do nothing to help her but give idle advice from a distance—a futile proceeding."[37]

Bob joined the family for Christmas, and the reunion smoothed over tensions that had built up during their separation. When he returned to the Burro Mountains, Isabella got an amazing letter from her husband, telling her how happy he was with everything. "You don't realize how much you've done for me," he wrote. Isabella, too, made an effort to show her appreciation. "Dads, dearest, let me say *to* you what I do so often say *of* you. One of the everlasting wonders that I shall carry through my life is your never having complained once, and the good cheer and interest you have, when too often you must have been unmercifully tired. . . . I bless you for your supreme courage, which I think the children begin to see too. . . . I think sometimes we don't say aloud (often enough) the good things we think." When school finished, Isabella and the children went back to New Mexico in time for roundup and its attendant chaos. The children were happily back in the saddle, riding with the cowboys, and their spirited mother took part as well. Bob bragged to a cousin that she had become "a wilder cowboy than either child." Isabella described the experience to Eleanor: "Suffering in all spots I stayed in the saddle from 6:30 am til 6 pm. House-keeping consisted in making beds when the men washed up for supper. I wouldn't have missed it for worlds."[38]

Bob was not doing well; only occasionally could he get up and dress. Isabella reported to Patty that he was "shockingly thin and a yellow-blue color. . . . He doesn't cough constantly [but] when he does it is of a dreadfully deep and nauseating quality. . . . Yesterday, after clipping a few hollyhocks, [he] sank white and exhausted into a chair." She added, "If I were as ill as he is I couldn't do anything but complain." Patty, who was taking care of eighty-eight-year-old Julia, was another concern. But Isabella determinedly "shoved a good deal behind me and have collected immense serenity and resource," she told her mother.[39]

Now it was Eleanor's turn to cope with an invalid husband. On August 14, Franklin Roosevelt contracted polio at Campobello. Isabella heard the news three weeks later but, surprisingly, delayed writing until nearly the end of the year, when she apologized remorsefully, "I can truly say that hardly an *hour* has gone by in

Left to right: Martha, Frank Cutcheon, Bobbie, Patty, Bob, Isabella, c. 1920

this many months, especially since Franklin's illness that I haven't thought of you *adoringly* and prayed for you too. . . . I shall just beg you to send me a little line of forgiveness and hope that 1922 will prove me a worthier friend." She shared her own hard-won insights, confident she would now be understood: "When great difficulties come to us in extreme youth we stagger along creditably because we are unable to see the whole truth and have abundant strength. When distress comes to us in older age we face up to it steadily and splendidly, partly through resignation and a sense of finish. When it comes to us at yours and my ages, I believe it is the hardest of all tests because ours are the years when clear perception has come and with it the intense desire to live while we may. . . . It is above all hard to mark time at our ages, no matter what spiritual interpretation we try to attach to the cause."[40]

That fall, their doctor diagnosed Bob with a kidney condition, warning that he was now a much sicker man. Bob observed wryly to Eleanor: "I could tell the good man I had been sick for quite a considerable time—and that it's 'old sing-sing, it's the same old thing'—but I suppose he wouldn't have seen the foolishness of it." He hoped to "thumb-nose" the doctor in the spring by rallying. Ignoring the doctor's warning that cold was especially bad for his condition, they all gathered at the Homestead for Christmas, when Bob rejoiced in a snowfall that made a "blaze of blue and white all around." Then he reluctantly agreed to return with the family to Santa Barbara, grumbling, "they don't trust me alone in the sticks."[41]

CHAPTER SIX ∿∿∿∿∿∿∿∿∿∿∿∿∿∿

"The Most Splendid Rainbow after the Storm"

THE NEXT TWO YEARS would be a time to try Isabella's soul, a time of unremitting illness and death. In the spring of 1922, her mother fell ill with flu and pleurisy, complicated by a weak heart. Isabella wired Unc: "Outlook very uncertain. Please tell her friends to hope with us." Unc sped out to Santa Barbara on the fastest trains, which, to his anxious mind, seemed excruciatingly slow. Isabella in her anguish turned to John, wiring: "Mother making splendid fight for life. There is hope. Help us with your thoughts." For the next four months, Isabella spent most of her time at the hospital, where her mother was alternately delirious and unconscious. Isabella wrote Eleanor during one of her vigils: "We slipped in and out of that valley so many times, hand in hand." To make matters worse, both children came down with whooping cough, and Isabella was nursing practically around the clock. By August 10, Patty had recovered, but she was still confused. Isabella, suspecting the doctors were overmedicating her, took her mother back to New Mexico in hopes that fresh air would clear her head. Within a month, Patty began to feel more like herself again.[1]

∿∿∿∿∿∿∿∿∿∿∿∿∿∿∿∿∿∿

Isabella did not have much respite. The family returned to Santa Barbara in mid-September for the start of school. Just two weeks later, after fourteen years of struggle, Bob Ferguson died. On October 3, he collapsed with sudden kidney failure. The following night, as he lay in fourteen-year-old Bobbie's arms, with Isabella and Martha by his side, Isabella said to him lovingly, "Bob, you've made me very happy," and he slipped away. They took him back to Boone on the train. When Isabella walked into the door at Dinsmore Farm, the first thing she saw was Bob's hat, hanging where he had left it eighteen years before, when he was courting her. Back in Santa Barbara, the children tried to bear up. Martha was too distressed to look at her father's room and moved in with Patty, who was staying in a house the Cutcheons had built next door. But Bobbie would not give in to his grief, remembering that his father had said, "No matter what happens, one must go on with the rest of the world." Isabella, too, tried to carry on. Six weeks after the funeral, she went to New Mexico to sell off cattle and arrange ranch affairs, where outdoor work and sunshine helped revive her.[2]

Back in California, Isabella settled into a quiet routine, eating supper with Martha at six and going to bed by nine, their only diversion an occasional baseball game at Bobbie's school. Answering an avalanche of sympathy letters, she reflected on her seventeen years of marriage. Many people commended her selfless devotion. Ronald Munro-Ferguson wrote Frank Cutcheon that he thought Isabella's love for his brother had "almost passed understanding." But Isabella explained to Olivia, "In your blessed generosity, you feel that maybe I did help Bob over some weary trails. Possibly I did. . . . But it is as nothing in the face of what he gave us. . . . I now find myself yearning to share [with those who knew him in his strength] the reality of his years of invalidism, when his courage knew no complaint."[3]

She apologized to Eleanor for her "inexplicable silence"— hardly inexplicable in light of her difficult year. "There is no excuse," she insisted, "the waters closed over my head." She contrasted herself with Eleanor, "forever capable of striding ahead always in the pace that circumstances call for." She tried to describe her loss: "It is as though my husband, brother, father and sick boy had left our hours desolate. No words can describe the emptiness after all these years, during which his spirit of progress, his desires and care for us, filled life's least nook and cranny." She longed for a real conversation: "Eleanor, it would help so if I might compare your notes with mine. One doesn't stand still in the thirties [Isabella was 36] tho I used to think one had one foot in the grave by then."[4]

Isabella could not stand still. John Greenway had been waiting for almost twelve years, ever since, he told her, she had "stepped bewitchingly from train Number One at Benson, right plump into my heart." He was constantly traveling on business between Mexico, New Mexico and various towns in Arizona, but after a discreet waiting period of three months, he paid a visit to Isabella in California and was smitten all over again at the sight of her demure figure in black at the Santa Barbara station. They drove over to the Cate school to see Bobbie. On their way back, John repeated the declaration of love he had made by the corrals a decade before, asking that they pledge their love "with our whole souls and hearts and bodies." Isabella was overcome: "The words you made me say . . . as our car sped into the desert—how reluctantly I said them in the fear of their power." Later a sunset would remind him of the color in her cheeks "when you flushed so deeply . . . the day we drove to Cate."[5]

She would not yet commit to marry him, although she wrote to him like a lover: "At the end of each letter I sit and wonder and wonder how I can tell any least scrap of my love, and then I know I can't and that's the magic part. We'll always be trying." This was not enough for John, who wanted at long last to make sure of her: "How long will you keep me in this suspense? Give me hope or drive me to despair. I have spoken and I await your word." Still, she hesitated.

For one thing, he would have to take her together with all her family connections—aging relatives as well as two teenaged children. She was especially anxious about Uncle Frank's reaction. After the two men met in March, Unc took pains to assure Isabella how very cordial John had been to him. Nothing could have given Isabella greater comfort. With her uncle's blessing, she happily agreed to be married. John rhapsodized, "If my love keeps growing like this, I don't see how I am to keep my equilibrium. . . . This is to be the greatest year of all the chronicles of time. Isabella Selmes [he conveniently drops her married name] married John Greenway. 1923. Isabella Greenway. Have you ever seen her? Do you know her? Did you ever hear a more beautiful name?" Day after day, John poured out the love and longing of years. Isabella cherished his letters, "read and re-read and stuck under my pillow."[6]

They were separated a fair amount that spring, as she was laid up with back trouble in February, and he had business engagements. She assured him that the separations were unimportant: "I shut my eyes and almost feel you," she wrote. "My very life vibrates at even the imaginary touch." Still, she found that "you have been away so long it takes a great deal of daring to sign Your Isabella." She realized that their separations made them all the more eager for each other. In April John managed another visit, to talk about their future. Love, Isabella believed, should inspire them to the utmost usefulness. She was deeply impressed by John's lofty aspirations. In one of her rare journal entries she prayed: "God grant that I may be worthy and that John and I may achieve great good. . . . So high, so marvellous, so perfect seem John's ideals." She wrote John that "what matters and makes us is what we earn—spiritually, mentally, and tangibly." She had another goal, too, to banish the "grim expressions, all lonely and faraway" that she sometimes saw in John's face.[7]

The one cloud on her horizon was her mother's health. Patty was again suffering from pleurisy, and although she tried not to mar

Chapter Six

Isabella's happiness, she confided to Corinne: "I want you to tell me just man to man, if down deep in your soul you ever have the bitterness, even a little of it, which fills mine? If you do, what do you do about it? We can only take each other's hands as we crawl near the brink, and tell the truth. . . . Bob used to say pleurisy was the cruelest pain there is, and I know what he meant now—I think of Bob very often these days and with a better understanding." Patty rallied a little in early May, when she and Isabella went to Burro Mountain, hoping for its healing effect on lungs. Isabella and John had snatched a quick visit when he boarded her train for two hours en route through Arizona to New Mexico. The Homestead had been neglected for more than a year, and Isabella's days were taken up with demanding people and tiresome tasks. She wrote him wistfully: "I'll be glad when it can all be left behind and you and I can be in the big spaces and silences of our love." John wanted to visit Isabella, but she put him off with the humorous protest that the place was so disorganized, he would lose faith in her as a housekeeper. He was disappointed but divined her real objection: They wanted to keep their intention to be married a secret for a while longer.[8]

Meanwhile, although he was eagerly making plans for their honeymoon, he also looked forward to having her opinion in his business and political interests. Disillusioned with the Republicans, John had become a Democrat. In 1922, he sought nomination as governor and led for thirteen ballots before he finally withdrew to permit the endorsement of a compromise candidate. He was amused when the *Arizona Labor Journal* endorsed him for the office, as "these were the people who were trying to put me in jail a few years ago," at the time of the Bisbee Deportation. He had also been approached by Arizona's two U.S. senators about building a dam on the Colorado River. The state needed more electricity; rates in some parts of Arizona were up to five times higher than in Colorado.

John Greenway agreed to consider it, writing Isabella that he longed for her advice.[9]

On Isabella's way back to Santa Barbara to fetch the children, John boarded her train for another two-hour interlude. Afterwards he wondered why he hadn't asked some of the many questions he had for her about business and politics. But he was enjoying himself too much to talk seriously. He sighed, "What wasters of time we are to love so and be so much apart. We must expect to live forever!" The fact remained, however, that neither of them was exactly young; John, at 50, was even a bit deaf. But Isabella, soon after arriving in Santa Barbara, caught chicken pox from Bobbie. John wrote with exasperation: "Please marry me so I can make you take care of yourself." Confined to the house, Isabella welcomed the opportunity to moon about: "This whole day have I tried to do [other] things . . . and it proved such a failure that I just settled quietly to myself and loved you without interruption!"[10]

Meanwhile, John was off again, this time for Washington to discuss the Colorado River project with Herbert Hoover, a fellow engineer. Greenway took the opportunity to tell his sister Sadie and her husband Billie Keller, living in Washington, about his engagement; his sister had already figured out that he was in love, he wrote Isabella. John also reported that the Southern Pacific Railroad had sent him a pass for Mr. and Mrs. John Greenway. Isabella wrote back in alarm: "Who and how many people have you told?" But she relented. "How happy it will be when all the world can know that I love you with every scrap of life in me." She had gone so far as to put his framed picture on her dressing table: "I feel so bold!"[11]

After his return, John organized a trip with his future family. He took Isabella and the children, together with a few others for propriety's sake, in the mining company's private railroad car to Mexico to inspect a new mine, the Ahumada. Teenaged Martha found it all very romantic. At night, they sat on the car's observation plat-

form, while the miners played guitars and sang under the moonlight, and John's cook told ghost stories. Martha and Bobbie were
getting to know their prospective stepfather under ideal conditions. And Isabella was in heaven being near her lover for days on
end. They visited a shrine in an underground cavern, where John
clasped Isabella's "warm palpitating loveliness" and kissed her. The
trip proved a success from another point of view; later the men
found huge pockets of high grade ore, one of them 2,100 feet long.
John attributed his luck to "that kiss."[12]

They had been gone only a few days, but on their return to New
Mexico, they discovered with alarm that Patty had taken a turn for
the worse. She could no longer see to read or write, her heart and
kidneys were failing, and the doctor warned that she might go at
any moment. But her mind remained alert. Isabella's engagement to
John was a great comfort; Patty could leave her daughter, knowing
she'd be well taken care of, emotionally and financially. The two
women spent their last days together talking as they had before Isabella was married, when they were all to each other. Isabella told her
mother over and over how wonderful she had been. Patty was ready
to go, glad to escape the indignities of old age. The night of July 16,
Patty dreamed, prophetically, of her old friend Theodore Roosevelt. The next night, at four in the morning, she died. "Mother went
so peacefully," Isabella reassured the Cutcheons. John promised
Frank he would look after the family, buying their tickets and going
with them as far as Chicago. Unc, too, was relieved that Isabella
seemed to have found a safe harbor, with a competent businessman
for a husband.[13]

Isabella took her mother back to Boone, her second visit to the
hilltop graveyard in less than a year. They placed Patty's ashes in
Til's grave, while Frank read some of her favorite poetry. Isabella
mused to Blair Flandrau's wife, Grace, "As I stood there with Bob's
grave alongside I realized what a long part of the road was behind
me." She tried to be philosophical. "A perfect relationship makes it

easier to let a person go," she wrote Corinne Robinson. "I feel that not one or twenty years could have given anything more entire in understanding and love than what we had." Still, she faced "the anguish of realizing that I hadn't a thought or hope or a least or greatest plan that was not entwined around her." And to John she admitted that "still I cannot believe that my Mummy is left in the hilltop graveyard. Such a sense of despair comes."[14]

After the funeral, Isabella took the children to New York, where they and the Cutcheons tried to comfort each other. Stunned by grief, Isabella fell asleep at all hours of the day. But love helped in the healing process. One day a tender note from John, who was wont to call her his Rose Bud, stimulated her to such an extent that she rushed to town and bought a pink dress and a hat with roses in it. She began to fantasize about their married life: "I give you a very proper kiss with no lingering qualities. As you go off to the mill, I shall sew some buttons on your coat." But then he'd come back "because you've forgotten something, and we'll have a real [kiss] that will last until noon." John sent Isabella a picture of a woman in a western riding costume, a divided skirt with cowboy boots, and urged her to order such an outfit for riding along the Grand Canyon on their honeymoon. Isabella wrote John that her sojourn in the East had convinced her that they were real Westerners. Easterners, she noticed were "so hampered with *plans*—which leave no opportunity for impulses."[15]

Isabella often saw Eleanor, whom she found "deep in politics, speech-making all over the state. . . . I don't doubt that she will end in Congress." Isabella divulged her secret engagement; Eleanor, in turn, confided in Isabella. Eleanor had defied Franklin's mother, Sara, who wanted Franklin to retire from politics after he was crippled by polio. Isabella noted that Eleanor herself was working in politics while Franklin struggled with his disability, "to keep a live interest in their home." Isabella told John: "The weight of the tragedy of this house almost suffocates me at times. But Eleanor carries

John C. Greenway

her head high and is a great woman and will go the whole distance of life triumphantly. Time will wipe out the criticism."[16]

Although the Roosevelts were good political partners, their marriage had suffered after the discovery of Franklin's infatuation with Lucy Mercer. And theirs was not the only unhappy marriage Isabella saw; it seemed to her that no one in the East was in love. "Won't it be fun," she wrote John smugly, "to show them how it can be done the whole way." She warned him to enjoy his independence because he was "about to marry a tyrant who won't allow him a minute's peace—and who will have to be loved at the most inconvenient moments!" Transcontinental telephone calls were still difficult and rare, so they poured out their feelings in letters. John's letters read like those of a love-struck adolescent. He noted the number of days until their wedding in early November and signed himself "the 'boy' who loves you." Their continued separation, so close to their union, was hard on him: "I feel it's been a case of out-staying and out-gaming Father Time." He worried: "I feel the balance of my allotted span will be all too short and we have been very wasteful of time." Isabella assured him that "when, at last, we are together we can make up for the ages wasted."[17]

In early September Isabella took the children back to California for the start of school. John promised to ride with them from eastern Arizona as far as Tucson, "and if you are very sweet, I may go to Gila." He went to Gila. Then he went east to lobby for his Colorado River plan, for which congressional approval would be needed. But he found himself sitting in meetings, trying to concentrate on a project involving fifty million dollars and fantasizing about Isabella. As November approached, he said, "It's like the last days of fighting after the Armistice was signed. . . . I've fought so long for you." He managed a visit to California, where he and Isabella stayed in Los Angeles with a mutual friend, as going to a hotel would have been improper. He was, he said, waiting impatiently for her "to haul down the flag and surrender," and made sure she knew he had ordered a room with a double bed for their wedding night.[18]

In mid-October they announced to their friends their plan to marry. John rode around Warren, a suburb south of Bisbee where the mine owners and managers lived, calling on his neighbors with the news. He reported to Isabella that most of them said, "From your changed appearance we guessed it weeks ago." Isabella was inundated with happy letters. A typical one read: "I was *very* glad to learn that the clouds had broken for you, and the sun, shining through, was showing such a lovely path for your faltering feet to tread. . . . To find a real love and this promise of happiness after one's early youth has gone is, I believe, almost a miracle." One woman called it "The Most Splendid Rainbow after the Storm." Many expressed the thought that John was "one of nature's noblemen." Some wrote to endorse her decision to remarry; in those days a one-year period of mourning was seen as rather brief. But Isabella had done much of her grieving during Bob's long illness. His doctor, Walter James, wrote, "No one appreciates better than I the many years of devoted affection and care you gave Bob, nor how thoroughly you now deserve the coming years of protection and care yourself."[19]

Isabella Ferguson and John Greenway were married November 4, 1923, in the Cutcheons' house in Santa Barbara with only family and a few old friends present. When the ceremony concluded with their kiss, the children let out a cheer. John had gamely attended a baseball game of Bobbie's the day before, and the children were much involved with presents, rice, and other preparations. Afterward, John and Isabella, two well-connected people marrying in midlife, sent out over 2,500 wedding announcements. More letters poured in from friends delighted by her prospect of happiness. "You certainly deserve everything good in this world and I believe that it is coming to you now. It renews my faith in the Lord," wrote Mary Eckles, from Silver City. Olivia Cutting, now married to

Henry James, a nephew of the author, predicted that Isabella would now have a life to satisfy her deepest needs—her craving not only for love and security but also for lofty ambitions. Even Bob Ferguson's brother Ronald was pleased with her remarriage, writing Frank that John Greenway seemed all that could be wished and hoping that he would be able to help her with the children's upbringing. But Hector Ferguson and Anna Cowles, Bob's champions, did not approve, Ronald admitted; they felt "that Bob had suffered some pain from knowledge of the attachment."[20]

After the honeymoon at the Grand Canyon—John later swore he would never get over the thrill of seeing her slippers by his bed, and Isabella gloried in his smile of satisfied ownership—the Greenways returned to Warren, Arizona. A group of youngsters held a "chivaree," the traditional pranks and serenading on a couple's first night home. Greenway invited them all inside to show them his war relics. Isabella, sitting by the fireplace in a green dinner dress, made a deep impression on the youngsters, too. Married life, she assured the Cutcheons, was blissful: "What a glowing wonder life has become." John wanted them to come and see for themselves how she was blooming. Isabella eagerly began to plan her third dwelling, a roomy, airy house in Ajo, a mining town in the southwest part of the state where John, as majority stockholder in the New Cornelia Copper Company, had opened a new mine in 1917. Ajo had vast quantities of ore, but it had taken an engineer of Greenway's experience and determination to find a way to mine it. He patented his process for extracting the ore and planned a pretty little town with a central plaza, a well-appointed school, and a hospital for the workers.[21]

John and Isabella were careful in their joy not to overlook Martha and Bobbie. At Christmas, the children arrived with friends and enjoyed a lively time with nine hounds, a half-grown mountain lion, two bobcats and countless coyotes. Soon there would be another child; Isabella became pregnant sometime in January 1924. She wrote Eleanor that she was basking in "a happiness that I find hard to believe . . . [and] now that we have hopes of a baby, the very world seems turned to magic." But marriage, even so long anticipated and cherished a marriage as theirs, could not prevent John from having to travel more or less constantly between Ajo, Bisbee, and the Ahumada mine in Mexico to supervise his far-flung operations. Separation only intensified John's feelings, making him appreciate how closely knit they had already become. But Isabella felt a bit bereft during his absences. A month later, with John in Mexico, she was thinking of visiting the Cutcheons and the children in Santa Barbara: "I feel like a meaningless quantity suspended in mid-air when not with John or all of you," she wrote Unc. She had never in her life lived alone; she had always been on call for one or another of her relations.[22]

As John's wife, she was expected to help with his extensive business entertaining and spent Easter in Warren with a house full of company directors. Isabella delighted in her new role, confiding to Unc: "I am getting much kick out of being an 'employee' and trying to do the right thing and never let a side glimpse even of my arrogant and intolerant self be seen!! John is quite nervous." It's doubtful that John was at all nervous. He loved to see Isabella win over his friends, which she did with ease. Isabella learned much in this wider sphere that would stand her in good stead later on.[23]

John had been for years a bit player in the political game and wanted to attend the Democratic National Convention in New York in June. He and Bobbie left immediately after Martha's graduation, while Isabella stayed on a few more days for Martha to take her entrance exams for Bryn Mawr College. Isabella had confessed to Eleanor that she was "somewhat overcome at having a daughter bent on college"; few women of Isabella's and Eleanor's generation and class had gone to college themselves. But she admired her daughter's ambition. In New York, Isabella found the Democrats fascinating. She and John had always been Progressive Republicans, but, like many other former Bull Moose Republicans, including FDR's future secretary of the interior, Harold Ickes, they had become so disillusioned with Harding and Coolidge that they changed their affiliation. Isabella told Eleanor, "With intense interest do I for the first time try to look deep into your Democratic party to which John has gone after supporting Col. R for 22 years." The Democrats were not at their finest. They slogged through 103 ballots as the delegates of William G. McAdoo, Wilson's son-in-law, and Alfred E. Smith, governor of New York, deadlocked. Finally, the convention compromised on a Wall Street lawyer, John W. Davis. The proceedings were enlivened when Arizona nominated John Greenway for vice president. Minnesota, where Greenway had earned a sterling reputation, seconded the motion. Altogether, he received thirty votes from eight different states. His political future looked bright.[24]

After the convention, Eleanor took part in New York governor Alfred E. Smith's reelection campaign, although Franklin, still struggling with his paralysis, did not. Isabella wrote Eleanor: "I picture . . . life as it must tumble over itself for you these days." Isabella herself was spending the summer quietly in Arizona, languid with pregnancy and heat. John was surprised to learn that a couple of Arizona newspapers, impressed by his vice-presidential nomination, had begun to promote him as a gubernatorial candidate. Friends circulated his nomination petition in five counties before he even caught wind of it. He was doubtful that he could be elected, given his role in the Bisbee Deportation. In any case, with his first child expected in October, he did not want to run for political office that year. But he participated to the extent of leading the Arizona "Davis-Bryan Victory Organization," making speeches every night as the election neared.[25]

At the end of August, Isabella went with Martha to Santa Barbara to await the baby's arrival, due September 25. John was in a fever of anxiety, scolding her for attending dinner parties, fearing it threatened her health (she was thirty-eight) and "the baby's very existence." He consoled himself for her absence by sleeping in her bed, "happy in the fragrance you have left." When Martha left for college on September 17, John arrived in Santa Barbara, bringing his cousin, Dr. Oliver Patton, for added peace of mind. Bobbie came from the ranch, lean and fit, for his final two years at school. But her menfolk could not console Isabella at this trying time as her daughter would have done: "She is the loveliest soul, and to have brought her into the world seems to be fulfillment enough for one woman," she wrote Unc. The baby was more than two weeks late, arriving at midnight on October 11 with the umbilical cord wound around his neck. But he was safely delivered, and Isabella presented a strapping "ten pound miner" to her delighted husband. Martha, more apprehensive than she had let on, wept with relief on hearing the news. Aunt Julia rejoiced that Isabella was back "safe and sound from your trip to the Valley of the Shadows." Bobbie announced he would be godfather to young John Selmes Greenway, known as "Jack."[26]

John left to continue campaigning, taking the opportunity to speak out on his plans for harnessing the Colorado River. Isabella approved of his activities with reservations, warning that a political life could be precarious. She loyally told John, "I'd give a lot to hear you speak," but was even more impressed by her contemporary, Corinne Robinson Alsop, who, with four children under fifteen, was running for the Connecticut State Assembly. Isabella read with dismay that Eleanor and two of her friends were touring New York in a car decorated to resemble a teapot, a reference to the Harding administration's Teapot Dome scandal. "Do you think E[leanor] has lost her mind?" she exclaimed to John. With her friends in the thick of the political fray, Isabella faced more humdrum challenges. Jack was rowdy, her milk was slow to come in, she came down with flu and badly sprained her ankle. Wryly, she noted to Olivia that she

The Greenway house in Ajo, Arizona

had suffered more from the ankle than from childbirth and that she had had to furnish the new house in Ajo on her back by telephone.[27]

John was eager to have her home: "Everything that comes up I find myself wishing to know your opinion." They were apart on their first anniversary, but he rejoiced that they loved each other "more than ever, with a better understanding of one another, and wanting to meet the other fellow more than half way." Isabella felt the same: "I used to dream of all it might be. What you have made it I couldn't have dreamed of." John reflected that they had "good health, a lordly income, and a big rosy baby boy. . . . I feel we are only fairly started on life's journey."[28]

Isabella, however, was not in good health. In January 1925, she began to feel poorly; by late February she had taken to bed, with a subnormal temperature, rapid pulse, and nausea. The local doctors could not diagnose her condition, so John took her to California in the company's private railroad car. Isabella was borne, dramatically if awkwardly, through the window of the car on a stretcher to a waiting ambulance. Weakly, she protested these elaborate arrangements, "which she regarded as a restraint upon her independence," Unc observed with amusement to Martha. John had to leave almost at once to meet with his directors. The Greenways' letters during this separation are crowded with assurances of love. "I think of you all the time. . . . I took a long ride this afternoon and I don't think you were out of my mind a minute," John wrote. She replied, "Oh John mine, what it is to love you. It is sunshine. It is music. It is feeling. It is living." A San Francisco doctor diagnosed her with thyroid deficiency and prescribed iodine. But it was not until the beginning of June that she was up and around, after ninety-eight days in bed. Though still very weak, her spirits rose. "Life lies ahead!" she exulted.[29]

John, doubtless after consultation with Isabella, had decided to leave the Calumet and Arizona Mining Company, effective June 1. He had felt for some time that he was in a rut, and pursuing the Colorado River project would allow him to divide his time between their home in Ajo and the Grand Canyon. Frank thought that John should curtail his plans on account of Isabella's health, but she insisted to her husband, "Your ambition and work mean just as much to me as to you; they are ours. . . . All *my joy* is in what you are doing out in the world." Despite her support for his activities, Isabella rather welcomed the idea of a change of pace and hoped that John would relax with her for a few months before starting a new project.[30]

Another possibility arose when the *Bisbee Daily Review* printed an exclusive dispatch from Phoenix showing John Greenway as the dark-horse front-runner to unseat incumbent George W. P. Hunt in the Democratic primary for governor. Hunt, a grossly fat man with a droopy mustache, along the lines of William Howard Taft, had been Arizona's first governor and enjoyed longtime support from labor. However, "Arizona Democrats are tired of radicalism," opined the *Review.* They thought the conservative wing wanted a day in the sun, and Greenway was a natural candidate. He had "large personal popularity, speaks well, has a superfine record in two wars, has large means, and, undoubtedly, would be backed to the limit by the mining interests with which he for years has had close association." The incumbents might make protests about "trusts" and corporate control, the paper admitted. "In the past this sort of argument has brought the votes of the Arizona mining camps, but it happens that Greenway is himself a miner and knows how to talk to a miner." Greenway's resignation from the Calumet and Arizona management "had all the effect that would be created by the impact of a brick on a beehive," wrote one admiring reporter. However, Greenway ultimately decided that he could make a greater contribution at that time by constructing the Colorado River dam. The future of Arizona's development, he believed, could be insured with a new source of power.[31]

By August Isabella was quite well again, and John was off on another trip. For once, he neglected to write for ten days, although he sent daily telegrams. Isabella protested: "How would you survive such an ordeal?" John was equally quick to take offense at any slight of their romantic love. In Ajo, Isabella had made it a custom to bathe and put on a fresh dress in the late afternoon to wait for him in the doorway when he rode up after the day's work. One afternoon she was delayed and sent a maid to meet John on his return. When he rode up and saw the maid instead of Isabella, he turned the horse around, rode off again, and did not come home until nearly midnight. The next morning at breakfast he said, kindly but firmly, "Isabella, we will never mention again what happened yesterday. But I do hope you have come to realize the responsibilities of a marriage."[32]

Chapter Six

In the autumn, Bobbie went off as a freshman to Yale. Martha had done poorly during her first year at Bryn Mawr and had returned on probation. In October the Greenways went east, too. Leaving Jack in Locust Valley with his Cutcheon "grandparents," they traveled to Washington to lobby for the Colorado River dam. They were still optimistic about the project, Isabella reported to Martha, "in spite of the fact that apparently *all* the governors of the seven states have dashed east to contest John's claim."[33]

While in Washington, John suffered a bout of severe indigestion, and they consulted John's brother-in-law, Col. William (Billie) Keller, head of surgery at Walter Reed Hospital, who diagnosed John with a large gallstone. Keller believed the gallstone had been present for some time, so there was no urgency to operate, but he allowed it might be advisable to have it out within the next two or three months. At first John wanted Keller to keep the information from Isabella, possibly because she was now pregnant again and, nearly forty, was at even higher risk than with Jack. Prudently, they sought out second opinions. Bob Ferguson's old doctor, Walter James, and another doctor advised against an operation as unnecessary, but two more doctors agreed with Keller that the gallstone might bother John later on if it were not removed.[34]

Faced with this hard decision, they traveled back to New England, stopping off to visit Martha. Isabella created a small sensation among the Bryn Mawr students, who lay "in shoals at her feet," Martha reported to Bobbie. But Isabella was anxious and distracted when she visited Bobbie, who, not surprisingly, was having a hard time adjusting to life at Yale. Afterward, she wrote him apologetically, explaining why she had been worried and preoccupied. She asked him to tell no one of John's medical problem but stressed that "I want always to keep my faith with you and Martha of entire honesty." At first, the Greenways thought the best course of treatment would be to wait and see. John was advised to lose some weight and to eat a bland diet. He began to feel better. But he wanted to be able to travel abroad, and his brother, Dr. James Greenway, agreed with Keller and the others who advised him to have the stone removed. Isabella was fiercely opposed to an operation, but, in the face of mounting medical consensus, she reluctantly gave in, although she continued to have premonitions of a bad outcome. They returned to New York.[35]

In early January 1926, as they sped cross-country on the train, Isabella poured out her misgivings day after day in her journal: "January 7: I find myself utterly broken. . . . Why, since it is all pronounced so simple, so normal. . . . Because I believe that any operation 99 times out of 100 offers a line of surprises and horrors beyond remotest conception. . . . It is in all probability the beginning of the breaking of John's beautiful body and consequently the changing of our relation from one of Health, Hope and Love to ill health, fear and affection. . . . I must not talk. *No one understands* and all *misjudge*. I must cringe and shiver and be knocked almost out . . . but keep standing up through the whole process, because I don't want to meet my end lying down. . . . I can go on, yes, but not with joy and hope. Just with dogged determination and dread. Maybe with kindness and goodness and understanding of others' desperation."[36]

Already John's illness had begun to affect their relationship. "We cannot share the same compartment travelling because John should sleep comfortably down below and will not permit me to sleep up. He is afraid to kiss me for fear he may get a cold that I might be getting." When she complains that they are drifting apart, when every moment matters, he says, "You are not lovable when you are like that." She added: "This is just the beginning. Wait until the horrors untold begin to come. Wait until Billy Keller takes command, and I am included only so far as a child might be and told what they wish to tell me. . . . I will just jot down the horrors as they come (if I have the nerve) to show how little one can dream of them."[37]

Chapter Six

January 8: "Five more days before John's body is mutilated and we do the irreversible. Oh, God, speak to me. . . . Give me something to go forward on, something to believe. . . . If John is going to be ill and broken, I don't see how any effort of living can be worth while." Having spent seventeen years in one marriage with an invalid, she shrank from facing it again. She tried to confine her misgivings to her journal: "Silence is your stronghold. . . . What you say in your fear, your horror, your jealousy, your premonition will be remembered and misunderstood. . . . This is the 8th. On the night of the 12th—5 days—I will probably know if John is going to live."[38]

The operation was a success. John woke up and saw his wife standing by his bed and, making a huge effort to speak, gasped out, "You are the woman for me—Oh, Isabella, how I love you." Unc, who had come east to be with his beloved niece throughout her ordeal, relayed many telegrams of well-wishers expressing relief. Jack's nanny sent daily bulletins about the baby direct to Isabella at the hospital, where she never left John's side. But she was still apprehensive. Finally, after almost a week, Isabella began to relax.[39]

On the morning of January 18, she talked to John after he woke up, then agreed to go out for the first time, to have dinner with Unc. While in the restaurant, she was called to the telephone: John was in serious trouble. She and Frank rushed to the hospital, where they found John in great pain. The doctors explained that a blood clot had come loose while they were changing the dressing on his incision and had lodged in his lung. There was nothing to do but to wait for the clot to dissolve or pass on. Hours went by, as Isabella and the nurses tried to make John comfortable with cold compresses. Sedatives had little effect; he continued to suffer. A few times he tried to talk to Isabella but could not manage to speak. Finally, early in the morning of January 19, he died while she held him.[40]

Letters of shock and sympathy poured in from their horrified friends. It was too cruel, after Isabella's years of hardship, that she would not have even a few tranquil years of married bliss. Martha and Bobbie hurried to be with her.

Isabella Greenway roused herself to deal with the aftermath, wiring Mike Curley, the superintendent at the Ajo mine, to prepare a burial site at the top of the little hill where John used to turn his horse and wave to her as he went off to work in the mornings. By January 23, after a memorial service in New York, Isabella was back on the train taking John's body to Ajo. Martha was with her. She had never really settled into college life, possibly because of her sketchy preparation, and she would never return. She and her mother shared a compartment on the train, where Martha was witness to her mother's final tragedy, when Isabella miscarried John's second child.[41]

PART TWO

CHAPTER SEVEN ∾∾∾∾∾∾∾∾∾∾∾∾∾∾∾

"The Life of You in My Veins"

I SABELLA GAVE JOHN GREENWAY a hero's farewell. His coffin was borne by World War veterans and Rough Riders, taking turns, twenty at a time, to the grave on their little hill. John's obituary had appeared in papers all over the country; editorials and the resolutions of many organizations attested to the high opinion in which he was held. More than three thousand of his admirers assembled from all over the country. A plane flew overhead and, silencing its engine for a moment, dropped red and white carnations over the grave and the mourners.[1]

Isabella Greenway was hard put to answer the flood of condolence letters. They arrived from miners in small towns in Michigan and Minnesota as well as Arizona, from the political elite in New York City, and old Rough Riders. Some sent poems and some requested photographs. People wrote who knew Greenway only by reputation, or who had met him only once and been awed, showing that he could likely have had a promising political career. Others wrote brokenly who had known him well. Some promised God's

∾∾∾∾∾∾∾∾∾∾∾∾∾∾∾∾∾∾∾∾∾∾∾∾∾∾∾∾∾

The funeral of John C. Greenway

consolation, while others protested that Isabella's fate was impossibly cruel. Some urged her to be glad and proud and thankful for what she had, reassuring her that nothing could take that from her. But Aunt Julia Dinsmore, who knew, admitted that "a sorrow's crown of sorrows is remembering happier times." From the start, Isabella strove to transform her anguish into a memorial to her husband. She saved all the tributes—letters and telegrams and newspaper clippings—sorted by day and tied with red ribbon, as well as cards from the profusion of flowers. By February, she could write that "The volume of love which comes from the hearts of his friends is the crowning glory of his wonderful life."[2]

John Greenway died when his romance with Isabella was at its height. It never had to bear the test of time. For the rest of her life Isabella would carry an idealized portrait of their two short honeymoon years together. Separations throughout their courtship and marriage had kept them wildly eager for each other. At first, his death may have felt like just another separation. For a long time, she continued to write as if he were still alive, only elsewhere. "How many years of our lives have we written!" she mused a few months after his death.[3]

"Heart of mine," begins one undated letter. "It rains outside over on our hilltop. Your beautiful body lies all cramped in a coffin in the pajamas and dressing gown I love—the slippers we were forever hunting—the big flag over the whole. And here I sit darlingest in the house we built so joyously to live in." He would live, she assured him, in her. "Your very being surging through my blood—the life of you in my veins." To Hermann Hagedorn, a close friend of Theodore Roosevelt and president of the Theodore Roosevelt Memorial Association, she wrote, "Living for me is kinder than I anticipated, because John is everywhere always."[4]

Isabella Selmes Ferguson Greenway, at forty, had been tempered in the fires of duty, service, passion, and loss. Her husband's will left her an estate worth nearly two million dollars, a fortune in 1926. What would this extraordinary woman now make of the rest of her life?[5]

First, she had her son, John's son, less than two years old, to bring up. Isabella, like her own widowed mother, would forge an uncommonly close relationship with this child. She had great hopes for him, as John's legacy. Shortly after Jack's birth, Isabella had written John that the baby must be made ready "for the great adventure of carrying on—for us." Meanwhile, many of their friends urged Isabella herself to carry on John's work. In his fifteen years in Arizona, John Greenway had come to be regarded as one of its foremost citizens. As his widow, Isabella came to the attention of many—miners, the governor, prospectors, high school students—who were impressed by her strength of character in adversity.[6]

Work was an anodyne for grief, and she plunged almost at once into John's affairs, as coexecutor of his estate with Dr. L. D. (Davy) Ricketts, a fellow mining engineer from John's Minnesota years. She set herself a fierce pace, writing her son Bob on February 14 that she had just returned to Ajo after forty-eight hours of traveling, mostly at night. Martha protested that if they could travel by day, they might see something of the country, to which Isabella replied, "we are too busy—we must work by day." When she heard that the state legislature was planning to earmark money to fight the Diamond Creek Dam, she descended on Phoenix in a passion to defend John's dream. Aided by John's male secretary, Howard Caffrey—whom Isabella was coming to know as "a brick in strenuous effort and real efficiency on the typewriter"—she offered to coordinate the efforts of the men who were carrying on the Diamond Creek project. Still, as she noted to Bob, Caffrey and the others "are fairly stewing over John's affairs. . . . I can't help thinking how most people fuss . . . and how few can create the affairs themselves." This would be the role in which she would succeed her late husband.[7]

She also fought to have Frank Cutcheon represent her, as the second largest individual stockholder, on the board of the New Cornelia Copper company board, and she negotiated a cattle-grazing permit with the U.S. Forest Service. These demanding activities left her feeling, she told Frank, "astonishingly well, and while I only sleep in irregular spells, the lack of it does not seem to bother me." Her activity surprised all her relatives, who apparently had assumed she would withdraw into grief. "I wish you would get somebody to write me—*not a letter* but a mere geographical statement of where you are and where you are likely to be," begged her Aunt Mary Selmes. Isabella confided to John, "How it amuses us, doesn't it, dearest, to see me trying to be vigorous and progressive and in touch with all things, so that your presence in its characteristic of carrying on and forward is ever the same."[8]

At first she leaned heavily on Frank, but soon she came to think John would have considered Frank's advice overcautious and began to go more her own way. She tried to enlist Bob—"I will be glad dearest when you take the active part in all these things," she wrote him at Yale—but he was evidently unwilling or unable to respond. She and her children were planning to go abroad for the summer; Isabella expected Martha and Bob to make their own plans, but they were proving hard to pin down. "I have released the reins," she announced to Frank, resignedly. "[T]hey are beyond me." This was especially true of Bob, who, at eighteen, evidently wanted to stand on his own feet. Isabella lamented that she was not able to get from Bob "the kind of reaction to my inquiries and interest in him that I would like." She ruefully supposed it was the result of shipping him off at the age of twelve to live among strangers.[9]

Suddenly, though, Bob was in need of her as never before. In early April, he had gone to Pittsburgh with the Yale polo team. There he contracted scarlet fever, which quickly evolved into an ear infection, and then congested lungs. The doctors had to operate without anesthetic to relieve the pressure of the pleurisy, leaving a huge gash in his back. Isabella rushed out to him on the train, with Jack, the nanny, and Martha following in her wake. But the Fates had not finished with her yet. The Cutcheons had started from Santa Barbara with Julia Dinsmore, to lend their help, as always. On the way, Aunt Julia, age ninety-three, died of complications from a broken hip. The Cutcheons sadly continued east bearing her ashes. Her great-aunt's home had been a place where Isabella could slip back into a child's role and relax, feeling protected and taken care of, a respite from being the person in charge. Isabella's Owny was gone and with her, a special refuge.[10]

Isabella had to resort to heroic measures in Pittsburgh, where she found Bob enduring appalling conditions in the hospital. He had been quarantined by the state, but nurses were using him to transport dead bodies, because he was still strong enough to help. Isabella bribed a nurse to get him out and they retreated to a hotel, where Bob convalesced for three months. Isabella tried to keep up a good front, writing cheerfully, "Bobbie, poor boy, seems to have everything wrong with him but housemaid's knee." She tried to steal a few moments to commune with John. "Heart of mine—together we live these days—these days of fathomless adjustment. You are everywhere. I put my hand out and yours closes over it. I lift my face and yours leans near. We kiss, again and again, and time and place slip past." The letters allowed her the old joy of sharing with him all the events of her day, "when any reaction that you would have was so far more interesting than any reality that called it forth —the nights in Warren when we were forever dragging our clothes between rooms lest we miss a moment." Although John had "seemingly gone ahead," her belief that they were together in spirit for eternity made her feel that "no deep harm can come ever again."[11]

The doctors assured Isabella that a trip abroad would be good for Bob, so in mid-July the family set to sea, bound for Great Britain. Martha and Bob went on to Scotland to visit their father's relatives, while Isabella and Jack relaxed in Bath. She now had leisure to write John often, confessing that she knew he must have been disappointed in her the previous five weeks, "a distracted person . . . battered, pulled, influenced, blinded by grief." She admitted that "Writing you, sweetheart, when your body is what this world calls 'dead,' makes me just a little self conscious." But writing to him helped her as nothing else could do. Although she had an uneasy feeling John would have wanted her to go to France to see his battlefields, she assured him that resting at Bath helped her plan for the future—"for the greatness you would have for me. . . . I can do it, darling, if you'll let me slip my hand in yours." She realized "I must

Isabella and John Selmes (Jack) Greenway, 1926

have two sides now, the side that is the head of a family, able to say no as well as yes, make all decisions."[12]

Isabella also had to face the fact that, at forty, she was still a relatively young and undeniably attractive woman who had always basked in male attention. She acknowledged that some of John's friends had developed an attachment to his widow. She was tempted to charm them, to show that John had married a worthwhile woman. But she was aware of "that curious danger line when Nature slips in a trick if you don't watch out. . . . When you aren't— no I can't say that, it hurts too much—since our new life, it is harder for me to adjust these matters to their right place, but it helps a lot that you always approved of men and women friends and had so many yourself. I take a childish pride in having your friends 'fall for me' . . . so long as they know I belong to you for all eternity." The prolonged period of quiet introspection had its downside: "It's terribly hard to have the leisure to think as I am doing now that I am alone," she wrote in early September. But she believed it was better to confront her grief and get through it. Still, a confident feeling was all too apt to give way to despair: "A paralysis holds me . . . a deep horrible nightmare." Several days later, she admitted it was hard to stay in the land of the living. "It's so much more natural to plan my burial clothes and our resting place in Montezuma than to be the well-dressed person you love with a happy, tidy, inspiring life. But after all, what are 25 years or so? Just a chance to pay you a fitting tribute. . . . Mine is the privilege of finishing *our life*."[13]

By the end of the year, Isabella had written a long list of detailed resolutions for "Living as John would have me." In addition to family life and health, work was of paramount importance, particularly for the public good. She realized she needed solitude to plan, because "a sense of destiny besets me. GREAT DESTINY. . . . *I feel I see beyond*." She knew herself well enough to understand she would achieve her goals through her ability to work with people.[14]

The start of 1927 saw Isabella embarking on a string of projects. She began to spend more and more time in Tucson, where she rented a house. It was a bigger town, with more scope for her activities. The Colorado River dam was proving a well-nigh intractable problem. Congressional action had put an end, at least for the time being, to any prospects of a dam on the Colorado. Water and water rights were contentious issues in that desert region, and powerful interests had lobbied to deny the project.[15]

A more feasible task had suggested itself in May 1926, when a proposal was made in the Arizona legislature that a statue of Brigadier General John C. Greenway be placed in Statuary Hall of the U.S. Congress. Starting in 1864, all the states had been invited to contribute two statues each honoring outstanding citizens. Arizona, which had won statehood in 1912, had not yet sent a statue. The first anniversary of John's death in January 1927 called forth more letters on the subject, one of which announced that the Arizona American Legion was joining with the Spanish War veterans to petition the legislature to pick Greenway. The proposal had its critics: Greenway had lived in Arizona only for the last third of his short life, and his role in the Bisbee Deportation was not universally admired. Alternative subjects—Frank Luke, a Phoenix high school boy who became a flying ace in the World War, or Marcus A. Smith, who had done the most to secure Arizona statehood—were suggested. But Isabella worked hard to coordinate support for John's statue, and the legislature finally approved his selection, appropriating almost $5,000. Isabella, with the warmth that would later stand her in such good stead as a politician, wrote the Phoenix Veterans of Foreign Wars: "While the Statue would be a glorious tribute, it cannot compare to the heart-warming response that brings about its creation."[16]

The veterans had come through for Isabella; now she wanted to do something for them. Inspired by Greenway's record in the World War, as well as by Ferguson's tuberculosis, likely contracted during his service in Cuba, she was concerned about the plight of more than five thousand disabled ex-servicemen who had settled in Arizona, many of them suffering from TB. She was moved to action when she and Martha visited veterans in a Tucson hospital. The men were making items for sale, but Isabella thought they would have better success making something more attractive. She asked them if they would be willing to copy toys and knickknacks, if she provided samples and offered to buy their output for two or three months. The men agreed. The next morning, a newspaper story announced that she had helped found a new industry. After she got over her surprise, she began to see possibilities in the plan.[17]

Isabella went directly to Tucson mayor John White and boldly asked for a rent-free building where she could start an experiment for the employment of disabled ex-servicemen. Within three days, an old church had been placed at her disposal. When she first proposed the idea, she later recalled, many businessmen advised her against it, warning that it would take enormous effort as well as considerable capital to launch such a venture. The chamber of commerce, seeing that she was determined, advised her to concentrate on furniture, cactus novelty items, leatherwork, and a few toys. The new project was dubbed the Arizona Hut, "hut" being the World War I Doughboys' term for a place where they could retreat from the trenches for rest and relaxation. By April, the Hut was selling goods made in the hospitals, and Isabella had found a shop in Boston, run by the wife of a retired general, to take goods on consignment. Eventually a number of high-end stores—Wanamakers, Bonwit-Teller, Abercrombie & Fitch, and Saks & Company—were persuaded by Isabella to carry Hut goods. Isabella ordered lathes, jigsaws, and an air compressor, turning the church into a "young bedlam," as she put it. The following year, the Hut set up a small factory on Congress Street, with a gift shop nearby. At the end of 1928, about forty veterans or their family members were employed in the business.[18]

With their usual synchronicity, Isabella Greenway and Eleanor Roosevelt had both embarked on furniture co-ops in the same year. ER, together with her friends Nancy Cook, Marion Dickerman, and Caroline O'Day, created the Val-Kill partnership: a newspaper, a school, and the Val-Kill furniture factory, which opened in 1927, directed by Cook. Eleanor hoped that farm families could be induced to remain in the community if they had a second source of income. The design of the furniture that both factories produced is quite similar, and it is likely that Isabella may have borrowed some of her ideas from Eleanor and vice versa.[19]

Isabella's third project was to buy a ranch in the northern part of the state, partly for respite from the grilling summers in southern Arizona, where the temperature routinely soared above one hun-

The Arizona Hut workshop

dred degrees, and partly as an enterprise for Bob. In March she found the Quarter Circle Double X Ranch, a beautiful spread near the Grand Canyon, six miles west of the little town of Williams. The property was covered in Ponderosa pine trees, with a backdrop of mountains. Dr. Ricketts and her Uncle Frank both tried to discourage her from spending money on a ranch, since the Ahumada Lead company was performing poorly. Isabella tried to fathom what John would have had her do. "Don't be afraid to act," she imagined him saying. "Davy and Uncle are old and childless." She thought John would support her against "a storm from Uncle" at the prospect of Bob ranching and would also agree that Martha was more apt to find a suitable husband in the West than among rich young men in the East. Martha had become so popular in Tucson, Isabella told Bob, that she had finally had to return to Ajo, "because I could not afford to rent a house big enough to hold Martha's beaux." Martha was demonstrating Western independence, a development that Isabella professed to welcome. She noted in her diary that Martha "tells me that I bore people talking of the Hut . . . that I have spoiled Bob and am responsible for his entire lack of manners to his family . . . and go at such speed that I am wearing myself to exhaustion. . . . What does it all mean?" she concluded, like many another mother of an adult daughter.[20]

Believing that John concurred with her about the northern property, Isabella bought the ranch and moved up for the summer, installing Howard Caffrey in an adjacent house to help with correspondence. She managed to keep abreast of developments in the Colorado River project as well as her other interests, but she neglected to write to Frank, prompting an outraged letter from him in September.

"I think that your activities might be an excuse for negligence of casual friends—whom you rarely neglect—but despite your penitence I have been and still am hurt by this summer's evidence that the entertainment of others, business etc. really take precedence over giving me the personal news that my affection led me repeatedly to ask for. . . . Can you blame me that I begin to feel that the relationship is rather one-sided?"[21]

Chastened, Isabella must have written him as he wished, for he answered on October 5, "My dear child: If you knew how happy a letter from you such as I received yesterday can make me, how happy that letter did make me, you surely would not grudge the effort or the demand on your time and I realize that both are considerable." Now largely retired, with many of his circle gone, he was increasingly dependent on Isabella's love and attention: "So, perhaps, even if it is hard to put aside a practically important thing for a purely sentimental one, sometimes you will think it worthwhile to give me happiness by writing to me." He did not, as he might have, list the many times he had helped her, from giving her a home and schooling, to advice and support during Bob's protracted illness, to being her mainstay in the dark hours after John's death. He appealed to her purely on the grounds that he loved her and wanted to be loved back.[22]

It was increasingly hard for Isabella to ignore practically important things. She was troubled by the continued poor performance of Ahumada, and she continued to lobby members of the Arizona legislature for the Colorado River project. But, she confessed to John, she feared she was "drifting into an ineffectual busyness. . . . I have the facilities to live remarkably, but I am not capable of using them. This is not worthy of you, John." She knew she needed more time alone to think, although it must have been tempting to bury her grief in constant activity.[23]

The Hut was growing *"appallingly,"* she wrote Bob early in 1928. During its first year it had sold approximately $37,000 worth of articles made by the vets and their wives. Isabella's part got good coverage in the press. Sometimes she was identified snidely as Lady Bountiful, other times by the more dignified title of "sponsor," but always she was associated with the enterprise she had founded. Her increased activities prompted her to make a permanent move to Tucson, although the change from tiny Ajo left her disoriented. An amused reporter noted that she was unable to give her new street address, remembering only that her home was on "Sixth." Such vagueness was apparently typical of Isabella: A couple of weeks earlier she had bought four blocks of land in the east part of town and spent an entire afternoon a few days later trying to locate her property. She had somewhat guiltily made the purchase while her family were all in Europe but rationalized that the investment was for rental properties to be furnished with Hut products. Businessmen had advised her against it, she admitted, but she proved them wrong by renting out the houses and increasing demand for the veterans' furniture. Isabella Greenway was becoming a force in her new community. In addition to her work with the Hut, she served on several charity boards, became a good fund-raiser, and was a trustee of the Tucson Desert Sanitarium.[24]

In April, her growing political potential was recognized when she was named Arizona's Democratic national committeewoman. After the Nineteenth Amendment granted women everywhere the vote in 1920, each state chose a male and female representative for the Democratic national committee. The national committee-woman was responsible for party organization and national policy. In principle, women and men had equal influence on the commit-tee, but in reality, the party just wanted the committeewomen to se-cure the women's vote. A committeewoman was selected by a male executive committee who usually picked women who would go along with their decisions. Some thought Isabella's appointment was purely honorary, a tribute to the accomplishments of her late husband. As Eleanor Roosevelt, by then codirector of the national women's committee of the Democratic party, would later observe, all too often a committeewoman was selected because of her wealth or social standing or the party service of a deceased husband.[25] But some Democratic national committeewomen, widows like Daisy Harriman from the District of Columbia and former governor Nel-lie Tayloe Ross of Wyoming, had carved out their own place in poli-tics after their husbands' deaths. In any case, calls later that year for Isabella to run for elective office contradict the interpretation that it was an honorary appointment.

"So here I am face to face with Al Smith," she wrote Bob of the likely Democratic presidential nominee, the governor of New York. She was heartened by the fact that Frank and other Republi-cans approved of Smith. Later that spring, she was summoned east to meet him. Isabella was disappointed to discover that Smith was a man of no physical distinction, decidedly insignificant of bearing, but she realized, she told Bob, that he represented the "predominat-ing tough city group who are a big part of America and deserve their turn."[26] She was trying to talk herself into enthusiasm for a man who was so different from her Western ideal.

In late June 1928, she went to Houston for the Democratic Na-tional Convention, taking three-year-old Jack along with her. She arrived a day early, to have time to scout around. She reported to friends: "We Democrats in our shirt sleeves . . . seersucker linens,

Palm Beach suits, Alpaca and thin kid shoes … little drawling Southern women bullying such big helpless men. Some of us chewing gum. All of us pouring rivers of whatever you Republicans call the summer wet by which we honest plain folk earn our living." But the political ins and outs were coming to interest her even more than the painterly details she had always adored. And she honed debating skills that she would soon put to use as an official champion of the Democratic Party, arguing with southern delegates appalled by Smith's support of repealing the Eighteenth Amendment that had ushered in Prohibition. "To hear these little town Southerners talk you'd believe enforcement has been practicable, and the world better," she marveled. The convention also afforded her the opportunity to meet important Democratic women like Nellie Ross.[27]

When Isabella returned to Arizona, it was more apparent than ever that her appointment as national committeewoman was a tribute to her political prospects. A woman at the *Phoenix Gazette* wrote Isabella urging her to run for governor: "You would have the army boys back of you—100 percent—and the women of the state no less so. We know what your business acumen is like, we know you for an executive. The mud will fly this fall among the men—and you, like Caesar's wife (to be trite) would be the one person in the race above reproach." More realistically, Isabella was approached to run for state senate from the Ajo district. While admitting she was flattered by the confidence so expressed, she denied to F. A. Nathan of the *Tucson Citizen* that she was a candidate. However, up in Williams for the summer, she began to reconsider and sent out a flurry of letters to test the waters. She feared that her background was inadequate but was overwhelmed by assurances of support. She wrote her lawyer, Cleon Knapp, "If I had any doubts about running for the Senate, to hear that a dyed-in-the-wool Republican like yourself would vote for me would be the final influence that would turn the tables." The Ajo Democratic committeemen also endorsed her candidacy. The decision was all but taken out of her hands when nomination papers for the September 11 primary were filed for her from Pima County in July. She wrote Nathan to say she had changed her mind.[28]

Nathan sent a lengthy, sobering response. Even though he was a Republican, he assured her he would put aside his party affiliation to support her, and he believed that she could be elected. However, he thought she first needed to understand that the Democratic Party in Arizona was split into two factions: the supporters of Governor George Hunt and the conservative anti-Hunts who would likely join forces with the Republicans. He concluded, "I do not believe it possible to straddle this issue within the Democratic party and it is a question whether it is good policy or not for you to get into this mess at the present time . . . not knowing what you may be anticipating for the future." He was one of several advising her to reconsider, which she did, wiring Hunt's county coordinator: "Kindly disregard letter mailed Saturday from Williams accepting candidacy deeply regret conditions have since arisen which make it advisable withdraw." She wrote Nathan that support from people like him had been very gratifying: "my career of four days in politics was worth that."[29]

She had already made her decision to back out when she received a long letter from Frank Cutcheon urging her not to run. Surprisingly, she had not told her longtime advisor of her quandary; he had learned about it from a letter Isabella had written Martha, who was visiting the Cutcheons in Paris, where Frank was a member of the postwar Reparations Commission. Why had Isabella not taken her uncle into her confidence? Was it because she could anticipate all too well his objections? They were not the considerations of hardball politics, as Nathan's had been, but the more conventional questions of a woman's duty to her family.

"I fervently hope you will decline the nomination," Frank wrote his niece. "You have more than enough to do with the things that are really obligatory and although that sort of thing may seem like a lark, you will find when you get into it, if you do, that it will take a pretty serious demand upon your strength and attention without adding to—perhaps subtracting from—your general usefulness."[30]

Discussing her dilemma in a letter to John at the end of August, Isabella mused, "I teeter on the brink . . . a sweep of fire is trying to get me to run for the Senate. . . . You seem to say 'politics is fraught with the untrue, an ugly battlefield for a woman. If she is to enter it must be in an armour of spiritual confidence, unassailable in its strength of selfless objective.' "[31]

Perhaps sensing that her day in elective office would come, Isabella dedicated herself in the meantime to her job as national committeewoman. She soon realized that the Democratic Party was even more fragmented than usual that year. In addition to the factions Nathan had described, many Democratic women did not support Smith, either because of his stand on Prohibition or because he was a Catholic. Isabella hoped, though, that some Republican women would not be supporting Hoover. So she suggested organizing Smith for President clubs, leaving the state and county Democratic clubs to work for local candidates. Isabella believed that "the result of every campaign should be greater strength within its ranks."[32]

John J. Raskob, chairman of the Democratic national committee, wrote Isabella about the importance of organizing the women. Relatively new voters elsewhere, the women of Arizona had been voting as long as the men, since statehood in 1912. Tom Robins, a New York friend of John Greenway's, thought Western women enjoyed an advantage: "The political power of the right kind of woman in your part of the country is enormous. Here it amounts to very little." Isabella was not going to be relegated to the mere rounding up of women's votes, however. She wrote Raskob to protest Smith's reported support for the Boulder Dam. "Our birth rights in the Colorado river are nearest the hearts of every Arizonan," she explained.[33]

Still, she knew turnout would be critical and accordingly asked the state campaign director for the name and address of every Democratic voter, the budget and expenditures for each county, and a method to check Democratic voter registration. In a sparsely settled state of 110,000 voters, organization was going to be a challenge. But her resolve to be organized was still liable to her characteristic scatterbrained lapses. One day she completely forgot an appointment with the state campaign director. Another time she wrote the president of the women's Democratic club in Tucson: "I am ashamed to tell you that I have written twice to ask you to put me in touch with Tucson's Democratic outlook, and have each time been called hurriedly out of town and stuck the letters in the car pocket or my own and in neither case remember mailing them."[34]

Isabella could do little in the way of organizing before the primary election on September 11 because the factional struggles of local candidates took precedence in the voters' minds. In mid-September she received the dubious suggestion from New York headquarters that she enlist "some prominent women in your community whose husbands are for Smith and get them to take a lead in organizing the women." More usefully, Isabella corresponded with Franklin Roosevelt about strategy; she planned to say that, although she favored Prohibition, she supported Smith because Prohibition was not working, and he thought people should vote locally on the issue. Such a vote, if in favor of Prohibition, would result in a greater commitment to the experiment, she reasoned.[35]

By mid-October Isabella was in full campaign mode, traveling throughout the state. She wired Bob: "Darling Republican doing best defeat your candidate . . . speaking different town practically every night until election with no improvement in eloquence." But the *Nogales Daily Herald,* which supported Hoover editorially, disagreed, writing that her speaking style was a successful combination of "sincerity, humor, straight-forwardness, and touching appeal." She used the argument about Prohibition that she had rehearsed with Franklin. Another issue for many voters was Smith's Catholic religion. Isabella claimed that his record showed Smith had not shown partiality to his coreligionists. A decision to vote for Smith was, she insisted, a "test rather of our own Christianity than his." Addressing the Democratic Women's Club in Tucson, Isabella declared that women's "innate goodness" ensured that "our consciences are our constitutions."[36]

Isabella Greenway was appealing to the traditional assumption that women were less interested in partisan activity than in social reform. But many women in the 1920s, including Isabella, were beginning to erase the line between reform activities and politics. As the election neared, Isabella wrote the women's director of publicity at the Democratic national committee about her efforts: "We are having wonderful mass meetings everywhere—processions, bands, bon-fires, constant speaking and such an amount of campaigning has never been heard of in the State of Arizona." But she warned that in the last two presidential elections, the state had gone Republican. She sent a copy of her letter to Eleanor Roosevelt, who headed up the women's division at the national level.[37]

Isabella and Eleanor were writing a new chapter in their "volume of friendship," Isabella's term for their quarter-century correspondence. Much of their communication at this time was limited to an affectionate scrawl at the bottom of form letters or telegrams. Perhaps defensive because of her friend's head start in politics, Isabella stressed that she knew the local situation better: "We did receive your maps—such humorous documents, we think of having them framed!!! . . . They are wholly impractical from a point of view of time, distance and roads." She also wanted Eleanor to appreciate how hard she was working: "Martha is planning to buy a stretcher to take me out of Arizona the day after the election and charge it to the Democratic party," she claimed. But Eleanor soothed her friend's feelings by continuing to ask her advice. As Isabella grew more confident of her abilities, they worked together more smoothly. The day after Election Day, Isabella wrote Eleanor, "Hasn't it been a grand scrap?"[38]

Despite Isabella Greenway's efforts, Arizona, like most of the rest of the states, went for Hoover, continuing an almost unbroken run of Republican presidents dating back to before the Civil War. The South, the Democrats' former stronghold, had been particularly troubled by Smith's Catholicism and stand on Prohibition; Hoover carried five southern states. But in Arizona, Democrats took comfort from the fact that all their local candidates won election. Men from all walks of life wrote Isabella to express appreciation of her work. A disabled miner said, "I feel so proud to see our Women come out in the open and take the battle up that the men have shown a Cowardly action toward's [sic]." Even Governor Hunt, who had been defeated, praised Isabella, saying, "No other woman in Arizona did as much for the success of the party." Women voters were more than appreciative; they were inspired. "I am aroused now as I have never been before since we have been given the franchise," wrote a woman who offered to help Isabella reorganize. Franklin Roosevelt, who had been elected to succeed Al Smith as governor of New York, also wrote to thank Isabella for her good work. She was modest in acknowledging these compliments, laughing that she had worked hard "as to mileage, physical endurance and speechmaking, with the ungratifying result that Arizona went stronger republican for the president than it ever has before."[39]

Among men and women alike, she inspired enthusiastic support, and people began to mention Isabella as a possible candidate for governor in 1930. Isabella protested that their suggestions were "overwhelming to a humble woman in the ranks of domesticity," but that her appreciation of the compliment was "as profound as if I deserved it." Despite her objections, there were signs that Isabella was keeping her options open, writing of Arizona's successes to national leaders and supporting the Arizona Democratic Party financially.[40]

Back in Ajo for Christmas, she sent out holiday cards featuring a photograph of John Greenway's bust in a clay sketch by the noted sculptor Gutzon Borglum, whom Isabella had commissioned to create the statue of her husband authorized for the U.S. Congress. Borglum was then at the crest of a remarkable career. He had created a number of heroic sculptures and, in 1924, had begun his most famous work of art, the presidential sculptures on Mount Rushmore. After dismissing a number of artists as "decorative" or "faddish," when Isabella saw Borglum's work, she decided at once he was the one to sculpt her late husband. She wrote to John, "Such a sense of relief . . . that he can and will do a great figure of your glorious body." After the Democratic Convention in Houston, Isabella had visited Borglum in his San Antonio studio, bringing John's photographs, clothes, and gear to represent his various roles as Rough Rider, copper miner, and officer in the Great War. Borglum later remarked that she knew more about her husband's appearance and characteristics than anyone he had ever dealt with in making a hero's statue. They chose to depict him in civilian engineering outdoor clothes, with a "stern vigorous expression," and speculated that the statue of General Greenway would be the first shirtsleeved figure in the august Rotunda.[41]

The year 1929 brought a respite for Isabella after the strenuous election year. She took time to make amends to neglected family members. Frank Cutcheon, overseas and homesick, was still warning that involvement in politics would lead her to neglect her real duties, although in Paris he had been surprised to find that over a third of those working with him on the Reparations Commission were women. He was unwilling, however, that his own Isabella should be distracted by her work to neglect him. He now wrote pathetically: "At last we have something in your own handwriting. . . . For months I have felt as if an arm and a leg had dropped off . . . when months go by without a sign . . . one can't help wondering what the matter can be." Isabella answered that his letter had been "like the sun coming out after a cloud which I know too well I

The statue of John C. Greenway in Gutzon Borglum's Studio, 1929

created myself." But she gently but firmly defended her activity: "It will be hard for some people to understand when I say the winter has been singularly full of contentment for me. . . . It has been one hundred percent strenuous with legitimate objectives that have had no note of tragedy in them, and, with the exception of two years of my life, this is the first time this has happened for twenty-three years."[42]

Isabella warned her uncle that there was a possibility she might run for governor. She had received letters of support from a number of prominent Democrats, one of whom wanted to run for governor himself but had said that he would defer to Isabella and campaign for her if she declared. She was not thinking of it, she assured her uncle, because "I have always believed that a woman with small children should be in a position to give them her best and if necessary her all." She had a practical reason, too, for this seemingly altruistic position: Most reasonable women would not vote for a woman with a four-year-old, knowing she could not give her time to public service without neglecting him. Isabella claimed she was passing along the news of her possible candidacy only "for the gossip element there is in it," but she might have meant to indicate that it was a decision she would revisit.[43]

Meanwhile, she had built a house in Tucson. Always happy when homebuilding, Isabella loved her new place, "pretty, convenient, warm, sunflooded, and private." Bob wrote Martha, "Before long we will have to hire a group of carpenters and plumbers to keep our mother from getting depressed in her old age." But, Isabella told a skeptical Frank, she'd had a "delightful sense of justification" in building it, because she had furnished it with Hut furniture and was getting inquiries from hotels.[44]

Former Wyoming governor Nellie Ross, now heading up the women's division of the Democratic national committee, contacted Isabella soon after the first of the year in 1930, insisting that it was important even in "peace-time" for Democratic women to develop their organization. Isabella agreed, stressing to a colleague that their job had just begun. By August, calls for Isabella to run for governor were increasing. Both Arizona's U.S. senator Carl Hayden and the editor of the *Prescott Courier* supported Isabella, reported one longtime female correspondent, adding, "All the women are for you." She concluded, "Our men are too badly split up. The women must do the job."[45]

Isabella heard along the same lines from Franklin Roosevelt. A friend of Franklin's, W. L. Barnum, had written him that the Arizona Democratic Party badly needed someone to defeat Hunt for the gubernatorial nomination, and Barnum thought Greenway could do it. Hunt's liberal supporters were disgusted by his notorious political machine, while conservative Democrats deplored his progressive tendencies, but Isabella Greenway could "compose these differences." Franklin was in a position to influence her, Barnum thought: "You know Mrs. Greenway better than I do.... Women are differently constituted than men. We may think we know them, but we do not." Franklin duly wrote Isabella: "Apparently people are getting rather tired of the factional disturbances caused by the perennial candidacy of Governor Hunt and feel that you would satisfy all factions. More than that, they say that you would make a splendid governor—and that, after all, is the most important of all." Isabella stuck to her resolve not to be a candidate, at least not while Jack was still very young, but she answered Franklin, "You cannot imagine what a thrill I get when I think that you and Eleanor can, for a moment, entertain a serious thought of me as a candidate for governor, when, after our lifetime relation, you know, too well, my inadequacy." She promised instead to "plan a very strenuous campaign of reorganization" in an attempt to resolve the factional difficulties. In any case, she was ineligible, because she had not yet resided in the state for the requisite amount of time.[46]

CHAPTER EIGHT

"More Women and More Money"

ISABELLA GREENWAY was not going to run for governor, but early in 1930 she met with her various political advisors to decide what to do as national committeewoman. She wanted to improve the party organization, beginning with Arizona's 318 precincts, with special attention to recruiting more women at the precinct level and aligning the women's interests with the men's. In addition to good grassroots organization, Isabella knew that a permanent party organization needed money. She hoped her workers could persuade one thousand Democrats to donate at least one dollar toward a general fund. Although it would mean a great deal of work, she believed that the act of making a contribution would increase support and interest. After the stock market crash in October 1929, though, she advised her workers to collect only what people were willing to give without pressure. She summed up her philosophy in a speech to the Maricopa County Democrats in Phoenix: "The Democratic party in this state needs more women and more money."[1]

A letter Isabella had received from the Greenlee County chairman shows what she was up against in recruiting women. She had asked him for the name of his female vice-chair, and he answered, "We are somewhat old-fashioned here and the women do not take an active part in politics." Eleanor Roosevelt wrote Isabella's male counterpart, Arizona national committeeman Clarence Gunter, that he needed to remedy the imbalance. Women were the Democratic Party's best hope to overcome the Republican majority, she argued. While Eleanor was being stern, Isabella adopted a conciliatory tone in letters to her county chairmen, saying that she needed the names of women vice-chairs so that she could report on the "splendid progress" being made in party organization. Under cover of this blandishment, she slipped in an order: "It has proved expedient in most places to have the Democratic men and women attend all meetings together, rather than work as separate units." By the end of March, although some counties still had no women vice-chairs, Isabella could report that at least in some of the counties, the women were working at all times with the men. The reorganization of the Democratic Party would be one of Greenway's most important political legacies.[2]

Isabella was convinced that good organization was key to solving the lack of Democratic unity and was prepared to do it herself. She made that point behind her usual smokescreen of modesty in a letter to Dr. Gunter: "You can imagine how over-whelmed I am by the expression of confidence from the Central Committee who are permitting me to do a portion of the State organization work in their behalf because, like you, they are too busy with their personal affairs to give it the necessary attention." She thought that reorganization, such as they had undertaken in Tucson, could help eliminate factions, winning back Democrats who had drifted away. She was similarly modest when addressing Judge R. C. Stanford, the Democratic state chairman. She thought there might be trouble if "my part in the whole is accentuated through the gracious tribute paid my small efforts," begging him to "take the initiative and responsibility, leaving me as nearly out of the picture as possible." She claimed she wanted to avoid the criticism attendant on any "personal prominence," but she might really have been worried about sexist resentment by the men of her leadership.[3]

Isabella was more candid writing to her old friend Mary Harriman Rumsey, proud that she had been able to create in the West something equal, if not superior, to anything in the East: "We are simply seething in politics. I can only parallel our home to Alice [Roosevelt Longworth]'s saloon [sic] in Washington, the only difference being . . . that in our parlor of Democracy we are consorting with the real people. Martha says she very much doubts if our variety are any more real than Alice's. I leave it to you whether Alice can produce anything as rugged as our good friend who runs the Pool Hall in Ajo, [and] another who is the conductor between here and Phoenix."[4]

Isabella's work prompted even more calls for her to run for governor. Charles Hardy, the Democratic chairman of Santa Cruz County, wrote: "Wherever I go I hear many favorable comments upon the possibility." Frank Cutcheon was very much disturbed by reports that she was inclined to accept the nomination. He argued: "I think you would help neither the party nor the State. . . . You have everything to lose and nothing to gain." She answered that she found his letter depressing. Far from discouraging him, however, this only stimulated his lawyerly mind: "Nothing better than your reply could demonstrate how little of the temper of the candidate . . . and how much of the temperament of the woman you possess. My little exasperating franknesses are as nothing to the sledgehammer . . . which you will invite if you offer yourself as a candidate— still worse if you come to hold an important office." He insisted that she was already "a very fine influence in Arizona and elsewhere in *many* ways." But he closed as always with the assurance of "a heart full of love."[5]

Chapter Eight

On April 13, Judge Frank H. Lyman announced he would be a candidate for governor, pleasing Isabella by saying that with an organization such as she was trying to perfect, the Democrats should be able to elect him. But former Governor Hunt was still a force to be reckoned with. Isabella met with Hunt to try to persuade him not to run against Lyman. He appeared equally interested in Isabella's plans. Warning that she should realize that "no Woman, no Mormon, and no Catholic could be elected governor of this State," he asked if she had considered a run for Congress. He seemed confident that conditions in the state were advantageous to him: hard times, unemployment, higher taxes, unbalanced budgets, and an unpopular Republican incumbent. Isabella did not think Hunt could be elected and was depressed at the prospect of a primary fight. But she professed to find her meeting with Hunt "intensely interesting to one not accustomed to the workings of the political mind."[6]

At this time Isabella had another project closer to her heart than mere politics. Borglum had finished the statue of John Greenway, and Isabella traveled to Washington to see it dedicated on May 24, 1930, the first figure in Statuary Hall of a World War I veteran. American flags draping the statue were released by five-year-old Jack, revealing a work that Isabella thought "daring . . . unique in its bold technique and interpretation." Isabella had been dreading the "sadness and anguish" she thought the day would bring but, listening to eloquent tributes from Arizona's senators, found it instead to be "singular in its note of triumph and strength—just as John would have had it." While in Washington, Isabella met with Mr. Jouett Shouse, the chairman of the Democratic executive committee, who praised the West in general and Arizona in particular for eliminating separate men's and women's organizations.[7]

Isabella spent the summer in Williams, but she was still eager to work. Her male superiors, however, were ready to rest. She wrote Judge Stanford that since they had gone to the trouble and expense of collecting the names of every Democratic voter in the state, they should offer them to local candidates who could not afford to collect them. In mid-August, braving temperatures over a hundred degrees in a world without air conditioning, she went down to Phoenix to open an office for 660 Democratic candidates throughout the state. In September, Lyman was defeated by George Hunt in the primary, and Hunt went on to defeat the Republican incumbent in November. Agriculture, in which the overwhelming majority of Arizonans were employed, had been in the doldrums since the mid-1920s. As the Depression wore on, Arizona Democrats benefited from disillusionment with the Republicans, as well as from improved organization. Isabella was disappointed that the Democrats were stuck once again with Hunt, but she tried, as always, to be positive, writing a friend, "I am told that the experienced politician feels the most heated campaign to have been worthwhile if a 'tendency has been created' for something better." But she admitted it was "a hungry reward for hard work and great desires." Perhaps Isabella felt rewarded by a female admirer who wrote, "The finest and most encouraging thing for the women of the party is the interest you have shown."[8]

At the same time that she was building her reputation as a politician, Isabella was developing business interests that added to her image as a person who could get things done. For several years, there had been indications that a stock market crash was coming. Cutcheon had advised her to sell her inflated stock and buy government bonds, so her finances were not immediately affected by the events of October 1929. She was therefore in a position to invest in a small airline company. John Greenway's military chauffeur in France, Charles W. Gilpin, had learned to fly during the war; afterwards, he had continued to work for Greenway. In the summer of 1930, Gilpin asked Isabella to help him acquire planes from a charter airline that had gone out of business, and they renamed the company G & G Airlines, for Gilpin and Greenway. One day in late August, Gilpin flew Isabella down to Nogales, on the Mexican border. The airplane had too little fuel for the return trip, and they were stranded for several hours. Isabella used the time to work out plans for an even more ambitious enterprise—the Arizona Inn.[9]*

For some time she had been worried about the fate of the Hut, in its way as much a tribute to John Greenway as the statue. The furniture co-op had never made money, but after the stock market crash, the trickle of orders dried up entirely. For some time, Isabella kept the enterprise afloat, but when it ceased operations, she was left with a great deal of surplus furniture. Afterwards she liked to say that she built the Arizona Inn simply in order to use all that Hut furniture. But she had actually been thinking for some time about the possibilities of a resort hotel, for sound business reasons. Although civic leaders advertised the Tucson climate as a tourist attraction, there were no luxury accommodations. Isabella had very firm ideas about what she wanted—cozy homelike cottages grouped around a central garden—and she collaborated closely with her Tucson architect Merrit H. Starkweather. Even during construction, she continued to make changes. She was especially eager to have windows that provided good views. She would lie on makeshift beds fashioned from trestles and boards, to get an idea of what the guests would see on awakening. When one workman had the temerity to suggest that she couldn't make a certain change, she retorted, "Don't you ever tell me I can't do anything!" He meekly complied. The signature pink of the adobe walls was obtained, according to a later account of Martha's, when her mother asked the painting contractor to come outside into the bright sunlight. Standing in front of a newly plastered wall, the fair-skinned Isabella pointed to her face, flushed in the heat. "This is the color I want," she said.[10]

Construction began in the middle of September and, remark-

*Isabella Greenway operated G & G Airlines, which made flights between Arizona, California, and Mexico, until 1934, during a very competitive time in the airline industry (Holmstrom, 15).

The Arizona Inn

ably, was completed three months later. Originally, the Inn comprised a main building and four cottages, accommodating forty-five to fifty guests. The Arizona Inn opened on December 18, 1930, with a sorority dinner dance for twenty-five couples, during which an important omission was discovered: Isabella had neglected to provide a men's room. She had to call in Ajo miners to blast out a space underneath the lobby for the forgotten facilities. Isabella wanted her guests to feel completely at home, and, to that end, she provided for as much privacy as possible. Never would she divulge the names of her guests, who included, according to Arizona Inn historian Blake Brophy, "royalty, world figures, the celebrated, the notorious, stars and starlets, and some of the best cowmen in the West." Ironically, the Inn would be a more lasting legacy than Isabella Greenway's pioneering political career, which was more notable at the time.[11]

After Isabella's political activities in 1930, Governor George Hunt apparently considered it advisable to treat her with respect; in 1931 Hunt named her to the commission planning Arizona's exhibit at the upcoming 1933 World's Fair in Chicago. He had evidently taken notice of her growing influence not only in the mining and growing hospitality business but also in the politically important fields of conservation and cattle. The president of the Arizona Game Protective Association had asked for Greenway's help in lobbying, and she was active in the state Cattle Growers Association. Speaking in February on "A Woman's Place in the Cattle Business," Isabella claimed "forty-four years' experience" (she was then forty-four years of age), dating from her parents' venture in North Dakota. Many years later, however, she admitted, "I've ridden a horse ever since I was a year old and I'm simply frightened to death every time I get on a horse. . . . Only prayer keeps me on, and I never ride except when it's absolutely necessary to see the cattle or to get to a dam or some other inaccessible place. . . . I have the cloth for my riding clothes faded in the bolt so they'll look worn. Owning an Arizona ranch, I should appear to be an experienced horsewoman."[12]

Isabella also continued to keep a close eye on the Ahumada mine, through what she called "one of the leanest years in the lead field." Her Arizona Inn was prospering; the *Arizona Daily Star* reported that "the place is packed." One element in its success was that guests really did feel like guests in a home; Abby Rockefeller wrote that she had thoroughly enjoyed her stay because "Your presence adds so much of interest and charm."[13]

Isabella was still Democratic national committeewoman, too, and Franklin Roosevelt called on her from time to time for support. Despite the official tone of one such wire, he signed it, "Love from us both." Isabella was working hardest of all on another project with political potential, the Emergency Relief Committee and Re-employment Association, of which she was the chair. By the end of March, nearly two thousand people looking for work had registered with the Re-employment Bureau; about half had found work, at least for a few days.[14]

Isabella's work had necessarily taken her away from her children. Bob had gone to Europe in the summer of 1930, where he complained he was not getting enough mail from his mother and proceeded to Northern Rhodesia [present-day Zambia] to spend the next fifteen months learning the mining business. Martha, too, had been abroad, getting a polish to her education with a stay in England. So in early May, with Martha and Jack in tow, Isabella abandoned her activities in Tucson for nearly six months to visit Bob in Rhodesia. The *Tucson Citizen* noted her departure, in "the luxurious Greenway car," on the back of which were tied a "roll of blankets, smoked coffee pot, sun hat, and frying pan," surmounted by a sign, "Headed for Trader Horn." Isabella was not one to do things by halves. She had been ill, and Olivia Cutting James wrote her hope that Rhodesia would not be too primitive to allow for a good convalescence. Olivia reasoned that Rhodesia might actually be good for recuperating, since it was "one of the few places (*as yet*) you have neither mines, hotels, houses, ranches or airplane lines of your own to look after." A month later, Isabella was installed in a white plastered adobe house on the outskirts of the Roan Antelope Mine in Luanshya, delighted to have all her children under one roof, even though it was of corrugated iron. She was proud of her number one son, who had made a good place for himself, she wrote a friend. But even so far away, Isabella could not escape the demands of her various enterprises, and cables flew between Africa and Arizona. Still, she was able to relax and enjoy herself. As always, Isabella brightened the social life around her, entertaining guests from morning tea to "sundowners" and dinner.[15]

Back in Tucson by late October, Isabella immediately plunged into the minutiae of her many interests; everything from the inventory of bed sheets in the Inn to the Governor's commission on the copper tariff demanded her attention. The Depression had hit the state's vitally important copper industry very hard, and Hunt had asked her to meet with his copper commission, a considerable step up from her appointment to the World's Fair. A *Tucson Citizen* editorial wryly described Isabella's contributions to deliberations about a key industry: "From the accomplished Mrs. Greenway, who recently visited the African mining region, Arizona is receiving firsthand information about foreign competition in copper. Pointing out that African producers are now delivering copper in New York for a lower price than the actual cost of mining at Ajo, she is sensibly trying, in her capacity as a Democratic leader, to interest her party in the Republican principle of tariff protection."[16]

Isabella had decided to forego political office for herself, at least for the time being, but she had become a force to reckon with. An old friend from Tyrone, New Mexico, seeing her again after several years, found she had "changed quite a lot, or perhaps I've simply seen a side of you which I hadn't supposed to exist. . . . You are really a rather high powered executive." He added admiringly, "Lord only knows what you will try next."[17] What Isabella Greenway would try next would be to help elect her friend Franklin Roosevelt president of the United States.

Her first task was to win over Lewis L. Douglas, brother of her longtime friend Walter Douglas. Lewis, Arizona's lone congressman (with a small population, the state was entitled to only one), was thought to be opposed to FDR. Isabella explained to Roosevelt strategist Louis Howe that although Douglas had not come out for Roosevelt, he was not supporting anyone else; she suggested that a meeting with Franklin would bring him around. She also fought against a "whispering campaign" that Roosevelt's physical condition could be a handicap in the coming election. She had known Franklin for more than thirty years and could testify that before he was stricken by polio, his strength had been average. Now, she insisted, he was unusually strong, with greater vitality than most.[18]

Eleanor Roosevelt wanted Isabella to meet with Molly Dewson, one of Franklin Roosevelt's principal advisors, for a strategy session. Dewson hoped Isabella could get the state delegation to the national convention pledged to Roosevelt, because Arizona came high on the list of states in the roll call, and it would increase momentum toward his nomination. Flatteringly Molly Dewson added, "Eleanor told me last night how much you count in Arizona."[19]

When Franklin Roosevelt became an openly declared candidate on January 23, 1932, Eleanor enlisted Isabella for the duration. First Eleanor had to caution Isabella that there were deep divisions within the Democratic Party. Al Smith had not declared his intentions but was suspected of pursuing a "block Roosevelt" strategy. John J. Raskob, Smith's 1928 campaign manager, had appointed his ally Jouett Shouse as chairman of the Democratic executive committee. In short, Eleanor said, in something of an understatement, the Democratic national committee "was not in complete sympathy with Franklin's candidacy." Historian Richard Oulahan would later put it more strongly: "The National committee was directed by [Roosevelt's] sworn enemies." FDR's preconvention strategy, therefore, was to avoid working at the national level, instead concentrating his efforts at the state and local level. Eleanor wanted Isabella to take charge of Franklin's campaign in Arizona. "Do write me," Eleanor urged her, "as to your ideas on the possibility of getting the Arizona delegates elected for Franklin." Somewhat abashed at the businesslike tone of her letter, Eleanor added a handwritten postscript: "Darling, all this is official. Willy nilly I am doing some work at political headquarters! . . . I love you always more and more. Devotedly, Eleanor."[20]

On February 8, Smith coyly announced that he would accept a draft for the presidential nomination. To keep that option open, Shouse proclaimed that "it would be wiser . . . not to instruct delegates to the convention in favor of any candidate." Roosevelt argued that he supported primaries because they prevented "the kind of national convention which became merely a trading post for a handful of powerful leaders." Lines were being drawn. Roosevelt's campaign manager Jim Farley was busy lining up as many commitments as possible all over the country, while Eleanor continued to beg Isabella to obtain an instructed delegation in Arizona. Isabella was willing to do all she could, but she made it clear she would have to be trusted to use her own judgment: "You and Miss Dueson [sic] may think we are not crystallizing our efforts out here; but I can assure you they are not out of our minds a moment," she assured Eleanor. Her strategy was to wait, "letting those who might not have *followed* us to Franklin, now be in a position to *lead* us to Franklin." The Hunt faction, of their own accord, had wired Farley for permission to start a Roosevelt Club, and branches were appearing all over the state. While "everything indicates the delegates will be 100% for Franklin," she noted that "Arizona has but once, that I know of, sent an instructed delegation, so a move to that end would . . . create immediate antagonism."[21]

Isabella went to Chicago as a member of the committee on arrangements for the convention, where she helped select Roosevelt's choice for temporary chairman, Senator Alben Barkley of Kentucky, over Smith's man, Jouett Shouse. Roosevelt's control over the committee appointments would later prove crucial for his nomination. Isabella herself was chosen to give one of the seconding speeches for Roosevelt, and Maricopa County committeeman Russ Tatum wrote to congratulate her on "the distinct honor you won for yourself and your State at the Democratic pow-wow. . . . It was a recognition of the force of your character and influence." In April Eleanor weighed in again on the importance of an instructed delegation. The Roosevelt headquarters, she said, were "afraid there is no man strong enough to get it through, so they have asked me to write you and urge that you do whatever you can to bring this about." She added, "It is wonderful to have all the men saying such wonderful things about [you]." Once again, as if surprised by the tone of her own letter, Eleanor added, "I never thought that you and I would be urged on on every hand in a political way but we certainly have seen many changes in our respective lives."[22]

Isabella could not resist such a plea. By the end of April she was writing Molly Dewson that she thought they would get an instructed delegation, although it was taking time. She had written all nine hundred precinct committeemen and women, urging them to study the candidates' records. Roosevelt had a good reputation as the progressive governor of a large state, which appealed to Westerners. Arthur Mullen, who headed the Roosevelt campaign in Nebraska, later wrote: "The Roosevelt boom was spreading like prairie fire through the West.... Men in Colorado, Wyoming, Kansas, Missouri, Iowa, the Dakotas, and Minnesota ... were hot as horseradish for the governor of New York. We felt ... that he was the one man ... who'd do, if he were elected, the things the West wanted done."[23]

The Arizona Democratic state central committee met on May 9, with Isabella leading the Pima County delegation. At the eleventh hour, she wired Farley for backup, asking him to telegraph two key men with his reasons for wanting an instructed delegation. Finally she prevailed and secured the delegates for Roosevelt. By then, FDR had amassed a little more than three hundred delegates, but he needed 470 more to be nominated. Al Smith, with a later start, had around 225.[24]

Even outside of Arizona, Isabella Greenway was being hailed as "a political phenomenon, if not a political genius." She used her new visibility to lobby for a copper tariff, wiring an influential Western senator on the Senate mining committee that, "It seems an error to penalize our copper miner because in prosperous 1929 he did not come to Congress imploring protective provision in the Smoot Hawley bill. Were you in the west there would be no need for argument.... Closed mines cold smelters and thousands of unemployed.... A refusal of aid means a grave injury to Democratic victory in the west this fall."[25]

The Democratic National Convention opened in Chicago on June 27 to nominate a presidential candidate. The Roosevelt forces were first on the scene, along with "big shots, little shots, candidates, delegates, national committeemen, reporters, photographers,

*Isabella Greenway, front row, third from left, and the Arizona
delegation to the 1932 Democratic National Convention*

lobbyists, gangsters, beer-runners, local politicians, curiosity seekers," according to Arthur Mullen, Roosevelt's floor advisor. "The
hotel corridors looked like the main street in a Texas oil town just
before they're going to bring in a gusher." Isabella was on hand with
Jack, seven, who, the *Chicago Tribune* noted, "addresses his ...
mother in adult fashion, as Isabella." By now, even Frank Cutcheon
had grown reconciled to her political activity and wrote to enlist her
support for an alternate Prohibition-repeal plank.[26]

Farley estimated that Roosevelt had 690 votes for the first ballot,
still considerably short of 770, the number needed for nomination.
Al Smith was confident he could stop Roosevelt. He expected to
win the support of the California and Texas delegations, who were
backing John Nance Garner, when the convention deadlocked. In
this scenario, he anticipated support from California delegate William Gibbs McAdoo, Woodrow Wilson's son-in-law, who had been
denied the presidential nomination after a bitter fight at the 1924

convention. That experience had taught McAdoo that it was vitally important for the Democrats to agree on a candidate. Almost any Democratic nominee could expect election in 1932; people all over the country were wearing lapel pins that said, "Anybody but Hoover." Pulled-out empty pants pockets were known as "Hoover flags."[27]

The first day was quiet, belying what was to come. The first order of business was for the resolutions committee to draw up the platform. The only activity that day was a demonstration when Alben Barkley endorsed a proposal to repeal the Eighteenth (Prohibition) Amendment. Will Rogers, writing in the *New York Times,* complained "The Democrats met, talked, agreed and adjourned. . . . The day was a total loss. . . . Here people had travelled hundreds of miles . . . and paid fancy prices to see what? To see 1100 delegates sit there and act like a lot of Republicans. . . . Cheered everything, hissed nothing—why it made me ashamed I was a Democrat. . . . Is it the influence of the female delegates that have ruined the reputation of the old 'hell raising, rip snorting' convention?" Women were still news at conventions.[28]

On the second day, however, partisan troops moved into position. John J. Raskob, the chairman of the Democratic national committee, wanted Jouett Shouse for the permanent chairman of the convention, with the important authority to recognize speakers, cut short debate, or adjourn a meeting at a crucial point. Roosevelt's floor leader, Arthur Mullen, considered Raskob and Shouse "definitely, decisively, devilishly anti-Roosevelt." The Roosevelt forces wanted Senator Thomas J. Walsh of Montana. When Al Smith did not speak up for Shouse, choosing instead to address the issue of Prohibition, Walsh squeaked by, 626 to 528.[29]

The convention did not reconvene until the evening of the following day, June 29. Reporters looking for copy fastened upon Isabella Greenway, whom they dubbed "Arizona's Sweetheart of Democracy," a testament to her comeliness as well as her popularity in the Grand Canyon state. Will Rogers, writing in the *New York Times,* observed that Isabella provided a link between the two Roosevelts, as the widow of two of TR's Rough Riders and a bridesmaid at Franklin's wedding to Eleanor. But H. L. Mencken, as usual, was less effusive: "The lady politicians, when they are allowed to second a motion and show off their millinery, sound like auctioneers."[30]

On the fourth day, June 30, the convention finally turned to the presidential nomination. Roosevelt was nominated by John E. Mack, who had nominated him for his first political office. Mack claimed that the "plodding hesitating utterances" of a friend of twenty-five years would be "a more welcome tribute than that of the most gifted tongue." Possibly, but the convention was not stirred. The demonstration that followed was tepid, and Mencken observed, "I can recall no candidate of like importance who ever had so few fanatics whooping for him."[31]

Isabella Greenway, who next mounted the platform to second Roosevelt, got a very different reception. Twenty thousand delegates, alternates, and spectators, led by the Arizona contingent standing on their chairs, roared enthusiastically. She asked the convention to pay "special attention to the next sentence that is to follow. In his personal life," her quiet allusion to his polio, "he has gallantly waged and triumphantly won a battle against Fate such as few men are called upon to fight." It was not his courage in fighting polio that impressed her most, however. She extolled his political beliefs:

> He has been attacked . . . because he believes . . . that the government . . . should extend its beneficence with equal hand to
> *all* elements of the people. . . . Mr. Chairman, it is because he so
> believes and so acts that Arizona believes in *him*. It believes in
> him because he is not afraid to say that hunger must be fed,
> that suffering must be relieved; because he knows that the failure of those who fail is the price paid to nature for the success

of those who win and that, in the last resort, the successful are but trustees for all; Because he believes that . . . the succour of the helpless comes before all other gain.[32]

For Isabella, who often rambled, it was a very succinct and focused speech. Perhaps that was due to help from Frank Cutcheon; a draft in his handwriting is among her papers. The *Arizona Daily Star* proudly reported that "her brief speech was interrupted three different times . . . and at the end it received enthusiastic applause."[33]

The second name placed in nomination was that of John Nance Garner of Texas, with William Gibbs McAdoo bearing aloft the California standard in the demonstration that followed. Al Smith was nominated next, on the grounds that he had earned the honor: "In 1928, riding the crest of the wave, the Republican party was unbeatable, yet our candidate polled 15 million votes—more than any Democrat ever received. . . . Now when the tide has turned, my friends, should he be cast aside?"[34]

Jim Farley, FDR's campaign manager, was hoping for a first-ballot victory. He wanted to offer John Nance Garner second place on the ticket if he would switch the Texas delegation to Roosevelt. But Garner, Speaker of the U.S. House of Representatives, had gone back to Washington, and Sam Rayburn, Garner's spokesman, thought Texas should remain loyal to Garner for two or three ballots. Farley thought he could hold onto the promised Roosevelt delegates for at least that long. The night wore on as various favorite sons got their moment of glory. Farley wanted to stop the speeches and start the balloting, but he came to realize "A thorough-going Democrat will give you his support, his loyalty, his vote and his money—but never his radio time." Finally, at 4:28 A.M., the first roll call was taken. It lasted almost two hours. Roosevelt got 666¼, with 770 needed to win; Smith 201¼ and Garner 90⅓, with 196 scattered among the others. In the second ballot, which lasted even longer, Roosevelt picked up 11½ votes; Smith lost 7; Garner stayed the same. Garner's strength was surprising, considering he had not campaigned. FDR and Garner forces wanted to adjourn to find out what Garner wanted to do, but Smith supporters in the New York delegation refused. A third interminable ballot resulted in a gain for Roosevelt of a mere 4½ votes; Smith lost a few more and Garner added 11.[35]

McAdoo had promised to call for an adjournment, but when Chairman Walsh looked his way, McAdoo was engaged in conversation. "For what purpose does the delegate from California rise?" prompted Walsh in a loud voice. McAdoo jumped up to move adjournment, which Arthur Mullen, FDR's floor manager, quickly seconded. Walsh banged down the gavel before Smith supporters could object, adjourning the convention from 9:15 A.M. until 8:30 that evening. Roosevelt's backers had eleven hours to find ninety votes, or watch the pledged delegates defect.[36]

Jim Farley, "dragged through knotholes of worry and wrung in wringers of helplessness," began to make deals. Governor Harry Byrd of Virginia wanted to be a U.S. senator; he pledged his support and Roosevelt later appointed a Virginia senator to his Cabinet, clearing the way for Byrd's election. The Mississippi, Iowa, Michigan, Minnesota, and Arkansas delegations all had to be kept in line. But Farley especially wanted to win over the California delegation, because of its size and its position in the roll call. Two of the California delegates, Thomas M. Storke, a newspaper publisher from Santa Barbara, and Hamilton Cotton, a Los Angeles oil millionaire, both among McAdoo's closest personal advisers, would be instrumental in turning the tables. And Isabella Greenway persuaded them to change.

Shortly after the convention was adjourned, Storke and Cotton were making for their hotel rooms to catch some badly needed rest, "two of the most haggard and wornout men you can imagine," Storke later recalled. At the elevator they were detained by New

York men hoping to persuade McAdoo to support yet another candidate, Newton Baker, secretary of war under Woodrow Wilson. Storke assured them that California was committed to Garner for at least three or four more ballots. Even after they reached their room, however, they were unable to sleep. The phones rang incessantly, telegrams arrived in a flood, and people pounded on their door.[37]

"Perhaps the most insistent visitor we had," Storke remembered, "was Mrs. Isabella Greenway, who headed the Arizona contingent." Isabella knew Storke from Santa Barbara. "Her tearful pleas ... finally induced Ham and me to accept her invitation to confer with Farley," Storke admitted. Isabella arranged the appointment for 4 P.M. Farley told Storke and Cotton that Roosevelt would begin to lose support on the next ballot unless California, which came early in the alphabet, swung over to him. Farley asked what McAdoo wanted in exchange and was told "Nothing." Storke and Cotton agreed to support Garner for vice president and sped back to the Sherman Hotel, where they quickly told McAdoo about their meeting, and urged him to call a caucus. In the meantime he had heard from powerful newspaper publisher William Randolph Hearst, who also agreed to Garner for the number-two spot. It only remained to be seen if Garner would accept. Garner did. He said he had received all the honors he'd ever had through the Democratic Party and could not refuse an offer to be their vice-presidential nominee. He admitted privately to Sam Rayburn: "This man Roosevelt is the choice of that convention. . . . Hell, I'll do anything to see the Democrats win one more election." Garner told McAdoo to release the California delegates to Roosevelt.[38]

The California delegates, though, were not so biddable. Storke estimated that more than half wanted to stay with Garner for at least one more ballot. They caucused for over an hour, as the clock ticked on toward 8:30. Three times Isabella called Storke out to urge him on. "I have never seen such an excited and nervous woman," said Storke, "as she begged, 'Please come over to our side, Tom! Let me tell Jim [Farley] that California is going to switch to Roosevelt on the next ballot. Please! Please!' " Finally, McAdoo got instructions to vote the California delegation for Roosevelt on the fourth ballot.[39]

Later, one of Roosevelt's friends would say, "Of the 55,000 Democrats said to be in Chicago, 62,000 are going to claim credit for the switch" of the California delegation. Jim Farley observed, "Various men have staked out an assortment of claims . . . that they brought about the nomination by directing one effort or another. Actually, the majority of the claimants did little or nothing to bring about the convention selection of Roosevelt." But Raymond Moley, later part of the FDR "brain trust," believed "the two persons who deserve more credit than anyone else were Sam Rayburn of Texas and Tom Storke of Santa Barbara."[40] Isabella never claimed to have done a thing. But if Storke deserves credit, so does Isabella Greenway, who persuaded him.

The Roosevelt nomination was still not out of the woods. Rayburn had to fight hard to convince the Texas delegation to give up Garner. Garner was also strong in Alabama, and Will Rogers was speculating that Arizona and Arkansas, too, might swing to Garner on the fourth ballot. All three, early in the roll call, could cause a rush away from Roosevelt.[41]

The delegates reconvened that evening, clean and relatively rested. A thunderstorm had burst upon the scene in the early hours of the morning, and the steamy heat had abated. Alabama declared for Roosevelt, and Arizona, no doubt gingered up by Isabella, held as well. Meanwhile, McAdoo had been delayed when the limousine he was riding in ran out of gas (some thought not by coincidence). He arrived at the stadium just in time to run up to the platform. "California came here to nominate a President of the United States," he declared. "She did not come here to deadlock a convention . . . when any man comes into a Democratic National Convention with the popular will behind him to the extent of almost 700 votes. ... " The Roosevelt delegation began to cheer, the galleries started booing. It was nearly thirty minutes before they could be quieted. Then McAdoo cast California's forty-four votes for Franklin D. Roosevelt. In the final count, Roosevelt won 945 votes. But the New York delegation, many bitter-enders for Smith, refused to make it unanimous.[42]

The following day, John Nance Garner was nominated as the vice-presidential candidate. Isabella and others expecting "purely honorary" nominations withdrew their names, asking the convention to approve Garner's nomination "by acclamation." Congresswoman Mary T. Norton of New Jersey had also been scheduled to receive a vice-presidential nomination. Veteran Arizona state legislator Nellie T. Bush, who had been designated to nominate Isabella Greenway, was bitterly disappointed. "I think it's just too bad that at least one woman won't get the honor of being mentioned at this convention," she said. "I feel it is a little bit conspicuous that all the women who had planned to put up woman candidates have been asked to withdraw." As for Garner, he later admitted that he had traded his position as Speaker of the House, "the second most important office in the nation, for one which, in itself, is almost wholly unimportant," an assessment he later refined to "not worth a warm bucket of spit." Why did he do it? "I'm a Democrat," he said. "I believe the country needs a Democratic Party in power at this time." A prolonged fight at the convention might have cost the party its chance at the White House.[43]

Roosevelt flew to Chicago and, in an unprecedented gesture, addressed the convention that had just nominated him. Sporting a red rose in the lapel of his dark suit, he announced, "I pledge myself to a new deal for the American people." The term *New Deal* did not immediately draw attention until it began to appear in Rollin Kirby's political cartoons. Roosevelt's unorthodox appearance at the convention was just the beginning. He told the press later that evening that he would begin his campaign at once, instead of waiting until August as was customary. Isabella's conspicuous role at the convention earned her some invitations to participate at the national level, but she preferred to concentrate on Arizona.[44]

The Depression deepened: By 1932, twenty percent of the work force was unemployed; those who were working often had their hours cut and wages reduced. Isabella's increased visibility on the political scene brought her many more requests for assistance—for clothing, bedding, books, work, investment, college tuition. She gave what she could, but over and over she had to write, "Like every one, my resources are greatly reduced, and my responsibilities increased, and I have to budget with the greatest forethought. I have practically no margin for the unexpected."[45]

A few days after the convention, Isabella Greenway moved up to the cool pine forest in Williams. Her idyll did not last long. She had to mediate between two men who both wanted to run Roosevelt's Arizona campaign, national committeeman Wirt Bowman, and the state chairman of the Democratic committee, C. E. Addams. Before she could even try to reconcile the two, Bowman stole the march by opening headquarters without informing either Addams or Greenway. Isabella was furious that the rival camps were duplicating and complicating the work, creating not only friction but higher costs. She planned to go to Phoenix in early September, she told Jim Farley, "to try to harmonize these two campaigns. . . . This appears to me the obvious fulfillment of my obligation as National Committeewoman." On September 8, a letter went out over the signatures of all three with guidelines for forming Roosevelt-Garner clubs.[46]

The high point of the campaign for Isabella was Franklin Roosevelt's visit to Williams during a whistle-stop tour of seventeen western states. Roosevelt's stop-off in Arizona created great excitement locally. The last president to visit the "baby state" had

At the Quarter Circle Double X Ranch, 1932. Front row, left to right:
Mr. and Mrs. James Roosevelt, Jack Greenway, Isabella, Franklin Roosevelt,
Eleanor Roosevelt, Anna Roosevelt Dall, Martha Ferguson.

been his cousin Theodore in 1912. FDR arrived in Phoenix on September 25, continued on to Williams and proceeded to Isabella's 110,000-acre ranch six miles west of town. Isabella accommodated more than one hundred guests for lunch in her small and rustic ranch house. Tables covered with red and white checked cloths were set out under the trees. Isabella, wearing a bright red hat, green silk dress, and white sports coat darted from one group to another. "I divide my time now between . . . cattle and Democrats; both of them keep me hopping," she was heard to say. "When I get old I'll settle down and do some quiet work, like raising oranges which grow calmly on trees." The colorful party at the Quarter Circle Double X Ranch had a serious purpose. At last Isabella was able to introduce Franklin to Arizona's congressman, Lewis L. Douglas.

Seated together at lunch, the two men made favorable impressions on each other. Afterwards, Douglas presented Roosevelt to the waiting crowd of three thousand.[47]

Following the inevitable speeches—Roosevelt announced that he supported a popular tariff on imported beef—a rodeo and horse races provided entertainment and color, "a madly whirling panorama of dusty cow ponies, leatherbrown ranchers with their wives and sunburned children, cowboys in widebrimmed hats, girls in riding breeches and vivid blouses," as the *Arizona Daily Star* reported. Isabella and Eleanor stole a few moments together amid the tumult. Later Eleanor wrote, "It fills me with pride to see you in your own surroundings and realize how people love and respect you. . . . It is an inspiration just to know you."[48]

Isabella Greenway spent a month campaigning for Roosevelt all over the state. She tried to appeal to Republicans, as well. Democrats had helped elect Hoover in 1928, she said, and now that the country was "facing ruin," it was up to the Republicans to help elect a Democrat. She would study a few pertinent statistics before each speech, so she would not have to use notes; her natural way of speaking, combined with sincerity and a sense of humor, appealed to her listeners. During the last two weeks she crisscrossed the state in her company's airplane, learning firsthand about the extent of unemployment in Arizona.[49]

CHAPTER NINE ⌇⌇⌇⌇⌇⌇⌇⌇⌇⌇⌇⌇⌇⌇⌇

Lady of the House

Afer the Roosevelt landslide on Election Day, an Associated Press reporter wrote that Isabella Greenway, credited with having played a major part in Arizona's Democratic sweep, might be in line for a Cabinet appointment, possibly labor or interior. Isabella, however, saw the election results as "not so much a victory, as an opportunity and a great responsibility." She set about at once to organize more relief programs in her community.[1]

First, though, she had a lot of catching up to do, especially with her children. Tucked in the back of Isabella's diary was a Western Union telegraph form on which eight-year-old Jack had scrawled "MA COME HOME." The fact that she kept it shows that she may not have been entirely comfortable with her absence from her young son's life. Still, Isabella was a person who celebrated the present, and at present all her children were together with her after almost eighteen months. "I have been surfeited with the joy of having my children home," she wrote one friend, "and have been brazenly negligent of everything I ought to attend to, and have danced incessantly and consorted wholly with the generation below me, which I find far more invigorating than politics."[2]

Next, Isabella turned to her neglected correspondence, apologizing and explaining that she had been "swamped" during the campaign. Mail was a constant problem for her; she had written to one dismayed correspondent: "You have good reason to believe that the desert allows of no flowing of ink. I can assure you this is not the case." Her friend Bill Mathews, editor of the *Arizona Daily Star* in Tucson, wrote her a "brutal" letter of advice about handling these responsibilities. He warned her that she must attend to her mail, pointing out that Eleanor Roosevelt handled much more, and that if Eleanor could do it, so could Isabella.[3]

Attention to mail was crucial for a politician, but politics for Isabella Greenway was only a means to an end. In 1933, her main objective was to alleviate the effects of the Depression. Franklin Roosevelt would not be sworn in until March. Isabella wanted funding from the Emergency Relief Division of the Reconstruction Finance Corporation to experiment with relocating destitute families onto the land, but by March it would be too late for anyone to make a success of farming in that year. At Franklin's suggestion, she contacted Henry Morgenthau, head of the Farm Credit Administration, but funds under the RFC were available only for relief of destitution, not for experimentation. She was discouraged over not being able to do something at once, because the number of destitute families in Tucson had soared in one year from four hundred to two thousand; statewide, the total was some fourteen thousand people.[4]

Political action seemed the best way for Isabella to make a difference in difficult times. She was on Jim Farley's short list of women being considered for federal appointments, but Isabella Greenway would not go that route. Presumably acting on inside advice from the Roosevelts, Isabella tendered her resignation as national committeewoman on February 8, to be in a position to run for Arizona's sole seat in the House of Representatives. This seat was about to be vacated. FDR alerted her by wire that "Lewis [Douglas] will go in as Director of Budget. Want you to know this on account future plans." When the Democratic state chairman telegraphed Isabella Greenway an offer to run for Lewis's seat, she didn't hesitate, although later she protested: "It was no easy task for me to make up my mind to toss my sombrero (or shall I say bonnet?) into the coming congressional race." On Thursday, February 23, Isabella announced her intention to campaign for election as congresswoman-at-large, representing the entire state.[5]

Isabella promptly engaged the Western Publicity Service. Her strongest suit, they suggested, was her friendship with the Roosevelts and the voters' belief that she could have more influence with the new administration than anyone else. They asked for photos of Isabella with the president-elect at the Ranch, as well as glossies of Isabella alone and with the three children. The *New York Times,* too, was asking for pictures, but Isabella coyly ignored all such requests, explaining that she had passed the time in life when pictures might be taken. She also resisted Western's suggestion that she supply them with human interest stories about her late husband, who was still a hero in Arizona: "I particularly do not want to use my husband's life in this connection, as his is already a perfect fulfillment, and whether I succeed or not is still unknown." She would have been less than human, too, if she had not hoped to stand or fall on her own merits. Likewise, she insisted that she meant "to hold my costs to such a minimum that any other candidate can meet them. The election would mean nothing to me on any other basis." Finally, although she felt that although "Mrs. John C. Greenway is the proper way for my name to appear on the ballot," she confessed, "I seem to be known as Isabella Greenway.... I think Isabella Greenway has gone almost too far to retract." The year 1932 had resulted not only in Franklin Delano Roosevelt's election to the White House but also in two new Democratic women winning seats in the House of Representatives, joining three incumbent congresswomen. Isabella Greenway was hoping to be number six.[6]*

George Hunt had been replaced as governor of Arizona by B. B. Moeur, who now appointed Isabella to represent Arizona at Franklin D. Roosevelt's inauguration and at a governors' meeting immediately following. Less than a week after announcing her candidacy, Isabella found herself on a train speeding east with Jack, "launched in an unknown ocean of political turmoil and wondering at the set of circumstances which finds me there," she confided to a friend.[7]

Back in Arizona after the ceremonies, Isabella prepared to chart her course on this tumultuous ocean. There was some doubt as to whether an election for Lewis's seat would be held at all. Because a special election could cost in excess of $100,000, at a time when funds were badly needed for relief programs, the legislature passed a resolution that the state dispense with its representative in the House for nearly two years. The *Arizona Daily Star* protested in an editorial that while Arizona had two "alert" senators, they could not be expected to look after important legislation in the House, "a large body where things can happen quickly." One of Isabella's supporters issued a press release arguing that a congressman was needed to help revive the copper industry; to promote tariffs on livestock, wool, hides, lumber, and citrus fruits; to restore army posts; and to secure federal grants for unemployment and other relief programs. The *Star* not only urged the election of a new congressman, they endorsed Isabella over her two opponents, Harlow Akers and Billy Coxon. Akers, copublisher of the *Phoenix Gazette*, was a one-term state senator who had challenged U.S. Senator Carl Hayden in the primary the year before and had come close to beating him. He was considered a strong candidate. Coxon, secretary of the Arizona Corporation Commission, was a former state legislator

---

*Isabella Greenway was the sixteenth woman to be elected to Congress. By the end of the 1930s, there would be seven new Democratic women, together with one Republican and two Democratic holdovers from the 1920s.

who had challenged Douglas in the 1932 primary. He was seen as a political radical who would pose little threat. The *Star* noted that while Congressman Douglas had needed six years "to reach a point of influence back in Washington," Isabella, a friend of the president and his wife, would have immediate access. But the *Star* concluded that her record as the person who had done more than any other for the Democratic Party and for the state of Arizona was enough to qualify her. Greenway received endorsements from most of the newspapers in the state, including the normally Republican *Prescott Journal*.[8]

In addition to her qualifications as a copper mine owner, a stalwart of the Democratic Party, and a friend of the president, Isabella Greenway had a strong constituency among veterans. Her effectiveness as their advocate was soon put to the test when, on March 16, Congress gave President Roosevelt extraordinary powers to slash government expenditures, including veterans' benefits, by $500 million in an attempt to balance the budget. Local vets, many suffering from tuberculosis, feared the likely cancellation of the "presumptive clause" that allowed a reasonable length of time to diagnose certain slow-developing diseases, such as TB, before determining whether those diseases resulted from war service. Bob Ferguson, for example, had not been diagnosed with TB for ten years, yet he was evidently ill for some time before that and likely had contracted the illness in Cuba. The American Legion claimed that some 90 percent of the veterans in Tucson who were drawing disability compensation could lose part or all of their benefits, which, in turn, would cut the city's income by almost $100,000 a month. Moreover, because many tuberculosis patients came to Arizona because of its healthful climate, the disability rating in Arizona was 57 percent higher than the national average. Isabella promptly sent the Speaker of the U.S. House of Representatives figures on veterans in the area who were receiving compensation or disability allowance. She was already acting like a member of Congress.[9]

Isabella Greenway was surely interested in the plight of disabled veterans, but she was also enough of a politician to realize that they were her core constituency. She sent out letters to ex-servicemen pointing out that they had always been "a deep concern with me. . . . Anyone aspiring to the privilege of serving this State in Congress should be in closest touch and understanding of every phase of the Veterans problem." She actually worried that her friendship with Franklin Roosevelt might be a liability, if the veterans thought she would not stand up to him for them. No one would be a friend of the administration, she maintained, who did not try to help the veterans achieve justice. She wanted to make clear, however, that her work on their behalf had not been undertaken for political gain, insisting that "the ex-service man owes me nothing whatever. I found solace and comfort in my work with and through them and feel more strongly today what I owe them than I did in 1918."[10]

By May Isabella was campaigning in earnest. In addition to her usual grassroots organizing, Western Publicity advised her to concentrate on women and on counteracting antifemale bias. Women might support her because she was a woman; men might oppose her for the same reason. A Tempe woman typified the first group, writing, "If we are to ever gain laws . . . favorable to women, then more women must represent us in the law-making bodies. . . . You will be capable of fighting for equal rights for women . . . the right of the married woman to work as well as the married man." During the Depression, the federal government and more than 60 percent of private companies discriminated against married women in hiring. To those who said it would be better to vote for a man than a woman, Isabella replied, "Only time can prove whether I am as able to be of use as a man. I would not enter this race if I had any doubts on this score."[11]

One problem for Isabella Greenway was the common belief that only one woman candidate at a time should run. A precinct committeeman from Parker promised to support her candidacy, "with the understanding that our own Nellie T. Bush is not to be in the race. . . . I am opposed to two women being in the race for the same office, as both may be defeated." Mrs. Bush, who had been slated to nominate Isabella for vice president at the National Convention, did not run but became a Greenway supporter, even returning from vacation to cast her vote for Isabella. Another woman, Grace Sparkes, from Prescott, was thinking of making the race herself. Isabella wrote Sparkes that she knew Sparkes would be a serious opponent, and would be grateful to know when she made her decision. Sparkes did not run.[12]

Frank Cutcheon had changed his mind about Isabella's running for office; he reasoned that she was now in a position to serve the state and had no right to refuse. She wired him: "Uncs darling. . . . Would you feel like dictating brief synopsis of my forty-seven years background and associations for pamphlet circulation amongst people of all walks of life. Entirely understand if too much effort only ask it because believe you know best way it should be done." Frank obliged, writing in his characteristically fussy way: "Although I have worked hard over it—practically three full days—it is not a satisfactory job. . . . I have bracketed in lead pencil certain statements which could perfectly well be omitted."[13]

Isabella wanted to avoid, during the Depression, the appearance of having been brought up in luxury. She told a supporter, "Until I was almost grown, I lived for the most part on a farm in Kentucky and daresay that I know more about 'living off the land' in its most elementary sense than a great many people who consider themselves people of smallest means." Alice Roosevelt Longworth would later mock this tendency of Isabella's, saying that she would begin to describe the Dinsmores' charming house outside of Cincinnati, but by the time she finished, it had become a wretched log cabin. Letters of support began to pour in, so much so the town clerk in Clifton warned: "Your greatest enemy is going to be the overconfidence of your friends." To those opposing her, Isabella wrote graciously: "Yours is a fair letter and its challenge is the kind that would make for better government if more people practised such sincerity."[14]

Meanwhile, Isabella continued to work for the veterans' benefits. On May 22 she wired Lewis Douglas, now Director of the Budget: "Conditions of imminent destitution amongst veterans." She wanted his help in urging Roosevelt to send someone unofficially to report on conditions in Arizona. She also wrote Franklin: "*EMERGENCY RELIEF* will be necessary after July 1st and until this problem can be solved justly for the government as well as the Veterans." She signed her letter, "Hurriedly and with love to you and Eleanor, In admiration, Isabella." FDR did even better than Isabella had hoped; he authorized Governor Moeur himself to report on the potential effect of the Economy Act on the veterans.[15]

Moeur's preliminary report noted that almost 90 percent of the disabled veterans in Arizona had enlisted or been drafted from other states; the most seriously ill TB cases came to Arizona because of its beneficial climate. Most of these men lived with their families at far less cost than if they were hospitalized. The effect of the Economy Act due to take effect July 1 would be to cut their stipends by more than half, reducing the veterans, the report said, "to a standard of living below that of the Mexicans and Negroes living in one-room shacks, without any sanitary facilities." No thought was apparently given to correcting the situation of the minority groups, but only of avoiding a similar fate for the Anglos. If the men lost their benefits they would most likely lose their homes, and become a charge on the state. Disabled vets made up 20 percent of Arizona's population; the remaining taxpayers would not be able to support them. Being forced to compete for work against healthy men would condemn these men to death. It was an important issue, and Isabella's access to the president was noted.[16]

Isabella's close connection with the Roosevelts was underscored when Eleanor arrived in Tucson in early June for a visit. She posed for the press with Isabella and a delegation of twenty hard-rock miners, then the two high-profile women debated how to help such men. Isabella advocated a higher tariff, because Africans were willing to work for pennies a day. Eleanor, typically, thought a better solution would be to help other nations increase their standard of living. Isabella countered that it would take Africans a hundred years or more to catch up, while American standards of living had to be protected now. After Eleanor returned to Washington, Isabella continued to lobby her about the veterans: "You know from our talks that all I have contributed is in the sincere belief that Franklin's goal is justice and that he has been ill advised in this human equation." Eleanor wired back: "Franklin insists justice will be done."[17]

Politics had to take a back seat for a while, though. Martha, Isabella's beloved only daughter, was getting married. The previous fall, Martha, now twenty-seven, had met Charles "Chuck" Breasted, thirty-three, son of the famous University of Chicago archaeologist, Dr. James H. Breasted, in Tucson. The Breasted team had unearthed Tut-ankh-amen's tomb nine years before, and some said Chuck had been plagued by the curse stalking those who had been present. He'd had two failed romances—an earlier engagement and a brief marriage—and had been hospitalized with a serious illness. He had met Martha while convalescing in Arizona, and his recovery was waggishly said to have been caused "not by the desert air . . . but by a desert heiress." The pair intended to have a private wedding at the end of June, but Eleanor Roosevelt had inadvertently announced their engagement while they were visiting at the White House in the spring.

The wedding took place on June 28 at the Burro Mountain Homestead where Martha had grown up. The ranch was splendid with white thistle poppies, red cholla cactus blooms, and a carpet of yellow flowers. Martha, wearing an unconventional gown of yellow and white checked gingham, and carrying a sunbonnet full of

At wedding of Martha and Charles (Chuck) Breasted.
Left to right: Isabella, Bob, Jack, Martha, and Chuck (indistinct).

flowers, entered the living room on the arm of her brother Bob and took her vows in front of the fireplace on which their initials were carved. The wedding feast was an old-fashioned barbecue, enlivened by a Mexican orchestra. Among more than two hundred guests, including Bronson Cutting, now a U.S. Senator from New Mexico, and their old friend Belle Eckles, was Frances Hand, a friend of Martha's from Bryn Mawr and the daughter of Judge Learned Hand. Bob had been smitten and had proposed several times, so far unsuccessfully. Isabella thought Franny might be weakening, though, and warned Jack: "Almost anything might happen in the way of an increase to our family." The nuptials over, Isabella dashed back to Arizona to campaign, with barely a month before the August 8 primary.[18]

Isabella's platform included her standard support for veterans' benefits and a copper tariff; even farmers placed the copper tariff first on their list of concerns, since the state would die without copper. She also favored "agricultural equality," a term she preferred to "farm relief." One of her two opponents, Harlow Akers, was campaigning for the Verde River Irrigation Project, expected to employ some 2,500 people. Isabella quickly moved to lobby FDR and his secretary of the interior, Harold L. Ickes, for this popular plan. She argued that agriculture represented the future in Arizona: "When you and I are gone and the resources of our mines are consumed, these great deserts will be flourishing farm lands."[19]

Isabella was bold about approaching Franklin but diffident about asking unknown voters for support. "Would you be good enough to let me know if I may count you among my true friends, and I would be grateful for the courtesy of a reply," she wrote to one. To another she asked to know "if you finally make up your mind to support me . . . although I do not want to press you in the matter." She was painfully thankful for support: "I am perfectly overwhelmed to hear what you have done for me in . . . making an address in my behalf," she wrote a Mrs. Frances Simonson. "It is really one of the most overwhelming acts of friendship."[20]

The campaign pace was becoming fierce, as can be seen from a page in her diary for July 5. She had meetings at 1 P.M., 1:30 (Valley farmers), 2, 2:30, 3, 4 (Mexican Democratic Club), 8, and 9 P.M. One weekend she noted that she "wrote letters all day and most of the night." One Sunday, July 16, she scrawled triumphantly across the page "Mine!" Isabella flew in a G & G plane around the state, an unusual activity even for a politician in those days but made necessary by the scarcity of roads in Arizona and made possible by Isabella's ownership of the airline. She conducted what one newspaper called a "hopping" (as opposed to the better-known "whirlwind") campaign. Some days she managed to hop to as many as five different towns, giving speeches in each. Occasionally, the papers noted, she "hopped into a storm and had to make an emergency landing." Everywhere she said, "Your platform and my platform, as well as that of every thinking American, is today the same. We all of us believe that good citizens should know the 'liberty of living,'" defined as "the right to work, to own your own home, to eat, to educate your children and leisure to participate in public affairs." She made her office in the plane, typing and all.[21]

Isabella missed Jack, who was staying in Santa Barbara with the Cutcheons, and tried to keep him abreast of her doings: "Here is your Mummy flying over the farms of the Salt River Valley on one of the hottest little summer days ever broadcast by a weatherman & wishing with all my heart I was with you. . . . I sometimes get so lonesome I wonder if it is all worth while." It wouldn't be, she admitted, unless "we can make some plans by which you & I will be together more than any other boy & Mummy in the world."[22]

Greenway for Congress clubs had been organized all over the state. Mexicans, African Americans, veterans, farmers, miners, and business and professional people each had their own organizations supporting her. So, interestingly enough, did the Republicans, who were not fielding any candidates in the primary; the *New York Times* noted that Arizona "after brief excursions into the GOP . . . settled comfortably into Democracy's solid Southern phalanx." One paper observed, "Mrs. Greenway is covering the state with her campaign like a blanket and pulling like a Missouri mule."[23]

When Isabella appropriated Akers' issue on the Verde River Irrigation Project, he turned to negative campaigning. He challenged her claim to presidential access, saying she had no "right to office based upon such a shallow reason." In a radio broadcast, he sneered, "If I am a weak sister, going there to play society, to associate with wealth, then, I beg of you, don't consider supporting me." Isabella retorted: "The Roosevelts have a lot of friends who are not qualified for Congress." She wanted the voters to focus on her merits. Akers also accused Greenway of owning copper mines in Africa, which she continually denied. As she confided to a supporter, "The eleventh hour is terrific from my opponents—it sickens me in its untrue and misleading phrases." She refrained from any negative campaigning of her own. Coxon's employer, the Arizona Corporation Commission, had come under investigation by the state legislature, and Coxon, never a strong contender, became too distracted to campaign effectively.[24]

Isabella Greenway wound up her historic campaign in Tucson the night of August 7. She was late leaving a rally in Phoenix, and her pilot steered the plane squarely over the waiting crowd in the armory, swooping down to within a few hundred feet of the ground. When she arrived, preceded by police with sirens wailing, she was greeted by thunderous applause. For once, she made no political speech, saying only that words were not adequate to express her gratitude. She had been looking forward to that night, she said, since February, "but I think now I have been waiting for it all my life." The next day Isabella traveled down to Ajo to vote. A fierce thunderstorm knocked out the telephone, so she had no idea if she had won the primary or not. She needn't have worried. The final results were overwhelmingly in her favor, with 70 percent of the vote. The women took special pride in her victory: "Aren't we women folks wonderful?" gushed one worker. "Every precinct in Yuma county for you except Quartsite which was managed by a man!" Eleanor Roosevelt told the press, "I didn't congratulate her, I congratulated ourselves. I am very glad to have her coming here." As the *New York Times* had indicated, the Democratic nomination in Arizona was tantamount to election.[25]

The *Philadelphia Bulletin* used the occasion to muse on the state of women in politics. The only woman senator, Mrs. Hattie W. Caraway, had been chosen to succeed her late husband, and several women had reached the House of Representatives by the same route. (Alice Roosevelt Longworth, as usual, said it best: "Using their husbands' coffins as a springboard.") But Representatives

Ruth Bryan Owen, Ruth Pratt, and Mary Norton, among others, had won on their own merits and became influential members. Isabella Greenway would be one of these. "Women have come into politics to stay," the *Bulletin* concluded. Isabella Greenway appeared in *Time* magazine the week of August 21, in an unflattering photo ghoulishly captioned: "She will join her husband at the Capitol," a reference to John Greenway's statue in Statuary Hall. They pronounced her "an able Democrat" and credited her with having "had a large hand in engineering the McAdoo switch" at the convention. Her fame had become not only national but international. The Paris edition of the *Herald Tribune* featured an article about "Mrs. Greenway Tuxon," and she was mentioned in the Irish press.[26]

Isabella's first reaction to her nomination was to be "happy & appalled & prayerful." She was amazed by the landslide, and humbled. She confided to Olivia, "The irony of public service seems to be that too often those capable of profoundly wise contributions haven't the cheaper qualities that win elections!" Then she retreated to her ranch to rest. Although she claimed to most well-wishers that she was not tired, perhaps "because I am so interested and eager to be on our way toward accomplishing something," she admitted to Olivia that "recoveries from operations, only daughter's weddings, election to congress" had taken a toll. She planned to spend the month of September in California with Jack, whom she assured "already we are doing a little good."[27]

Isabella returned to Arizona a week before the October 3 special election. The Republicans had nominated a candidate, H. R. Wilkinson, at the last moment, and the Socialist, Dillworth Sumpter, was not expected to be in the running. Isabella's main challenge was to get a good turnout, but she hesitated to hire people to drive voters to the polls, because she had already been criticized for her spending during the primary campaign. In some ways she was acting as if she were already elected. On September 26 she sent the president a telegram arguing for the Verde River Irrigation Project: "Public works only relief for desperate unemployment." Out of a population of less than 500,000, Arizona had 140,000 men and women on relief. Isabella planned go to Washington immediately upon election to lobby for the Gila and Nogales Flood Control Projects and to see about the copper code.[28]

Copper, Cattle, and Constituents

ON THE MORNING of Election Day, October 3, Isabella, although not normally a pious person, wrote in her diary, "Oh God with all my heart I ask for help & pray as I never have before in behalf of a suffering people. . . . Give me beauty of soul & mind & health of body and let me dedicate them one and all to mankind." It was the last entry in her 1933 diary, before, as she might have said, the waters closed over her. All day a series of short radio announcements implored people to turn out. "Arrange *now* for a way to get to the polls to cast your vote for Isabella Greenway for Congress." Despite the lightest turnout on record, Greenway swept to victory, four to one against her closest opponent, Sumpter, the Socialist candidate. Her next election would be only thirteen months away. Mindful of that fact, she prepared form letters for eager job seekers: "My dear——. Thank you for your good letter in which you (recommend) (endorse) (write in behalf of) *name* (applicant for) *position*. It will be a privilege to be of any help I can in this connection." Three days after the election, she prepared to leave for Washington, dodging delegations bearing petitions for various projects as she tried to pack, answer constant phone calls, and deal with a flood of mail. Finally, with Jack and the Cutcheons, she boarded the train east. Meanwhile, telegrams were arriving for her at the White House, with more petitions.[1]

The Nogales Flood Control Project was her first order of business because almost half of the Santa Cruz County residents were on relief. She put in twelve hours of work on her first day—"the hardest of my life"—but told a reporter, "When I stepped across the threshold of my office I was too excited for words. . . . You see, I've never had a job before." Later that day, Isabella went alone to Statuary Hall to commune with her husband's statue in the dim afternoon light. In spite of the workload, she still had energy for the Washington social scene, lunching at the White House and visiting with Eleanor who often walked her dog over to the Willard Hotel where Isabella was staying. She also renewed her friendship with Mary Harriman Rumsey, who had worked with Isabella in their debutante days at the New York Junior League and was now chairman of the Consumers Advisory Board. Isabella kept the common touch, though. One evening she took a cab to the White House for dinner. As they arrived, she looked at the other guests and remarked to the driver, "I don't think I'm dressed up enough for this occasion, but I'm from the sticks and wouldn't know any better." The driver asked her where she came from, and she answered, "Arizona." "I'm from Ajo," said the driver. "I put in the ore crushers there for General Greenway." Isabella promptly leased his taxi for the duration of her stay in Washington.[2]

Because Isabella Greenway was different, she made good newspaper copy. Gossip columnists described the newcomer as "the most colorful personality" on the scene. One rhapsodized: "Of generous proportions, Junoesque in stature" (she was 5′8″), Isabella in a pink gown suggested a "full-blown rose." Another thought she had "a luscious personality with the patina that sorrow lays on noble souls." Men adored her, but, as Martha later observed, so did their wives. Daisy Harriman, a popular Democratic hostess not exactly renowned for her kindness, remarked, "There never was anyone like Isabella. She is a fairy-book person." However, Isabella was not a passive princess but a hardworking congresswoman. Ten days after her arrival in Washington, the Public Works Administration announced approval of the Nogales Flood Control Project. She reflected, "It is good to think of what this means."[3]

Copper was the basis for Arizona's economy, and Isabella discussed the need for a copper code with anyone who might be able to help her get results. She talked oftenest to Harry O. King, deputy administrator of the National Recovery Administration (NRA) in charge of codes for the nonferrous metal industry. King, a Chicago native who had moved to Bridgeport, Connecticut, where he excelled at turning around failing companies, was said to be well informed on the industry. Handily, in Washington, D. C., King lived next door to Isabella's friends, the Lewis Douglases, where she could easily confer with him.[4]

Caught up in efforts to lobby for irrigation projects and a copper code, Isabella stayed on in Washington all fall, amidst "chaos and bedlam," she informed a political ally. "Everyone is moving—furniture, files and people being dumped from one building to another. Whole projects!!! lost apparently or forgotten forever. . . . Distinguished statesmen are to be seen prayerfully engratiating themselves with stenographers and office girls in the hope of trailing some major project involving ten to twenty millions that may have passed into entire oblivion in any one of three blocks of buildings." She saw one bright spot: "the *motive* prompting this warfare . . . the determination of every hand to right the world for the helpless and suffering." By November 2 the Verde River Irrigation Project on which she had campaigned had funding of $4 million. The Arizona Democratic Association wired from Phoenix: "People hilarious all day climaxing with parade in evening." Isabella suffered "waves of homesickness," longing "to share things with the friends that matter."[5]

At once she began to lobby for a new project to improve existing irrigation canals, projected to employ nine thousand men. But, as she confided to an old farmer friend: "It would be easier to cut corn on your ranch than to do the work in this office and I am not sure I do not wish I was doing it." On November 10, however, Isabella had an excuse to drop everything for one day as she rushed to New York for Bob's long-hoped-for wedding to Frances Hand, a tiny, private affair in the Hands' home in New York. Bob had finally thought to offer Franny a large sapphire ring, a Ferguson heirloom that seemingly won her over; ever after, it was known in the family as "The Persuader."[6]

By mid-December, two months after Isabella's assault on the capitol, Interior Secretary Harold Ickes reported to Roosevelt that over fourteen thousand Arizona men had been employed in public works programs, with another three thousand expected to be at work by January 1. This would go a long way toward providing for an estimated twenty-one thousand unemployed. As Isabella prepared to return home, she asked Ickes for permission to release the information, feeling that it would be especially welcome over the holiday.[7]

The attractive widow was reported to be getting along well with the notorious curmudgeon; their banter made news. At one early afternoon meeting, she arrived to find Ickes looking worn and weary. "I hate to talk to a man before he has lunch," she said. He retorted that he never ate lunch. "You should," Isabella protested, producing an apple from her large handbag.

"This isn't the Garden of Eden, you know," protested the secretary.

"That makes it perfectly safe," the congresswoman replied.[8]

Even before her inauguration, Arizona's sweetheart was proving to be an effective member of congress.

Chapter Ten

Isabella Greenway was sworn in as Arizona's sole U.S. Representative on January 3, 1934, along with eight other new House members, including one other woman, Marian W. Clarke (R-NY), elected to succeed her late husband. Eleanor Roosevelt was in the gallery, imperturbably knitting, as usual. Alice Roosevelt Longworth, dazzling in her trademark blue, sat across the huge chamber in the opposite gallery, peering through her lorgnette. Isabella Greenway, dressed simply in a cocoa-brown wool dress, had gathered with other Democratic congresswomen to the left of Secretary of Labor Frances Perkins in the front row. When the new members were sworn in, Isabella turned to smile and raise her hand in salute to the president's wife, whose knitting needles had finally stopped as she gazed down upon the scene.[9]

Isabella Greenway had hoped for an appointment to the Labor Committee, a request the Associated Press found droll, since she had been a debutante among New York's social elite. Isabella was also interested in the Interstate Commerce Committee. But there were no vacancies on either, and she was appointed to the Public Lands Committee. Nearly two-thirds of the state of Arizona was government land—Indian reservations, forest reserves, national parks, military reservations, and public domain. The Arizona Cattle Growers' Association promptly began to lobby her on the issue of the Taylor bill, sponsored by Rep. Edward Taylor (D-CO), which would give control of the public domain to the secretary of the interior, Harold Ickes. He would then divide all public land on which no valid claim existed into grazing districts, to prevent overgrazing and soil erosion. Stockmen from western states, particularly Arizona, where the public domain represented nearly a fifth of the total acreage, vigorously protested legislation that might deprive them of free access to public grazing lands. But Isabella argued that programs for flood and erosion control might be at risk unless there was some control of grazing. Greenway was also assigned to the Indian Affairs Committee.[10]

In Congress, Isabella found herself the target of intense lobbying and quickly became adroit at the indirect answer to a plea for support: "Thank you for your good letter . . . drawing my attention to . . . " she might say. "I will follow it up and keep you advised. I hope I may give it the wholehearted support you suggest." Trickier was negotiating with other politicians. She thought the majority leaders were ill-advised to pressure the Democratic Congress to rubber-stamp administration bills: "Democrats, unlike Republicans, will not stand for it." Certainly, she, Isabella Greenway, would not stand for any effort to get her rubber stamp on legislation.[11]

Still, on the first administration bill, she fell into line, voting for a 15 percent pay cut for federal employees as part of the Economy Act. Arizona Senator Carl Hayden had persuaded her that they had to support their "Commander in Chief" in "the war against hard times." Support meant not only voting for the bill but also agreeing to a rule that barred amendments, known as the Gag Rule. Hayden concluded, "I have to choose between throwing him to the reactionary wolves who would utterly destroy his Administration or to serve with discipline under his banner." Isabella clearly faced the same choice and made the same decision, but reluctantly and only because it was the test vote of Roosevelt's strength. Veterans were disappointed in her vote, but, as she philosophically observed, the veterans' mistrust was "an irony which I have long become accustomed to." However, veterans' letters and editorials criticizing her vote may have stiffened her spine to oppose Franklin Roosevelt in the future.[12]

The most urgent of Isabella Greenway's concerns was to revive Arizona's copper industry. Immediately after her inauguration, she met with the NRA staff and the consumers of copper. Producers and consumers agreed a code was needed to stabilize the price of copper, and Isabella believed it was better to work for a reasonable compromise that would get the mines open than to stand around complaining if they couldn't get everything they wanted. In addition to official meetings, Isabella used Washington back channels, stressing to the president that he needed to use the threat of an embargo to keep foreign copper from infringing upon the U.S. market. She also worked closely with Harry King, who headed the copper code deliberations. Harry enlivened the dry proceedings for Isabella with a private tongue-in-cheek assessment of the parties to the copper code: "The term 'Squeaky Wheel' includes all those vocally evidencing a craving for a little grease. . . . 'Silent Sow' includes all those who expect to get the swill when the wheels are squeaking the loudest. . . . 'Chisler' sometimes herein abbreviated as 'SOB,' means any other member of the Industry who obtains a benefit."[13]

As secretary to the strong nonferrous metals bloc in the House, Isabella testified for a reduction in criminal penalties for misstatements in the registration of securities with the Federal Trade Commission. She argued that prospective mining was a speculative enterprise, that nine out of ten of the great mines in the country, copper, silver, and gold, had been developed after several failed attempts. When the FTC commissioner asked the Arizona congresswoman: "You would not put $1000 in an enterprise that does not even keep book after issuing stock?" she laughingly answered: "I have done it many times."[14]

Isabella's relations with the White House were still very cordial, and she was often invited for evening parties. But her maiden speech in the House of Representatives took issue with the administration's Economy Act. It was a stirring appeal for restoration of veterans' pensions, especially for Spanish American War veterans, and of hospitalization benefits. "I am a Democrat anxious to make the Democratic administration successful," she insisted. She supported necessary economies but accused her colleagues of political expediency in cutting the veterans' benefits. Tubercular vets, she said, had been turned out of hospitals built with federal funds with "temperatures of 101, ill, cadaverous, with hectic spots in their cheeks; and those people today are walking the streets of my home state begging for work." She urged Congress to work "honestly and without party lines" for a solution.[15]

Her speech went a long way toward rehabilitating Isabella with the veterans. One wrote that her first speech was "a disputation of the argument . . . that your social relationship with the President's family would impose upon you the necessity of submerging your views to his." She was still smarting from having been urged to vote for the Gag Rule as a pledge of party fealty. "The Gag Rule should never have been presented under the guise of an Administration demand," she protested. This suggests she did not blame Franklin himself for the pressure. Isabella tried to walk a fine line between preserving her independence and benefiting from her special access to the president. She was hopeful about bringing Roosevelt around to her point of view, writing several constituents, "The President indicates he has an open mind about the fact that there are injustices to correct in the veterans' legislation."[16]

Isabella was one of the Roosevelt family's most intimate friends in public life during their early years in the White House. She did worry, she wrote Franklin, about "the tales that are reported to the White House about my activities" by highly placed members of his administration, assuring him they were exaggerated. "It is inevitable that you and Eleanor will frequently be embarrassed with doubts about my loyalty," she admitted. She hoped "that eight years from now we will come out on the other side of this ghastly experience—happy and united." Franklin wrote back reassuringly that no one had been talking to him of her activities. "Honestly I think the greatest reform that could be accomplished in the House of Representatives at the present time (strictly between ourselves because the Executive must not speak of such things) would be a thirty day embargo on cloak room gossip," he said. Because of Isabella's well-known friendship with the Roosevelts, she was often asked to intercede with them. While she was not above mentioning something casually to Franklin when seated next to him at dinner, she made it her policy never to try to arrange appointments with him for others.[17]

The press made much of her opposition to another administration proposal. She was the only House Democrat to vote against a bill authorizing the Army to carry the mail, citing a number of accidents, some of them fatal. When praised for her stand, she replied modestly, "It didn't take as much courage as you might think, for the reason that my conviction was very strong." She noted to another supporter, "I am 'on the spot' a good deal between independent conscience and no political habits." One commentator suggested she was "the most dangerous foe the administration has in the chamber," explaining that, because her colleagues considered her almost a member of the president's family, "when she bolts, they feel free to do likewise."[18]

But Isabella supported Eleanor wholeheartedly in her project to build a furniture factory in Reedsville, West Virginia, to augment the Subsistence Homestead project located on 1,100 acres near Morgantown. Because no private industry could be lured there, the U.S. postal service had agreed to establish an experimental factory to make wooden furniture and post office equipment. Speaking on the floor of the House, Representative Greenway argued that the Ludlow amendment opposing it was "a far broader issue than a furniture factory, the leading lady of the land, or the purchase of one particular commodity." Insisting that "I am speaking about a matter that I know a little about," and hinting that for others in Congress, this was not the case, she sketched the parallels between unemployed miners in Arizona and unemployed miners in West Virginia. She knew, she said, that successful subsistence homesteading had to be complemented by some other earning capacity. She admitted that the idea of a "governmental laboratory" was "radical," but claimed that "the experiment being made is as much in behalf of private industry as it is in behalf of the unemployed."[19]

She received a round of applause, but Rep. Samuel Pettingill

Left to right, Mary Harriman Rumsey, Eleanor Roosevelt,
Isabella Greenway, at the White House

from Indiana denounced it as "state socialism," arguing that the
furniture business was very competitive, with a low return on investment even in prosperous times and that government competition would be unfair. The proposed plant would cost $525,000 to
employ 125 men, a per capita investment of $4,200. The govern-
ment could not afford to employ the eight million unemployed at
similar rates of investment. Isabella was unconvinced. Like Eleanor, she had a passionate interest in both furniture factories and
homesteading. "I don't think there is anything in the entire New
Deal that is any more important, in its national future than this," Isabella declared. However, many congressional Democrats joined
with Republicans to deny the project funding. Representative
Greenway was more successful in securing $500,000 for home-
steading in the Salt River Valley outside Phoenix. In addition to
vegetables for themselves, residents were urged to produce pyre-

thrum, an insecticide made from a flower of the chrysanthemum family, to replace Japanese imports. And she introduced a bill to enable disabled World War I vets to prove up their homestead claims without improvement or cultivation. This bill became law.[20]

Much of Isabella's time was spent not in crafting legislation but in responding to the concerns of anxious constituents. Business people objected to taxes: A tax on telephone and telegraph use was condemned as a "burden on recovery"; the tobacco industry argued that if people stopped buying cigarettes because of a high tax, the government would lose more money. A two-cent increase in the price of gas brought protests from businesses and individuals alike. Private citizens turned to her for everything from dental care to avoiding deportation. And of course, many wrote begging for jobs.[21]

Most desperate of all were homeowners afraid of losing their homes if they could not pay the mortgage. Isabella referred individual cases to William Wayland, the overworked state manager of the Arizona Home Owners' Loan Corporation, for refinancing. She used her trademark combination of warmth and persistence to get action: "How badly I feel about continually imposing these inquiries . . . upon you, is hard to say! Especially in the face of the wonderful way in which you have carried on and all that you have achieved. But . . . I think you understand . . . that there is no alternative except to follow these through." Wayland and his limited staff were working fifteen to seventeen hours a day, seven days a week, and were still three months behind. At the end of March, Wayland collapsed and would not return to work for nearly six months. But Isabella took heart from her efforts: "Is there any position more exhilarating than being able to help people save their homes?" she asked after two applications had been straightened out.[22]

Farm foreclosures were another serious problem. She was working hard for a bill to refinance farm loans with Federal Reserve notes, but she was reluctant to stray too far from the party line, hav-

ing already resisted the administration on veteran and airmail legislation. She did, however, urge Eleanor to work on Franklin: "If
Franklin can hold this ever-increasing Farm Union bloc, built
around this bill, by investigating the facts ... it might *save* a complete break." She added gratefully, "I am relieved to know how you
are handling this."[23]

At the end of her third month in office, Isabella wrote Jack an
assessment of what "they" had achieved so far. "We have accomplished our two weddings & two new children [her son-in-law and
daughter-in-law]. We have also helped open Ajo & returned the
Spanish War Veterans their pensions." Jack added: "And elected to
Congress." They both signed the document, which Isabella titled:
"Partners in Personal and Political History." A door closed on her
old life on March 31 when Sir Ronald, Lord Novar, died in Scotland. Newspapers made much of the fact that her son Bob could
have succeeded to the title but had chosen instead to remain an
American citizen.[24]

Isabella was working harder and harder. She wrote declining an
invitation to dinner on March 22, her forty-eighth birthday: "Vital
matters for my State have made it impossible for me to have the
pleasure of much personal life.... Work has kept us on into the
night for the last weeks." She apologized to constituents for not being able to answer mail in a timely fashion. The Arizona congresswoman was receiving an average of 135 letters a day. But she took
time to write to a man on a general delivery route in Winkelman,
Arizona: "Let me know if your pump is re-established and the well
is again functioning, because those are the things in life that
matter."[25]

It was not just the number of problems she faced that weighed
on her but also their magnitude. She apologized to a friend, "This
cannot, alas, be the letter I would like to write you, due to unspeakable congestion, with a fight on in every committee to which I belong." In particular, the Indian Bureau bill and the Taylor bill wor-

ried her, as she was "uncertain of their entire soundness, although I don't doubt there is merit in both of them." She finally voted against the Taylor bill, writing Harold Ickes directly of her decision. She regretted having to deny him a bill that would have placed the public domain under his jurisdiction, but added, "Possibly I shall be able to help you in the broader picture, as I am very sincere in my conviction that the public domain grazing should be administered by an expansion of the now existing agency." She signed her letter to the notorious curmudgeon, "With warm best wishes." Eventually the bill was so modified that only eighty million out of 183 million acres were affected.[26]

The Indian question was also a vexed one for Isabella. Early in the year, representatives of various Native American organizations, including Anna Wilmarth Ickes, Harold's wife and a longtime advocate for Indian rights, met to urge repeal of the current system of allotting land to individual Indians, recommending instead measures designed to restore traditional communities under modern conditions. The allotment program had failed to foster the intended individualism in Native Americans and was fast destroying the native society. The resulting Howard-Wheeler bill, approved by the administration, would reverse the fifty-year policy of assimilation, dating from the Dawes Act of 1887. It would provide new government land to the Indians, bar whites from reservations, vest title to tribal property in the tribe, and forbid the sale, taxation, or attachment of tribal lands. It would extend credit to Indian farmers so they would not be forced to lease their lands to whites, and improve access to higher education. The bill was wildly controversial. Critics said it infringed on the rights of individual Indians and promoted anti-Americanism, creating an experiment in "communal" living that bordered on Communism. It would be costly to American taxpayers and undo the "progress" that Indians had made toward "civilization," most notably after they were granted citizenship in 1924. The administration fought back. Harold Ickes hinted that any Indian Service employee who opposed the bill should resign. Indian Affairs Commissioner John Collier took his crusade to the airwaves, arguing that white business interests opposed the legislation from selfish motives and that opposition to the bill arose from racial prejudice. Isabella, a member of the House Indian Affairs Committee, took a middle ground. She believed a preliminary experiment should be tried on one tribe before such a drastic change was made, she wrote Franklin. As a committee member, she also resented Collier's "propaganda."[27]

Somehow, despite the long hours, crushing responsibilities, and constant demands, she managed to retain her joie de vivre. Working ten-hour days, she would have dinner sent up to her office, then roller skate with Jack in the hallowed halls of Congress before going back to work. Her spirits got a lift, too, when finally, after months of wrangling, a copper code was signed on April 26. Her work, she wrote, was "a joy . . . on account of my beloved John." Every day, she visited his statue, where she "saluted all that is best in a great life like his."[28]

She was also coming to admire the man with whom she had worked so hard. "Mr. King has been very remarkable in the way he has handled this problem and through his diplomacy he has brought [the miners and the operators] to a readiness to agree never before known in the history of the industry," she wrote the administrator of the NRA. She, too, had taken a leadership position, herding thirty-four congressmen from fifteen mining states to hearings. And she had been outspoken in her criticism of an early draft, describing the proposed code as "lukewarm dishwater." Afterwards, Isabella professed to be ashamed of the disparaging phrase but noted with glee that "it has been quoted in the press generally across the United States." Just when she began to despair of getting the code signed, she returned to her house one night to find it filled with roses from the president of Anaconda Copper, a token of his capitulation. Ajo would be opened in July for partial production, she promised the superintendent, Mike Curley, adding: "Jack has just been in to see me. He says he will be in Ajo the day it opens."[29]

Isabella was still enjoying "the novelty of everything." She could laugh at criticism, like that in a letter she forwarded to Lewis Douglas: "I voted for Mrs. Greenway for the reason I thought she would stand by President Roosevelt. Can't we find another Lewis Douglas in Arizona?" When she received a complimentary letter she was ecstatic: "I do the best I can," she answered, "but in spite of it all, I blunder and like every one make mistakes; so a letter like yours, evidencing approval of some of my efforts, is indeed appreciated." But she reacted differently when a labor union official wrote critically: "With your influence, finances and background it should not take much nerve to have a principle to fight for. It's an experience. Try it." She answered sharply, "I acknowledge your letter but regret that it is so lacking in courtesy and confidence."[30]

Another strategy for full employment was public works. Isabella made an impassioned plea on the floor of the House for a road bill to give work to some of the forty-two thousand unemployed heads of families in Arizona, almost a quarter of the voting population. She urged her fellow congressmen to "vote for a bill that gives our friends who have no way of earning their living, a program affording the right to earn as men like to," drawing a round of applause. Afterwards, she admitted, "I was so excited I almost died. I am not used to talking." Arizona received $13 million for road construction over a three-year period. Work projects could be combined with another of her interests, conservation. She lobbied the National Parks director to create the Organ Pipe Cactus National Monument near Ajo and urged the Forest Service to rehabilitate the scenic drive up to San Francisco Peaks in Flagstaff, not far from her home in Williams. As one of the few women in Congress, she also received requests regarding women's issues, especially to overturn the section of the 1932 Economy Act discriminating against married women in government service. Isabella resisted gender partisanship, however, replying coolly that she believed everyone in Congress was "open to the appeal for help when injustice was at hand."[31]

Before Congress adjourned at the end of June, Isabella had one more triumph. For months she had been involved in the dispute over mineral rights on the Papago reservation. Her mining friends did not want the rights to revert to the Indians. Isabella hoped to see a bill drafted that would permit mining and still protect Indian occupancy of the reservation, arguing that mining provided much-needed employment. The House Indian Affairs Committee, at Isabella's suggestion, refused an amendment proposed by Ickes restoring the mineral rights to the United States. She worked hard with the committee to draft an acceptable alternative, even to the extent of taking coffee and sandwiches to midnight sessions to keep her gentlemen colleagues in good humor. The amendment passed and was adopted at the House-Senate conference in mid-June, occasioning Isabella "terrific excitement." She was also successful in helping farmers—both white and Indian—on the San Carlos Irrigation Project, with a bill to eliminate interest on the construction costs. This bill passed easily and the president signed it on June 5. Isabella crowed, "I am still so new at this job, I almost die of excitement when a bill of mine goes through." She wrote "My dear Franklin" (when she took issue with him, he was "Mr. President") to thank him. "We are just so happy about this, I can't resist telling you the good [news] and the relief it has brought."[32]

As the congressional session drew to a close, Isabella began to turn her thoughts to her second campaign. Her campaign the year before had been for the remainder of Lewis Douglas's term; now she would run for a whole term. No one expected her to have any difficulty. She must have gotten particular satisfaction from a scrawled note: "While I have never been in favor of supporting women in politics, I will have to admit that I think you have done much better than the average man." A campaign worker wrote reassuringly that "your fences are hoss high, hog tight, and bull strong." It was just as well; Isabella didn't think the work in Congress was going to abate long enough for her to get home to campaign.[33]

When Congress adjourned, an exhausted Isabella took Jack to Long Island to stay with the Cutcheons. But after an invigorating swim in the Sound, she dragged herself back to Washington for another month to tend to matters that had been shelved in the rush to adjournment. It was no small sacrifice, and when the Associated Press reported she was vacationing on Long Island, she wired the Arizona papers asking for a correction: "I am remaining in Washington indefinitely." Adverse press publicity always made her cross. An Arizona newsletter reported that she had ten assistants, claiming this "opened a few eyes as to the reasons for the high cost of government." Isabella protested that she was allotted two "paid secretaries"; the others were paid personally by her, in order to try to meet her responsibilities. Arizona had only one representative, she reminded the editor, and "many new programs and new departments." She claimed she didn't even like flattering publicity. "It makes me unhappy to have it put in print that I have achieved all sorts of things, which I was nothing more than a humble participant in. . . . It . . . apparently is the penalty that a woman pays while there are still so few women in national life that they are focused on out of all proportion."[34]

She was glad to take credit, though, for work on two bills Roosevelt signed after Congress adjourned. He had, "with some reluctance," signed the Frazier-Lemke farm mortgage bill, amending the bankruptcy laws to enable farmers to obtain a five-year moratorium on their debts. He also approved a railroad pension bill, praised by the *Washington Post* as "another broad stroke on behalf of the 'forgotten man.'" Isabella recalled that "the railroad legislation coming in at the 11th hour gave us all nervous prostration until the president's signature was actually on it. We telephoned and telegraphed and rounded everybody up on a petition."[35]

In the summer lull, she was able to follow up on requests from constituents. But this merely emboldened applicants to ask for more. A woman wrote to thank her for help in getting their home loan and then asked for help in finding employment for her husband. The never-ending demands were getting Isabella down. She wrote Jack: "Your letter ... made me the happiest Mummy who ever woke up lonely in a hot town in a lonesome four-poster." Because she was staying behind to do extra work, foregoing rest with her family or the chance to campaign, criticism at this time hit especially hard and, on at least one occasion, roused her to stinging sarcasm. A priest from the Bureau of Catholic Missions complained that she had refused to see him, when the senators "invariably" saw him promptly. She answered: "Your letter will be kept as a stimulant against the happy relaxation sometimes induced by kindness and understanding. I have worked faithfully and effectively in behalf of the Indians this year. . . . In making it clear how signally you feel I have failed you have given me an illuminating experience for which I am truly grateful."[36]

Fatigue may have played a part in her exasperation. Even though Congress was no longer in session, she found "life has been incredibly congested, to the point of its being really a physical stunt to get through the days and nights." Finally, at the end of July, she and Jack set out cross-country by car, stopping in Chicago to visit Martha and Chuck. The city was uncomfortably hot, and an article in the *Chicago Tribune* made things even hotter. The paper was published by Roosevelt arch-enemy Robert R. McCormick, who lavished no love on Roosevelt's friends. Greenway, described as a "wily, solitary Congresswoman," was said to have "gotten more for her state than any man in the whole congress." Arizona was "getting back in easy money more than 36 times what that state's citizens paid in federal taxes last year." What may have surprised Isabella more than the *Tribune*'s attack on her share of the New Deal "swag" was the author of the article, John Boettiger, who would soon marry Isabella's god-daughter, Anna Roosevelt Dall, then in Nevada obtaining a divorce from her first husband.[37]

Equally surprising may have been a letter from Harry King. He complained that he had been contending with a mountain of mail but promised, "If I ever get a minute's time I am going to write you a real nice letter thanking you for all you have done for me and telling you exactly what I think of you." The letter had been typed by a secretary, but he added a handwritten p. s.: "I have for a long time been trying to get up the courage to ask you for a photograph of yourself. . . . It would be a real source of inspiration."[38]

Harry King was not her only, or even her most passionate, admirer at this time. Gutzon Borglum, the sculptor of John Greenway's statue, had become very attentive. Although Isabella had been working with Borglum off and on for almost seven years, when she arrived in the capital to take her seat in Congress, he suddenly saw her in a new light. Perhaps because she was now in a position to help him with funding for his chronically debt-ridden Mount Rushmore project, or maybe just because she was lovely and he was lonely, he subjected her to a barrage of ardent letters. She answered few of them, prompting him to conclude: "I shall think of you always as a Moss Rose, because you have all its richness," but, he added, "the Moss Rose is all thorns." Borglum was married, and though Isabella, after eight years of widowhood, was likely flattered and intrigued, she did not allow any indiscretions. But she continued to help him politically, serving on his Mount Rushmore commission and interceding for him at crucial points with the Roosevelts. And she kept his love letters in a large manila envelope marked "Not to be opened until after my death and the death of my children."[39]

CHAPTER ELEVEN

"The Lonely Goal"

I N MID-AUGUST, Isabella Greenway began her second campaign in a year. This time she could run on her record and on Roosevelt's. Maintaining that "the policies and programs of this Administration apply particularly to the development of Arizona," she claimed to be in the best position to ensure that they were enacted. To stress the point, she wired the chief of the Bureau of Public Roads in the U.S. Department of Agriculture: "It would mean a great deal to this state and particularly at this moment of election if we could get Arizona's road program giving employment approved." He promptly reassured her that the bureau had passed the Arizona highway program.[1]

Isabella Greenway's only Democratic opponent in the primary was Frank Hilgeman, an extremist who advocated wealth redistribution (any "fortune" in excess of $1 million was to be given to the U.S. Treasury), public ownership of railroads and utilities and the liquor trade, and universal military conscription. He opposed the Farm Bureau, the Agricultural Extension Service and large parts of the USDA and was not expected to be any kind of a threat. Isabella was not campaigning in the usual sense, she said, but rather "conferring" with her constituents. There was no need for her to run hard; she could have had almost any political office she wanted. U.S. Senator Henry Fountain Ashurst, who had served in the Senate since statehood in 1912, even offered to retire in her favor. Isabella Greenway easily won her primary on September 11, polling three times as many votes as Hilgeman. She was not complacent about her victory. "To evidence my appreciation, I know of nothing except to serve the state in such a way as to insure our return to sound prosperity," she explained to a well-wisher.[2]

Greenway was personally popular but worried that confidence in the administration was flagging. In a letter she drafted to Roosevelt strategist Jim Farley, Isabella suggested that the country was on the verge of "social unrest": The unemployed got no food "while farmers are being paid not to plant the very things these people need." But she had enough residual Republicanism to fret about the budget not being balanced, "because confidence will never be restored while our government is borrowing continuously." She also wanted Congress to investigate complaints of excessive governmental regulation; reemployment, she argued, could not happen without private industry. The letter, though not sent, reflected her thinking.[3]

Alarmed by "undiminished" unemployment, she did send a letter to Harold Ickes, asking him to reconsider the Verde River Irrigation Project, which had bogged down while being transferred from one department to another. Delay of the project, she told Ickes, was "shaking public confidence in this administration." Worse was to come: On October 4, the $4 million earmarked to begin the Verde Project was rescinded by the Public Works Administration because of doubts the investment could be made to pay. Isabella's shrill protests to Ickes drew only the maddeningly calm response: "I know the situation in Arizona is very bad, but I also know that it is not any worse in Arizona than it is in a great many other States." A week later, disgruntled desert homesteaders near Phoenix hanged and burned effigies of Greenway, Ickes, and Moeur to protest their blasted hopes. Isabella's effigy sported a long, flowing dress and a massive tumbled wig.[4]

Gone were Isabella's jaunty remarks about not campaigning. When the Democratic state central committee of New Mexico asked her to come speak for their candidates, she replied that her own campaign demanded "much strenuous work and travel." In the last year, she explained, she had worked in four campaigns against seven opponents and put in six months' service in Washington. In the last six weeks alone, she had crisscrossed her state twice, she wired FDR. But on the hustings she was beginning to advocate policies that diverged from the president's: taxation of income, instead of homes and property; old age pensions; and a revised federal agriculture plan. "I think we should stop plowing under agricultural wealth," she said bluntly. She authored a plank in the Democratic state platform urging the Department of Agriculture to pay the farmer the same amount for food that he was being paid for not planting, to make food available for needy families.[5]

Isabella Greenway could point with pride to the copper code on which she had worked all spring. Harry King sent her a letter full of statistics about copper orders, but added: "I was told the other day that I had 'surrendered to the wiles of the remarkable Isabella Greenway' and had written a code under which Arizona was the only state that benefitted by it." Arizona mines had opened, while those in Montana, New Mexico, Utah, and Nevada had not.[6]

Just before the November 6 election, former Governor Hunt published an appeal to his friends in the Democratic Party to support Isabella's Republican opponent, Hoval Smith. It was Hunt's last strike against her. The seventy-five-year-old former governor would die later in the year of a respiratory ailment. Meanwhile, Isabella nervously urged her supporters to get out the vote, especially among the women's Democratic clubs. But the general belief was, as one columnist put it, she would "be re-elected at a hand-gallop." And she was, by a majority of more than thirty-three thousand. Answering letters of congratulations, she wrote, "I was so lucky . . . but I never forget where good luck lies—in the hearts of one's friends." To Eleanor, she waxed eloquent: "I am off on that devastating course through which one occasionally emerges to see one's traditional soul, on a far horizon, clean and sweet as of old. . . . To come through, friends with oneself, is perhaps the lonely goal that is the way of wisdom."[7] Over the next year, Isabella would find it increasingly difficult to remain friends with herself and with the Roosevelts at the same time.

The end of the year was a time for taking stock. In her 1934 diary she wrote: "From 18 to 37 I struggled. 37 to 48 I *dared*. I must assimilate these chapters into *Results* . . . [in] the last lap—48 to 70—22 years." First of all, she vowed to care for her children and her aging aunt and uncle. For herself, "use & enjoy my body," taking care of it "as it wanes." She also wanted to "accumulate money & order my scattered affairs . . . create a political organization beyond defeat and for use."[8]

True to her promise, Isabella Greenway put her family first. In early January 1935 she delayed her return to Congress, pressing though that was, to spend ten days in Chicago to wait with Martha for the birth of her first child, somewhat overdue. The baby, a boy, arrived on January 13, and Isabella hastened back to Washington.

In her second year, Isabella Greenway had lost none of her allure for the media. NBC invited her to give a national radio interview, together with another close friend of Eleanor Roosevelt's, Representative Caroline O'Day, who had just been elected from New York. Bess Furman of the Associated Press kept calling the office trying to get the name of Isabella's new grandson (eventually called David). Another reporter for the Associated Press ran a lengthy interview with Isabella on January 26, noting that the "brown silk in her gown [was] no warmer than her brown eyes, her face serious with mental concentration" as she outlined her hopes for the coming year. She was also profiled in a *New York Times* magazine article in April. The author wrote her afterwards to say he "felt we were hitting nearer to real things than often happens in congressional conversations." He apologized for including information about her friendship with Eleanor, explaining that the *Times* had insisted on "800 words of explicit treatment." An editor at the Dodge Publishing Company asked Isabella to write a book "to be published within the next twelve months." Isabella Greenway was not concerned about her press coverage, however. She worried about the difficulty of maintaining a statesmanlike vision of national affairs in the midst of pressing problems.[9]

One of the most immediate problems facing Congress was revision of work-relief programs, especially for those who were not able-bodied. Florence Warner, secretary of the Emergency Relief Administration in Arizona, wrote Isabella advocating health screenings to eliminate "slackers" trying to take advantage of the relief programs, as well as to identify those with chronic illnesses such as tuberculosis, for whom, she said, "A few days arduous work may undo years of treatment." Warner desperately hoped Congress would adopt a health insurance plan. She herself, as a self-supporting woman, wanted health insurance, but although she had researched extensively, she could not find a plan that covered women. Warner seemed to accept the argument that "women are too serious a risk," but hoped the women in Congress would take action. Unemployed women were relatively invisible, but they, too, needed work. Ellen Woodward, director of women's work for the Federal Emergency Relief Agency, FERA, advised Isabella that, in addition to traditional jobs in offices and libraries, women could also repair furniture, make road signs, and serve as "emergency homemakers" in families where the mother was temporarily disabled.[10]

Chapter Eleven

Road work was extensively used for federal relief projects. Governor Moeur wrote Representative Greenway that Arizona's unemployment situation was becoming critical, and he wanted to be able to hire day labor instead of contract, in order to employ more men. Moeur suggested that he could not depend on the other members of the Arizona delegation; notes in the margin of his letter to Isabella indicated that Senator Ashurst's help had been negligible, while Senator Hayden was avoiding the issue altogether. Greenway replied to Moeur that she had received a "perfunctory" answer from the Bureau of Roads, but she planned to persevere. Finally, the bureau agreed, if the State would pay any cost overruns. Once again, Isabella was proving herself the person who got things done.[11]

Of course, Isabella's persistence in getting an answer where her colleagues did not may have been at least partly due to her ability to hire enough staff to chase down all these requests. Howard Caffrey, in particular, drafted many letters evidently requiring extensive research, and wrote lengthy memos for Isabella that demonstrated shrewd political analysis. But nobody could have looked after the affairs of an entire state without help. In addition to lobbying for work relief programs, Greenway had to attend to a host of other problems: labor and management relations, a bonus for the veterans, fences to keep cattle off the Arizona highways, and turf wars on the reservations. Isabella informed one correspondent that "we are really working eighteen out of most twenty-four hours." By mid-March, when critical legislation was being considered, she calculated they were "something over six thousand letters behind in my office." She confessed that she sometimes neglected her "understanding friends . . . while I struggle with the less understanding." The work, she said, was "almost insurmountable." It must have been especially hard for a single mother.[12]

At this time Isabella Greenway was grappling with an issue that would become a defining one during her tenure in Congress—social security. In President Roosevelt's annual message to Congress on January 4, he had announced that "social justice, no longer a distant ideal, has become a definite goal." By 1935, many European countries, beginning with Germany in the 1880s, had adopted social insurance laws, but the United States lagged behind. Some states offered pensions to their workers. Veterans and federal civil servants, public employees like police and teachers, and about 15 percent of employees in private business also enjoyed pensions. Most people stopped working only when they fell ill or were fired. Of an estimated seven million over age sixty-five, half required help, mostly supplied by relatives. About 700,000 were on the public rolls. In mid-1934, Roosevelt had charged Secretary of Labor Frances Perkins with drafting legislation to present to Congress. She deemed an old-age pension "politically almost essential." Unemployment insurance was also needed. So was health care, but Roosevelt recognized that would not be feasible. On January 17, 1935, Roosevelt presented his social security program, providing for the federal government to contribute up to $15 a month, on a dollar-for-dollar matching basis, to any state pension paid to persons over sixty-five.[13]

In March, Isabella Greenway led a group of House Democrats to try to persuade the president to defer all other social security legislation for that session, in order to pass the old-age pension provision. She argued that "the country is on fire for its passage," but feared that the entire social security bill was so controversial, it would all be defeated. Franklin put Isabella "on the spot," she later told Eleanor, by asking her to vote for the bill as a whole, which she felt she had to agree to do. Isabella was also worried that it might take up to two years for state legislatures to enact their side of the provision, and she offered an amendment granting pensions of $20 per month starting July 1, 1936, to people sixty years or older who were currently on the relief rolls. In the end, her amendment was defeated, and the administration plan passed easily.[14]

Undeterred, Isabella wrote Jim Farley in her capacity as the secretary of the Democratic congressional campaign committee. She said the Democrats were hard put to explain why an old-age pension bill "ingeniously excludes any possibility of giving pensions to old people except in a very few instances for almost two years." She added, "The Republicans are intelligently building on this at this moment." She apologized for arguing about "the political phase of what should be only a humanitarian and economic problem," but she hoped Farley would support Senate efforts to amend the bill to give pensions to the needy at once. Meanwhile, she defended Roosevelt to her constituents, pointing out that "there have been a great many Presidents heretofore who could have had legislation in behalf of old age and that Franklin Roosevelt is the only man actually driving it through."[15]

Isabella was afraid that her well-publicized stand against Roosevelt's bill might affect her friendship with Eleanor. In the draft of a letter that may not have been sent, she wrote to explain that she no longer came to Eleanor "with all the flood of matters about which we are all thinking and working"; because Isabella was a member of Congress, Eleanor might be seen as being unduly influenced by political pressure. It would be "just one more thing . . . about which something (and usually difficult) has to be done," Isabella realized, adding, "I'm not a step further away in my adoration."[16]

The press of problems continued without letup. Unemployment was still a grievous problem for her state. Farmers, too, were struggling. The farm loan bill, a.k.a. the Frazier-Lemke Moratorium bill, had been found unconstitutional and Isabella was now supporting a new Frazier-Lemke Farm Mortgage Refinancing bill. By the end of May, Isabella was longing for home and an end to constant work. She was hanging on, she said, to the "hope and conviction that lurks among us all here in Congress that we will be home by July 3."[17] It was a vain hope.

Another piece of unfinished business was the Taylor Grazing

Act. Isabella Greenway spoke on the floor of the House of her decision to vote against the bill, citing twenty-four years' experience
raising cattle. The bill would give federal control of some 173 million acres to new departments. She argued that more effective planning could be accomplished if grazing control were left under the
Department of Agriculture, while responsibility for erosion and
flood control was vested in a new bureau in the Department of the
Interior. The measure passed but succumbed to a pocket veto in
September.[18]

Isabella also lobbied effectively to keep a four-cent levy on imported foreign copper from expiring on July 1. Had it done so, copper being held in bond in the country would have been declared
duty free, vastly increasing the surplus and undoing the work of two
years. The extension was passed and signed by Roosevelt on June
29. The *Phoenix Republic* quoted the chairman of the Arizona Copper Tariff Board as saying that Representative Greenway had "lent
all her tireless energy" to the campaign of educating her fellow congressmen on the issue. She was immensely popular at home, the
president of the Reserve Officers Association wrote her, "held in
high esteem by everyone," unlike Hayden and Ashurst. She needed
these morale boosters to keep working through the oppressive July
heat. Although Greenway had been told in May that Arizona's unemployment was around fifteen thousand, July statistics showed
the number to be nearly forty thousand. The proportion had
shifted, too; now more than five thousand, or one-eighth of the total, were women. This startling discrepancy was due in part to
changes in registration requirements.[19]

At the end of July Isabella took Jack to New York to visit another
new grandchild, Bob and Franny's daughter Frances, called Patty.
Jack stayed on with them for a break from the heat while Isabella returned to the steamy capital. She felt bad about their separation, assuring him: "I miss you like nobody's business. It's amazing what a
close corporation we are. The rising sun means to me *you;* the day-

light hours reflect *you* & the sun going down just spells *you* in another form." She particularly missed him at night, "when you are too sleepy to be responsible & yet you are very sociable and cozy." She recognized the separation was hard for him too: "Your blueness quite got me last night. . . . I admired the philosophy you summoned when you spoke of the ranch and said 'but that we cannot have yet.' I'm just determined to be ready to spread out wings and *fly* the moment this poor old weary Congress swings the gavel of adjournment." She sent the letter special delivery so he would have it the next day. Two days later, Jack replied, "Mother, Theme of my days—I am fine. . . . The only thing that I could possibly desire is Y-O-U who are in all probability cooking to a frisel."[20]

The session was grinding to an end. "There is almost an undercover stampede to get away," Isabella noted on August 1. She rejoiced that the year's road budget would complete the paving of "every foot of Route 66 across the State," which she hoped would stimulate business along the roadside. She could also be proud of her work to get Civilian Conservation Corps (CCC) camps in her state; Arizona was hoping for approximately twelve thousand enrollees in almost sixty camps. Due to Isabella's efforts, Arizona received a higher than average allotment. Finally, at the end of August, Congress adjourned until January. Isabella and Jack fled to Williams, vowing to stay on "until the snow flies."[21]

Even on her first vacation in over three years, Isabella Greenway continued to work. The transfer of the FERA public works to the Works Progress Administration, and its various road projects, demanded a great deal of attention. She wrote Franklin Roosevelt, vacationing himself in Hyde Park, of her worry that some of Arizona's programs might be canceled. Harry King, who had moved back to New York after the copper code was adopted, came to visit on what was ostensibly a working vacation. When he returned home, he wrote, "I wish I could find some possible excuse for getting back." By mid-November, Isabella was down in Tucson, working harder than ever. In addition to lobbying for various job-creating public works, she made speeches to assure her constituents that the New Deal was achieving results, anticipating a hard battle in the 1936 election. But she was a realist. Addressing a nonpartisan audience at the Rotary Club, she said, "I hope the Republicans will not try and say that everything the Democrats have done is wrong, and that the party in power will not endeavor to convince a thinking public that everything this administration has done is meritorious and right."[22]

Isabella returned to Washington in January 1936, but this time alone; Jack, now eleven, had gone to Massachusetts to attend boarding school. Perhaps she worried that her two older children had suffered from too little formal schooling and wanted to be sure Jack would be well prepared. He later revealed that the separation had been a great wrench. Insecure, he told his mother he'd had a dream "in which you married H[arry]. This gave me a terrific shock and I merely wanted assurance that it was far from the truth."[23]

At the beginning of her third year in Congress, Isabella Greenway was more popular than ever and received many invitations to speak. Most she declined, explaining that a day or two away "might be two days when most of interest to Arizona would be at stake. . . . While we are in session I can never make a date." But she was eager, as always, for impromptu fun, as when she and Florence Kahn, a fellow congresswoman from California, dressed as hotel cigarette girls and crashed a stag dinner party of seventy congressmen.[24]

Isabella was unusually lighthearted during this time, perhaps because she had taken an important decision—to announce her retirement from Congress on March 22, her fiftieth birthday. The year before she had assured the *Phoenix Gazette* that she intended to be a candidate again in 1936. But during the next twelve months, she had changed her mind. Her press release stated simply that she would not be a candidate for reelection, "because various other responsibilities demand more of my time." A second press release elaborated on the short announcement: "I'm the head of my family and our interests are very scattered and right exacting." She had, she said, let her affairs "go to sixes and sevens from pressure." Furthermore, she explained, "When I came here the times were so critical, but now I feel that Arizona's better off; the mines are opening and the farmers in better shape." She pledged to stay active in state, national, and party affairs, adding gratefully: "I don't believe any woman ever has been given . . . as much as this—being the first woman ever to represent an entire state in Congress as representative at large." Ruth Hanna McCormick had represented the state of Illinois at large from 1928 through 1930, but she had not been, as Isabella Greenway was, the state's sole representative.[25]

Isabella denied that she was leaving to get married, to run for governor, or, at fifty, to take up philosophy. The Associated Press reported that she "met the marriage rumors, both general and specific, first with a convincing and serious denial and secondly with a laugh. . . . 'I would be an unhappy woman indeed,' she said, with a dimpling cheek, 'NOT to have the compliment of conjecture thrown about even my fifty years.'" She stated that, despite considerable pressure, she was not a candidate for governor. As for philosophy, at fifty, she admitted: "You come face to face with the fact that you're crazy to live. You begin to budget your resources, with an eagerness akin to greed. . . . The refreshing part of the milestone is the revelation . . . convincing us the intense pleasures come from the simpler things." Success, she had come to believe, should be measured by energy invested rather than by mere tangible results. Her decision to retire was met by dismay. Typical was the reaction on the editorial page of the *Tucson Citizen*: "We cannot agree that the work of reconstruction . . . is completed. . . . None will deny that Mrs. Greenway will be happier in the direct management of her private interests. All will regret her decision to return to private life when there is so much to be accomplished in public affairs."[26]

Isabella with David Breasted

Some commentators speculated that she was leaving Congress because of her many policy differences with Roosevelt. But in her press release, she stated, "I'm proud to have been allied with the courageous experiments of this Administration. President Roosevelt and the Democratic Party need four more years at least in order to begin to complete and establish those policies which should become permanent through merit, and eliminate much that is not succeeding." Her son Jack Greenway later suggested a different reason. "She was exhausted," he said. "Everybody who wanted somebody to go and trace out their lost veteran's pension, they spread the word how good she was and she got thirty referrals. She wasn't in the business for that and she was just plumb exhausted." Because she was Arizona's sole representative in the lower house, all the desperate people in a desperate time turned to her, and she did her utmost to help them.[27]

Greenway's congressional correspondence bears out Jack's observation. The secretary of the Arizona Cattle Growers' Association had written Isabella the year before: "Whenever anybody in Arizona wants anything, he always says, 'Write to Mrs. Greenway about that.' It is a wonder to me if you ever have time to attend the sessions of Congress." Nevertheless, the woman added two typewritten pages of her own requests. Isabella had received few letters of thanks for her efforts. She answered one: "You have written me one of the nicest letters I have ever received since I became a member of the group of public servants. It is the kind of a letter that is an oasis in the desert of TRYING." But now she got a gratifying number of letters from grateful and disappointed constituents. "Oh! Oh! Oh! What *will* we do now," wrote a Tempe woman. The male secretary of the Casa Grande chamber of commerce wrote that there was probably no "member of your constituency who opposed your election any more than myself." He had come to realize he had been wrong and wished she would reconsider.[28]

Another compelling reason for her decision was the worsening health of the man she regarded as her second father, Frank Cutcheon, who was suffering from debilitating attacks of angina pectoris. And despite her denials, Isabella Greenway may have wanted to devote more time to another connection, her deepening relationship with Harry King. One astute correspondent wrote later that spring: "A little bird told me, so here's all the luck in the world and how's for a piece of the cake?" The Kings had left Washington and moved to New York in 1935, but Isabella now had a place in New York City herself, an elegant apartment at 840 Park Avenue, three blocks from Martha's family and two blocks from Bob's. Meanwhile, she had several more months of hard work ahead of her, which she had pledged to finish.[29]

Unemployment in Arizona had swelled as disappointed people, fleeing their own barren states, were turned away at the California border and retreated to transient camps in Arizona. Men forced to leave the camps had broken into stores to take food. In the camps, no one was actually going hungry, but crowding imposed an increased risk of tuberculosis. Arizona officials begged Isabella to do what she could to extend federal relief programs. Harry Hopkins protested that the 3.8 million people already employed under the Works Program were 10 percent more than the original legislation had budgeted to cover. Greenway was one of the first signers of a House petition to earmark funds in the Relief Appropriation bill to continue Public Works projects. In a gesture more to show her convictions than with any real hope, on May 31 Isabella introduced in Congress a "stamp-scrip" plan for the District of Columbia. The program would stimulate buying by issuing date-stamped scrip that had to be spent before it expired. She pled with congressional colleagues to help her pass "this, my last piece of legislation." Franklin had encouraged her to pursue the idea, and she was "*ever so grateful,*" she told him, for all the time and interest he had given the project.[30]

The tone as well as the subject of her note to him undercut the supposition that she was leaving Congress because she was at odds with the president.

Though her stamp-scrip plan failed, Isabella Greenway left several legislative legacies. One was the copper code and the opening of the mines. Another was the social security plan, on which she had concentrated a great deal of her attention. The first checks for the aged, the blind, and dependent children were mailed on February 13, 1936. Isabella felt the plan was far from perfect, however. She wrote a constituent: "It is particularly impractical in a state like ours where the old people outnumber, in normal ratio, the rest of the population. . . . I am told to meet Federal contributions in that bill would practically double the entire cost of government of our state." Her interest in homesteading also had paid off. While homesteading as Isabella and Bob Ferguson had known it was on the wane, due to inaccessibility, lack of water, and poor markets for agricultural products, resettlement had been modestly successful. She also worked to make existing farms more modern. At that time, only 30 percent of farms in Arizona had electricity, and Isabella introduced a bill to provide electric power from the Coolidge Dam to farm families in the Casa Grande Valley. Roosevelt signed it into law on June 26. Isabella also continued to work on grazing rights, recognizing that a balance had to be struck between the needs of the cattle growers to make a living and the fact that, in many areas, "the carrying capacity of the range is entirely exhausted." She fought for the Navajos against mandated stock reduction for erosion control, noting that many families did not have enough animals even to take care of their own meat requirements and were being supplied with tinned meat from cattle slaughtered during the drought.[31]

Water was crucial to Arizona's economic well-being, and Isabella and her staff had worked hard for water development projects, albeit with disappointing results. The Parker Gila Project continued on-again, off-again, as Secretary of Agriculture Henry Wallace continued to raise objections. Farmers sent him bushels of produce—dates, pecans, oranges—grown on land the government deemed "unproductive." The Verde River Irrigation Project did not go through, due to high per-acre costs and possible water shortage, and Isabella received a great deal of criticism for the failure of the project. One correspondent accused her of having been under "sinister influences" to condemn it, a charge she hotly denied, concluding, "A letter like yours, in its injustice to me, is one of those broadening experiences, which through developing tolerance, make public service worthwhile."[32] It must have seemed to her that she had made the right decision a month before to retire.

CHAPTER TWELVE ∾∾∾∾∾∾∾∾∾∾∾∾∾∾∾∾∾∾

"At Home with the Right to Stay There"

ISABELLA WRAPPED UP her three years in Congress by mid-June and headed west, rejoicing to her Aunt Mary Selmes that she and Jack were "jubilantly ... at home with the right to stay there." Though Isabella was looking forward to retirement, she dutifully kept working right up to the end of the year, pleading for extensions on homestead claims, such as that of a disabled serviceman's widow with two small children: "I hope there is some means whereby these requirements may be waived in such unusually distressing circumstances."[1]

Once she had left Washington, she decided not to see Harry King while he was still married. His relationship with his wife, Mildred, was deteriorating, however. They had separated, and he had told her he wanted a divorce. He wrote Isabella that he had been confronted by Mildred's angry father: "He said I told him I loved Mildred twenty-two years ago and I was either a liar then or now. I feel terribly sorry for him, he is all upset—and I don't blame him for

∾∾∾∾∾∾∾∾∾∾∾∾∾∾∾∾∾∾∾∾∾∾∾∾∾∾∾∾∾∾∾∾

thinking it is all my fault. He will be happier that way." Harry objected, though, to Isabella's request for some distance. "Three or four years ago this might have been worth considering. Today it would only prolong the agony. The only reason it has come to a head now instead of long ago was the desire not to hurt Mildred's mother. To imagine for one second that you had or have had anything to do with it is too absurd. If I had never met you it would have been the same. Except that your kindness, generosity of thought has kept me from possibly precipitating this sooner." Still, he tacitly admitted the wisdom of her decision. "I love you my darling too much to take even the slightest chance at spoiling anything. My willingness to stay so far apart for so long at this time proves that. This loneliness and yearning is dreadful—and only possible because it is right."[2]

Isabella devoted her attention to her Uncle Frank, refusing all other commitments with the excuse: "Family matters are closing in." She spent several weeks in Santa Barbara, where she found Unc sitting up in anticipation of her visit. She also took responsibility for her aged Aunt Mary Selmes and for Julia "Mammy" Loving, now in her eighties, suffering from arthritis of the spine. Isabella sent Mammy a monthly allowance and wrote often to keep the old woman's spirits up. When Frank traveled to Long Island in September, Isabella moved back east at the same time. Jack, now at the Fay School in Southboro, Massachusetts, with Harry King Jr., wrote his mother: "My darling, Your regular letters are the brightest things in my life." He had apparently become reconciled to her relationship with Harry Sr., adding: "When you see him next give him my dearest love." But Jack must have found it hard to share the person who had considered him the center of her universe for so many years, and he wrote again a few days later, "I love you more than anything else God ever created & admire you extravagantly." Down in Washington to close their house, Isabella answered Jack reassuringly: "I loved you so while I packed your books, clothes, toys, important pa-

Jack at boarding school

pers, pictures and keepsakes. And all the time I kept thinking what happy times we've had here in Washington and that the next move is toward your career!!"[3]

Isabella stayed near Frank Cutcheon until his death on November 12 of a heart attack, at the age of seventy-two. Afterwards, she went back west to Santa Barbara to console his widow, her Aunt Sally. Twelve-year-old Jack wrote in his curiously adult manner, addressing her as "Dearest Isabella":

"I have been with you in mind all the long way of your sad journey. I am sure this is a great ordeal for you but . . . we must rally around the poor little old lady and do everything we can. I am sure that would be Uncle's desire if he were here."[4]

At the start of 1937 Isabella Greenway was beginning a new life. Although Frank had been one of her main reasons for leaving Congress and now was gone, she still looked forward to devoting more time to her family. She settled into her Park Avenue apartment, with easy access to her young grandchildren, and visited Jack at school every other week. "My cup is full with the joy of getting to know my family again," she exclaimed to more than one person. She missed being in the West but had a "terror of putting four days' train travel" between herself and Jack in the event of an emergency.[5]

True to form, she began her new life by writing a long, reflective memorandum to herself, taking stock and planning. She was pleased with Jack and Bob but concerned about Martha's health and marriage. Isabella had grown disenchanted with Chuck Breasted, whom she found, on closer acquaintance, to be rude and critical. However, she reminded herself, "She (*not I*) must unravel her personal life: don't interfere & don't worry." Her program for Martha included "love, tact" and "money in reserve to save her."

As for Harry, "The time has not yet come to decide on marriage." She craved the approval of her children, noting: "At present Jack likes & loves H—but dreads my marrying." Furthermore, "Harry is not independent enough financially to make marriage practicable. He and I and our children could not be happy unless he was supporting me fully." Isabella believed that Harry, forty-two, nine years younger than she, needed an occupation. About him, she resolved: "Enjoy, love, & keep in close touch but apart." Despite her resolutions, their affair could not be put on hold indefinitely. First, there was speculation in the press, which Isabella continued to deny: "I had a good laugh over the inquiry about my being married," she wrote a friend. "It must mean that the columnists have temporarily run out of names. I have no plans of that sort." Jack had also heard rumors at school that his mother was going to marry

King. But he was less anxious now that he was building a new life for himself that did not include his mother. She may have read with mingled feelings of relief and sorrow a letter in which he described all the activities that prevented him from writing more often: school work, chess, skating. "You can see," he concluded, "that I am not writing you more for a good reason. The very fact that I do this is proof of our great relation."[6]

Although she was caught up anew in family matters, Isabella could not altogether abandon the interests that had compelled her for so long. In early February, she visited Washington to lobby for the renewal of the tariff on foreign-mined copper. Her friends in Congress gave their former colleague a gratifyingly warm welcome. She stayed at the White House for several days, putting the lie to stories about her retirement being due to a rupture with the Roosevelts. Staying with Eleanor "as an old friend and with no politics in the picture was an unspeakable joy and relief. . . . The President was blooming . . . and apparently enjoying the controversy that is shaking the United States on the subject of the Supreme Court," she reported to a friend. Isabella took on small assignments, like heading up the Arizona Historical Memorials committee to celebrate the 1940 quattrocentennial of Coronado's expedition. She relished her ability once again to ask friends to drop in on her in New York, to have dinner and take in a play. In the West, where she retreated for the summer, she alternated between her cool mountaintop in Williams and Tucson, where she was expanding the Arizona Inn. Isabella stayed in Arizona until Thanksgiving, apparently untroubled now by being separated from her newly independent younger son.[7]

As 1938 began, rumors about marriage continued to swirl, with Isabella Greenway's name linked to several others, including that of General Douglas MacArthur. Most persistent, of course, were the rumors about Harry King, especially after his divorce from Mildred became final in late 1937. Isabella continued to deny them all, protesting that "at the age of 51, I consider it an enormous compliment," but insisting "I have no ideas of marriage."[8]

Isabella did a little charity work in New York and Tucson, but she was often on the road from one place to another, to such an extent that her administrative assistant Howard Caffrey wrote her in mid-May, "Your wire was welcome news this morning, for the deduction it gave us that you were still here among us mortals on earth." She was beginning to miss the excitement of her years in politics. In her journal, she took stock of the eighteen months since her retirement. "Why am I down?" the entry begins. "Because you are backing up stream or marking time—or you think you are." The "last constructive thing you did" was leaving Congress on January 1, 1937. She acknowledged that she had devoted a good deal of time and attention to her family. In addition, she had spent an "infinite" amount of time to discover she loved Harry and "an infinite amount of time to trying to help him up and back." She concluded, "The above might be called repairing & sustaining life's fences." She had been doing real construction, too: rehabilitating her Santa Barbara residence, roofing the ranch buildings, working on the house in Ajo, adding to the hotel and renovating a house in New York. Most mortals would consider that a great deal to show for eighteen months, but to Isabella, building was apparently as natural and as unremarkable as breathing.[9]

"The Human Equation," as she put it, continued to preoccupy Isabella for much of the summer. She went west, leaving Harry in her New York house, haunted by her presence. He was suffering from the heat, over one hundred degrees, but especially from "the loneliness that overcomes me when we are apart for more than a week or so." Isabella granted him a fortnight's reprieve to visit her at Williams. He planned to stay in bed the whole way out on the train, he told her, "because I don't expect to sleep a minute while I am there. I just want to look at you every minute and kiss you and hold you close and look at you again." The visit must have reassured him; on the train going home he wrote, "When I left you before it's been like a trip to the unknown. Now I know where I am going. Let's always be like this. The last two weeks have been heaven."[10]

Chapter Twelve

Harry may have thought he knew where he was going, but Isabella continued to worry that an alliance with Harry might complicate already difficult family relationships. A month later, en route to New York on the train herself, she analyzed her problems with her children: "M. indicates that she shares Chuck's point of view about me . . . in part & from time to time. . . . He has told me I am vitriolic, that I crush & discard from my life the major relations." He had cited Unc as an example, which gave Isabella great pain, although she tried to convince herself that there she was "guiltless." She had had "pleasant & restrained relations" with Bob for years but knew that he often criticized Harry to Jack, who reported: "Harry bores him and Frances and he'd hate to see you bored the rest of your life and I think he's fair to warn you now—rather than let you down later when you have married Harry." Jack observed, "He's too shrewd not to know that I tell you most of the things he tells me and he uses me as a means of telling you what he thinks." But Jack, too, could be a problem. "Poor Jack," Isabella noted, "he wants to be loyal and it's hard on him not to. He can still hurt me more than anyone." She concluded: "I must accept the fact that my children truly do not admire & approve of me, that their love, if there, is of habit. . . . But this is usual . . . and has no bearing on my relation to them and my responsibility. They have none *to me and I all to them*. And it should be so." She was still struggling to come to a decision about Harry: "If I marry Harry it will be because I love him and enjoy being with him. I think he is intuitively kind, generous and unselfish. I think he is able and should succeed and be a fine . . . influence in Jack's life. If he is none of these things it will be hard and I must face the consequences alone."[11]

Small wonder she was down!

Harry was doing his best to recruit Jack in this struggle, writing him, "I salute you as a real son," and signing his letters, "All my love." And despite Jack's capacity to hurt his mother, he was more often very tender. In his letters he expressed himself in a surprisingly florid style for a thirteen-year-old boy toward his mother. "Cherie," he wrote her in February, "I am in ecstasy over your coming," and signed himself, "With inestimable love, Thy Son." He must have been proud of her when she gave a well-received speech on Prize Day at his school. She in turn was exceedingly proud of Jack, who had made a very good record. In the fall, he entered the Phillips Academy in Andover, Massachusetts, where he roomed across the hall from George Herbert Walker Bush. There, too, Jack did well, earning honors in all his subjects, an unusual accomplishment for a student in his first year.[12]

By the start of 1939, Isabella was moving closer to a decision to marry Harry King. They began by remodeling two adjoining brownstones at 132 East 92nd Street, between Park and Lexington, gutting the insides and refacing the outsides. She had helped Harry toward the financial security which had been one of her conditions for marriage; together they had launched the Institute of Applied Econometrics, where he served as president. He was also a director of several corporations. As for her children, she had apparently chosen to ignore their misgivings, as well as those of many acquaintances, one of whom characterized him as "a vulgar Adonis." However, another old friend, Elizabeth Sherman Lindsay, wrote reassuringly that she loved Isabella's "beau."[13]

Isabella Selmes Ferguson Greenway married Harry Orland King on April 22 in the parlor of their new house, attended only by members of their immediate families. Jack, fourteen, served as best man. Isabella wrote Sally, far away in Santa Barbara, that she sorely missed the person who now represented "Mother, Father, Uncle— the world that was my grown-up world when I was a child." She added, "I pray it's best." Harry's daughter Saranne later evaluated the Kings' marriage. "He adored her," she said simply. At the wedding ceremony, she recalled, "He gave her the ring, she kept John Greenway's ring on and she put my father's over it.... She worshipped John Greenway. As my father worshipped her." Still, Saranne thought they had a successful marriage. "She was great to him. I never saw them fight or anything, but she was much the dominating figure in the marriage. . . . My mother was so dependent and he really needed a dominating person in his life. . . . That's why he was so happy with [Isabella], one of the reasons."[14]

Unlike her previous husbands, Harry did not like to advise Isabella on her financial concerns. After they had been married almost a year, Harry wrote protesting that "too much business is getting into our lives. . . . After all we are in love and married and not incorporated." Five days later, he begged, "Now Darling do one thing for me. Don't work so hard and tensely. We have everything to be happy about and a great future." What did Isabella think of this? She had been beset by problems and business from the age of nine. Was the invitation to take it easy a burden lifted, or a rejection of her entire way of life? Would she feel blessed and tended to, or succumb to the depression of ennui? Harry was also different in objecting to even the shortest separation. When he left her on an extended business trip in March, he wrote, "This is the last time I am going through such a performance. Four nights and three days on a train —alone—without you and endless more days scattered all over the country—just doesn't make sense." A month later Isabella was away. "I'm terribly lonely," Harry wrote plaintively. "It hurts so much to be in love."[15]

The balance between home and work was one that occupied the attention of women all over the country. The Depression had cost many women their hard-won jobs, but as it began to lift, women once again dared to pursue careers. The *Tucson Citizen* ran a graduation story that began "Career or no—the question is as familiar to young women all over the country as the one asked by Hamlet in his soliloquy. . . . Tucson girls . . . of the class of 1940 probably are still debating this question with themselves." The article offered Isabella Greenway King as an example of nationally renowned women who maintained happy homes.[16] As Harry's letters suggest, Isabella

The wedding of Isabella Greenway and Harry O. King

herself was still trying to find the right balance in her new marriage. By October, she discovered a cause that would make use of her political skills, an activity that Harry could share.

Franklin Roosevelt had been nominated for an unprecedented third term. Isabella claimed to see this as a "danger signal and a demonstration of misused power," she told the press. Isabella and Harry King joined the New York national headquarters of Democrats for Wendell Willkie, the Republican nominee, explaining that "loyalty to country takes precedence over loyalty to party." Isabella was offered the position of associate director. She may have objected to FDR's challenge to tradition, but she was likely also influenced by her new husband, who was a Republican, even though he had worked on the New Deal. Now disillusioned, Harry believed "that the system that made ours the greatest country in the world is far better than the collectivist state that the New Dealers have tried to force on us."[17]

Isabella, like many, also objected to Roosevelt's support of the Allies in the growing European conflict. She had always been a pacifist, hating war because of the anguish she had endured when John Greenway was overseas with the AEF. She used to say to Jack, "*I think that if the Congress knew that the first thing that would happen is that somebody would set up a machine gun in the podium in the House . . . and went B-r-r-r- once around that room, killing one full round in there—this war would not occur!*"[18]

Isabella supported Willkie because she hoped he would do more for full employment. It was not hard for her to support a man who had been a lifelong Democrat and had only recently changed his own party affiliation, and she noted that "Circumstances have . . . blurred the clarity of party leadership." She was right: Henry Wallace, a Republican, was running as FDR's vice-presidential candidate. In addition to her work on the national committee, she served as chairman of Arizona Democrats for Willkie. She traveled to Tucson in mid-October, to explain her position "so there will be no misunderstanding between her and the people she knows and loves best," wrote the *Arizona Daily Star*. But her "explanations" were more like campaign speeches for Willkie. She visited every county, speaking three or four times a day.

"All the powers needed to create a dictator have been granted," she said. "Our President has appointed the majority of members of the supreme court, 5 out of 9; he is head of the army and navy; one-fourth of the inhabitants of this country receive entire or partial government benefits, directly or indirectly, from his subordinates." Congress had passed laws giving him "the absolute power of a dictator."[19] She neglected to mention that she herself had helped enact many of those laws.

Isabella now wrote Eleanor: "Here comes another chapter and one I don't like the experience of." She explained that her chief objection to FDR was the third term, adding, "You would, I know, do what I am doing if you felt as I do." She hoped that her participation would be reported on impartially, "and that our lifelong family relations will be safeguarded." But she knew that in a political campaign, others might exploit their differences. She closed with "A heart full of love always and an understanding that surpasses all words and will survive in spite of everything. Devotedly, Isabella."[20]

Eleanor replied, "I am, of course, sorry to have you openly on the other side, but I realize you have to do whatever you think is right." She stated her own objections to Willkie, but added, "of course, as far as I am concerned political differences never make any differences in one's own personal feelings." But she sighed to another friend: "I'm a bit weary of having her reasoning always so pure but I know she thinks she is doing the right thing." The American public, wary of abandoning a proven leader at a time of danger, voted overwhelmingly for Roosevelt. Willkie carried only ten states.[21]

CHAPTER THIRTEEN ∞∞∞∞∞∞∞∞∞∞∞∞∞

"*She Was Unique*"

THE APPROACHING WAR had defeated Isabella's candidate, but it also provided her with the opportunity for more public service. In 1941 Isabella was drawn into work with the American Women's Voluntary Services, enlisting women throughout the country to aid national defense efforts for the conflict that most agreed would eventually come even to the United States. An army was being conscripted for the first time in peacetime. AWVS was in the tradition of women's voluntary organizations in past war times, like the Sanitary Commission in the Civil War, or the Land Army in World War I. They mobilized and trained women in fire fighting, air raid precautions, radio code, first aid, map reading, convoy driving, and motor mechanics, among other things. AWVS sent volunteers to the Aircraft Warning Auxiliary Corps (spotters, plotters, switchboard operators, and couriers); police and fire departments; armed forces; draft and rationing boards; air raid wardens; and salvage (an educational campaign on the need for saving grease, scrap metal, rubber, and rags). They also supported a Land Army; in California,

∞∞∞∞∞∞∞∞∞∞∞∞∞∞∞∞∞∞∞∞∞∞∞∞∞∞∞∞∞∞∞

thousands of women went into the fields to replace the interned Japanese. Women worked in victory gardens and canteens; hospitals; day care (to free mothers to work); and recreational services for men in the armed services. They provided legal advice to service men through the Women's Bar Association. By May 10, 1941, seventy-two AWVS units had been established in twenty states, as well as Alaska (not yet a state). It boasted over thirteen thousand members, about a tenth of whom were in New York taking training courses.[1]

The American Women's Voluntary Services, modeled on a women's organization in Great Britain, had been established in January 1940 by Alice McLean. Isabella admired her hugely: "I used to think that Theodore Roosevelt had the greatest capacity for endurance that I have ever known. I later decided that President [Franklin] Roosevelt's wife has. I have now decided that Mrs. McLean has. All of us faint, reel and pass out of entangling details again and again to find her standing firm." McLean persuaded Isabella Greenway King to serve as chairman of the board of AWVS and over the summer Isabella went west to organize new units, primarily in California.[2]

After the Japanese attack on Pearl Harbor on December 7, 1941, civilians found their lives as much transformed as the soldiers'. Women flocked to volunteer. A story in the *Saturday Evening Post* describing "Eight Hour Orphans," children abandoned by working mothers, left chained to automobiles in trailer camps, or in dog houses in back yards, prompted the AWVS to consider training women to run day nurseries. AWVS received national recognition when the *New Yorker* profiled Isabella (who could not have been best pleased by their caricature drawing of her). On her office desk, the article noted, were "two letter files labelled, respectively, 'Confusion' and 'Trouble.'" Part of the trouble was occasioned by the refusal of AWVS to meet with unionized office workers. The organization was open to women of any color or creed, and included Mary

McLeod Bethune, director of Negro Affairs for the National Youth Administration. Isabella was shocked that "what was supposed to be a patriotic organization" could refuse to take in women who happened to be in a union.[3] Class differences were apparently more divisive than race.

Isabella tried to get government recognition for the AWVS, but, after she had "gone to the mat" with Eleanor, she accepted that the government would not officially recognize any agency except the Red Cross and the Office of Civilian Defense. Still, a number of government departments, like Treasury, gladly accepted their help. The AWVS stepped up recruitment, finding that women were willing to work "if . . . made to feel that they are a definite part of the war effort." An AWVS uniform helped. One organizer warned that if women were not persuaded to volunteer in large numbers, "total conscription of women will come," as it already had in England.[4]

Isabella took a leave of absence for most of the summer to be with Jack, who had just graduated from Andover and was planning to go to Yale, his father's alma mater, in the fall. In fact, she had asked to resign but was refused. By fall, the organization needed her contacts and powers of persuasion more than ever. Nine months after Pearl Harbor, the AWVS had mushroomed from a prewar membership of thirteen thousand in twenty states to 250,000 in thirty-one states. They were entirely supported by contributions; there was not even paid membership. Isabella begged for donations and organized benefits. Her political savvy was needed, too. The government had finally recognized their efforts, inviting them to participate in an official campaign to enlist every family for the Fight for Victory and Peace.[5]

Isabella moved to Washington, D. C., where Harry, no doubt feeling that there was never going to be the cozy domesticity he had imagined, had taken a job as a "dollar a year man," heading the copper division in the War Production Board. "I am wondering how you arrange to carry your responsibilities and still be a wife in

Washington," asked Isabella's friend Mildred Bliss, who, as mistress of Dumbarton Oaks, knew all about being a busy Washington wife. But Isabella seemed to be thriving on work; Sally Cutcheon observed that Isabella looked better than she had for a long time.[6]

Isabella worked for the AWVS in Washington, but it was by no means her only activity. She also served on the Committee for Constitutional Government, a nonpartisan organization dedicated to keeping the government from assuming extraordinary powers that might endure after peace was won. Her interest in this group doubtless reflected the stand she had taken during the 1940 campaign. Isabella was a member of its advisory board, which included the Rev. Norman Vincent Peale, newspaper owner Frank Gannett, and author Booth Tarkington. Once again the reformed New Dealer was fighting big government. But she retained her liberal credentials by supporting the American Arbitration Association, where she served on the executive committee with Frances Kellor, a noted social reformer. They hoped to contribute to postwar planning, including international commercial arbitration. At the beginning of 1943, Isabella resigned from the AWVS, no longer able to carry on for the New York-based organization while living in Washington.[7]

Isabella may have relocated for Harry's sake, but he could still be disappointed when her work took precedence over their relationship. A note written on February 24, 1943, "at the office, 5 P.M.," rebuked her for slighting him. "My darling," he wrote, "I came down five minutes after you left and could and would have been here in two minutes had I known. I could never leave you without a good-bye even for a day. The only real happiness I've ever had has been with you and I love you so much that I don't think I could take anything short of the complete understanding we have always had. I am hurt and down but I adore and worship you." Perhaps to placate him, Isabella's name on the AAA masthead changed from Mrs. Isabella Greenway King to Mrs. Harry Orland King. Eventually, Isabella solved the problem of Harry's conflict with her work by combining them; by 1945 Harry was serving as the president of the American Arbitration Association. They moved back to his home in Bridgeport, Connecticut, where Isabella could be near Jack at Yale. She resumed calling herself Isabella Greenway King.[8]

The center of Isabella's emotional life was probably still her younger son. At eighteen he had enlisted in the Army Reserve Corps and spent a year, 1942 to 1943, training with the Army Air Force at the University of Virginia at Charlottesville. He then entered the USAAF Training Command School at Yale, preparing to be a technical officer in communication. But by the next year, he began to experience a "terrible introspective gloom," and left school to join up. He discussed his decision at length with Isabella on a visit home to Bridgeport, sitting on the end of her bed, with the sound of the sea in the background. She would have tried to be strong, true to John's ideals and the Rough Rider traditions, but afterward she confessed that it had brought back the terrors she had felt for his father: "fear again crept in and gripped my soul." She had no such worries for Bob, who was serving in Australia near Sydney in the Home Economics division, shipping food to MacArthur in the Philippines. Jack was equally fortunate. After leaving Yale, he went to Ohio and then to Texas for further training in cryptography. Finally, in April 1945, he was sent to the Aleutian Islands near Alaska. "This hasn't been grim . . . compared with going away to boarding school at 12," he wrote. "Living conditions are luxurious compared with the . . . winter camp on the Ranch."[9]

Jack and his mother kept up a brisk correspondence. He wrote his mother particulars of army life, explaining, "I always open my heart with complete frankness and right now this is very much with me." He apologized for the "trivial nonsense" in his letters, "but I do so love to write." He was still effusive: "Here is another installment, darling, of love on my private 'pay as you go' plan of being your son, and I hope to remain helplessly in debt always." In another sense, though, their roles were changing. He asked whether

Jack in World War II

the home in Bridgeport was working out "as far as your privacy and peace of mind" were concerned. "It is the one issue that I have felt that you sometimes fail to meet squarely," he wrote. "The one thing I couldn't stand, being away as I am, is to think that you were getting into any sort of a tailspin." Twenty years of age and a soldier in the army, he now assumed the role of his mother's protector as she neared sixty.[10]

During 1945, Harry wrote a family newsletter to circulate information about their far-flung family. His son Harry Jr. had participated in the Normandy invasion, and his return home occasioned a prolonged celebration. The newsletters give glimpses of wartime America, as when the Kings bought two steers because meat was so severely rationed they had been without it for weeks. But their family life still included the great and near great of the age. Harry played golf with Gene Tunney. Jack was an usher at the wedding of an Andover classmate, attended by Lieutenant George H. W. "Poppy" Bush, who had returned after having been shot down in the Pacific and reported missing for five weeks. The Kings dined on several occasions with the journalist Westbrook Pegler. One of his articles had been critical of Eleanor; Isabella, Harry reported, "lit into Mr. Pegler in her inimitable way, and gave him a few of the facts of life as to what a fine person Mrs. Roosevelt really was."[11]

On April 5, the newsletter noted, the well-known society portraitist Elizabeth Shoumatoff visited their house for cocktails and told the family that she was off the next day to Warm Springs, Georgia, to paint President Roosevelt's portrait. No train accommodations were available, and she had to borrow gas coupons from friends to make the long drive. She observed that "the president has changed a very great deal since I did his portrait two years ago—the one in which he wears his Naval cape." She looked into the distance and said, "You know, it is a very strange thing, but I have a feeling that they think this may be his last portrait. . . . I *must* go and do it. It will be very interesting, but . . . very difficult."

A week later, on April 12, Martha and Chuck were working out of doors, enjoying an unusually clear day on Long Island, when their nine-year-old son David ran out of the house to announce that Roosevelt was dead. The president had collapsed and died of a stroke while Madame Shoumatoff was sketching him. For the rest of the evening, listening to the radio, Chuck reflected on the "innumerable ways in which this man's life had affected all of us—especially in the family. His relationship and that of his family to ours would make a story in itself."[12]

Two months later, Isabella lunched with the widowed Eleanor at the Biltmore in New York, where the former First Lady shared with her old friend the problems of packing up the family belongings at the White House after a twelve-year residence, as well as taking care of various grandchildren while their fathers were at war. Jack observed to Isabella that "Aunt Eleanor" had withdrawn from the public scene "with a magnificent dignity and unobtrusiveness. . . . Sometimes I think of her as strangely miscast. . . . Perhaps she should have . . . led a private life instead of a public one."[13]

The momentous events of early August 1945 disrupted the family to such an extent that their wartime weekly missed an issue. When the newsletter resumed, Harry wrote: "The news of the atomic bomb burst on the world and August 6 and 7 were filled with a sort of dazed reaction that something cataclysmic had happened in the history of the world." He and Isabella were in New York City on August 14 when the announcement that Japan had surrendered came over the radio and "the town went wild." Harry and Isabella "listened to the announcement at least ten times," then stopped at St. Bartholomew's church before going out to dinner.[14]

"I still can't believe any of all the things that are happening," Isabella wrote Jack on August 23. "The habits of the last $4\frac{1}{2}$ years have become imbedded." She would wake in the night and turn on the radio, "and then I give myself a big fight talk & say 'Get back on the beam & try to live as you used to & feel as you used to & *do* as you used to.' It's just bewildering." She was instantly aware of the political implications: Congress would be "bombarded" with relatives demanding their men home and parents protesting the drafting of their sons now that the war was over. Truman wanted new recruits for two years' service to release those who were in. Isabella marveled that they could now fill their cars with gasoline whenever they wanted and could buy cheese for the first time since the war started. "It is like coming out of ether and overhearing bystanders whispering that the operation was successful!"[15]

Isabella was beginning to think about postwar life. She wrote Jack a flattering letter, saying that to her and to others as well, he represented the inspiration of the future. She confessed, "The only times I get low are when you aren't apparently as *self*-inspired to the same degree you inspire others." She may have felt low because she thought she had failed to instill sufficient ambition in John's son, or perhaps because, for once, she herself felt undecided. She wanted to go to Tucson to look after the Inn but also needed to sell their house in Washington, D. C. Harry was starting a fiberglass industry and she wanted to be on hand for that, too. And she was needed in Williams to see about having the grazing permit expanded. Meanwhile, she had the Bridgeport house and the house in New York to run. "It's wonderful to fancy myself important but I certainly do carry the sack of small nothings that oil the family wheels and are the repairs & replacements that keep us on the highway," she wrote Jack a month later.[16]

On October 11, Isabella wrote a loving testimonial to her son on his twenty-first birthday. "You *are* your Father's fulfillment & you and I must—in being vigorous & happy—along our ways realize we are carrying on as he would love and revel in." She wrote him often, everything from family gossip to politics. She was very impatient for his return. "Darling—for Heavens sake when are you coming home!" she wrote on Armistice Day. Jack may not have been as eager to come home as his mother was to have him. "His time in the service was a very important thing to him," one of Jack's oldest friends, Deezy Manning Catron, later said. "He was out in the big world. . . . I think that when he came back he didn't want to be crushed." Isabella could be overwhelming for family members. Her grandson David Breasted later observed that she "sucked all the oxygen out of a room," dominating everyone in it.[17]

With the war over and Jack safe, Isabella turned to the concerns of her family and businesses. She spent more time in the West, very much involved with her Inn. During the war it had remained open, even during the summer; the Inn had been classified as an "essential industry," because it served the nearby Davis-Monthan Air

Base, where the Army Air Force was training, and the University of Arizona, where Navy personnel were taking classes. Isabella's girlhood friends Elizabeth Sherman Lindsay and Laura Chandler came for a visit and were lost in admiration of their friend's accomplishment. Elizabeth wrote to Olivia Cutting James, praising the Inn with its blooming native plants and delicious food. "The service is the greatest proof of Isabella's genius," she said, but it was her old friend's executive ability that amazed her. "She pretends to be vague and maintains that all detail is done by others. . . . *All* her 'staff' were seemingly dull routine people until she made them into administrators. Her ex-chauffeur is now contractor, engineer and head gardener. Her ex-stenographer is bookkeeper of the Inn. Her ex-Secretary is her man of business and a first-class executive. *She* says they do everything and they each say *she* does."[18]

In 1947, Sally Cutcheon died in Santa Barbara, and Isabella inherited the Dinsmore Farm. She tried to keep up the old farm traditions, sending beef cattle from Arizona and making jams and jellies for the Arizona Inn. The farm manager's daughter, Emma Seburn, was awed: "She was just beautiful. . . . When she was out here on the farm, she just let her hair blow, and she always had a big hat to stick on her head."[19]

In 1948, Isabella Greenway King was once again roused to focus on the national scene. This time her concern was inflation, and she conceived a plan for women to pledge not to pay more than agreed-upon prices for essential commodities. She sent copies of her proposal to John L. Lewis, president of the United Mine Workers of America; Secretary of Agriculture Clifton Anderson; and even to Harry Truman, closing her letter to the president with "warm friendship." (They had served together in Congress.) Anderson blandly assured her that his department and the Department of Commerce had "discussed various voluntary plans. . . . We hope to have such a plan in the near future and are confident that it will include many if not all the suggestions contained in your wires." Her plan drew mixed reviews in Arizona. The Tucson Business and Professional Women's Club unanimously endorsed her idea, but a letter to the editor of the *Arizona Daily Star* called the plan "visionary and impractical," speculating that Isabella had "an ulterior political motive."[20] Isabella no doubt wanted to help solve a critical problem, but she may also have hoped for just such recognition, after several years of comparative obscurity.

Jack returned to Yale and graduated in June 1949. Isabella had lived in Bridgeport while Jack was nearby, but when he moved to Tucson to enter law school at the University of Arizona, she spent less and less time in Connecticut. Though her involvement in politics was now over, she still retained her love of building and constructed a number of cottages around the Inn over the next several years. By now Harry was more comfortable with her absences and enjoyed her letters during their separations. "Darling ... what a writer of the English language you are. You really ought to devote all your time to architecture and writing," he told her.[21]

By 1950, Isabella was beginning to feel her age, sixty-four. A fall on a slippery rug in Connecticut had "really knocked me out," she admitted to Jack. She was often breathless, probably from the onset of congestive heart failure. Martha would come over and walk the floor with her when she couldn't get her breath. But Isabella avoided doctors, thinking them mostly "useless." Jack was concerned about her condition but put it down to worry. "It is obviously impossible that all the people who serve as objects of your concern be reformed. Therefore the problem is to stop worrying about them (or us)," he advised. She self-prescribed a Broadway play and reported to Jack: "I went feeling that my body was like an automobile. That the battery was dead, the spark plugs missing, the carburetor clogged & the starter jammed—& I laughed myself into circulation." She paid a last visit to Boone County. On the day she

Isabella Selmes Ferguson Greenway King in her Tucson house

was leaving, the manager's wife found Isabella stretched across her bed—the bed she had been born in—crying hard.[22] Perhaps she realized she would not be coming back.

Isabella's health deteriorated slowly over the next two years, but while she withdrew almost entirely from public and political life, she never lost her deep interest in the state's affairs. Meanwhile, Jack became active in state politics, as county chairman for the Democratic Party.[23]

Isabella continued to suffer from congestive heart failure, and in November 1952 she had a heart attack. But she recovered sufficiently to go back to New York in the summer of 1953 to visit the Ferguson children and grandchildren. There she had another heart attack but returned to her beloved Tucson home as soon as she could be moved. Although weak, she was cheerful and enjoyed the company of her children. On December 14 she suffered a stroke from which she did not recover. She died four days later, on December 18, the twenty-third anniversary of the founding of the Arizona Inn, her most lasting legacy, and was buried at the Dinsmore Farm, where members of her family had been buried since 1836.[24]

Among the many letters of condolence Jack Greenway received, three stand out for the historian. Morris Udall, a young Pima County attorney who would go on to a brilliant career in the U.S. House of Representatives, wrote: "In a time when intellectual honesty was all too rare, she displayed it ever. I've always felt toward her a lot of the veneration which Englishmen display toward the queen." Carlos Ronstadt, president and general manager of the Baboquivari Cattle Company, later known as the father of singer Linda Ronstadt, confessed, "I loved her dearly." He added, perceptively, "My heart has been sore since her first illness, because I knew she suffered because she could not do for others what she thought she must." Corinne Roosevelt Alsop wrote simply: "She was unique."[25]

CHAPTER FOURTEEN ⟶⟵⟶⟵⟶⟵⟶⟵⟶⟵⟶⟵

Isabella's Legacies

OR MORE than twenty years Bob and Frances Ferguson lived in the little brownstone "Bandbox" at 135 East 69th Street (now number 145) where they brought up their three children: Frances, always known as "Patty" (1935), Robert Harry Munro Ferguson, called "Bob" (1937), and Phyllis (1938). Martha and Chuck Breasted settled in the Cutcheons' Locust Valley property on Long Island where Isabella and Bob Ferguson had been married. The Breasteds had four children: David (1935), Macomb, "Mac," (1939), Isabella (1941) and Sarah Grace (1946).

The seven cousins grew up hearing tales of Bob and Martha's youthful adventures at the Homestead: how they ran wild and got lost and made their pocket money by trapping and skinning animals and selling the pelts to an outfit in St. Louis. The two families spent long summers at the Quarter Circle Double X Ranch in Williams.[1]

Isabella built her last house, a spacious, two-story dwelling next door to the Arizona Inn, around 1950, as a home for Martha and her family, and the Breasteds moved to Tucson.

⟶⟵⟶⟵⟶⟵⟶⟵⟶⟵⟶⟵⟶⟵⟶⟵⟶⟵⟶⟵⟶⟵

Bob and Martha with their children, 1941. Front row, left to right: Frances Hand Ferguson, Bobby Ferguson, Phyllis Ferguson, Patty Ferguson, David Breasted, Martha Ferguson Breasted, Macomb Breasted. Back row: Bob Ferguson holding Isabella Breasted. Missing: Sarah Grace Breasted, who was not yet born.

Jack Greenway, too, settled in Tucson. He became director of the Inn at Isabella's death and remained so until he died in 1995, but Jack was never a hands-on manager. Isabella had not wanted him to spend his life as an innkeeper. Jack took a law degree in 1954 and served as chairman of the Arizona Democratic Party in the 1950s and 1960s, as well as Democratic national committeeman. He was also active in social and community causes. He never married.

Isabella Selmes Ferguson Greenway King was buried in the family gravesite at Dinsmore Farm. Harry King died in 1976 and was buried in Connecticut. In 1995, John Greenway's body was moved from Ajo to lie beside Isabella, and Jack was interred there, too. Martha, who died at the end of 1994, asked that her ashes be placed in the grave of Julia Loving (Mammy). Bobbie, who had died ten years before, was buried with his father.

At Isabella's death, Jack Greenway inherited the Quarter Circle Double X Ranch. In the mid-1970s he sold it to my mother, Bazy Tankersley. Bazy is the granddaughter of Mark Hanna, a notable Republican senator and campaign consultant at the turn of the last century. So I thought it passing strange that my Republican mother had a photograph of Franklin D. Roosevelt on her living room wall, until I learned that the photo had been taken at the ranch in 1932, when FDR and Isabella were campaigning.

Isabella Greenway was the first of several extraordinary Arizona women in politics, but she was years ahead of her time. Nearly a quarter of a century after Isabella's death, Margaret Hance was elected mayor of Phoenix in 1977. Rose Mofford, secretary of state beginning in 1977, became Arizona's first woman governor in 1988 when Governor Evan Mecham was impeached. Similarly, Arizona's second woman governor, Secretary of State Jane Hull, took office in 1997 when Governor Fife Symington resigned after a jury convicted him of fraud. In 2002, Janet Napolitano was elected governor in her own right. In 1981, Sandra Day O'Connor, who grew up on a ranch not far from the Burro Mountain Homestead and then became a Phoenix lawyer and judge, was appointed to the U.S. Supreme Court by President Ronald Reagan. Finally, in 1992, almost sixty years after Isabella's election to Congress, Arizona sent a second woman to the U.S. House of Representatives, Karan English.

Isabella Greenway's legislative legacy included funding for Route 66 and WPA work for Arizona's parks, her contribution to passing the landmark social security bill, the relief afforded heads of families through road works and other construction projects, help for Arizona farmers, the revival of the copper industry, and disability benefits for veterans with TB, which was passed over Roosevelt's veto. Rep. Greenway helped hundreds of constituents negotiate the thickets of the new federal bureaucracy, especially with regard to mortgages. When she retired, Isabella also left behind a well-organized and newly invigorated Arizona Democratic Party.

In spite of the many tragedies of her life—the loss of her father when she was nine, her mother's poverty, her first husband's terrible illness, her second husband's unexpected death—Isabella remained resiliently optimistic. Like her friend Franklin Roosevelt, she emerged from these trials a strong, compassionate person, with empathy for the unfortunate and hard-won skills to help them. Through it all, she retained her sense of fun and her zest for adventure. As her friend and political advisor Tom Robins put it, she had "an extremely intoxicating effect" on everyone she met, which was no doubt responsible for much that she was able to accomplish. Peg Richmond, who married Chuck Breasted's half-brother and thereby became a member of the close-knit Red Heart clan, noted that Isabella had the ability to make everyone she met "feel like they were the most important person in the world." Isabella admitted that she was sometimes disorganized; she pled guilty to the charge that she became effective "only when intolerable pressure from self-created chaos" drove her to action. But one perceptive friend noted that Isabella saw in every problem "a multitude of OPPORTUNITIES."[2]

Although Isabella Greenway's path-breaking political career received more attention in her lifetime, her most lasting legacy has been the Arizona Inn, run since 1995 by her granddaughter Patty Ferguson Conroy Doar. The family-owned and -operated Inn has retained the reputation for intimacy and charm that Isabella worked from the start to establish. In 2003, it was listed in Condé Nast *Traveler's* "Gold List: The World's Best Places to Stay" and *Travel & Leisure's* "The Greatest Hotels in the World."[3] *Traveler* observed: "Top-of-the-line" service "always comes with a smile." The Inn's master carpenters continue to repair and reproduce the Hut furniture that inspired Isabella to create this Tucson institution.

Isabella Greenway (in white dress) with Eleanor Roosevelt at the Inn, 1933

Five years after Isabella's death, Eleanor Roosevelt visited Tucson and stayed at the Arizona Inn. "It seems strange," she wrote her friend Lorena Hickok, "that she should have died and I should still be flourishing."[4]

The Inn is flourishing still.

NOTES

NYT   *New York Times*
 OC   Olivia Cutting
 OCJ   Olivia Cutting James
  PS   Martha (Patty) Flandrau Selmes
  RF   Rebecca Flandrau
RHMF   Robert Harry Munro Ferguson
 SBS   Sarah B. Selmes
  SC   Selmes Collection, 1021, Arizona Historical Society
 SFC   Sarah (Sally) Flandrau Cutcheon
  TC   *Tucson Citizen*
  TR   Theodore Roosevelt

INTRODUCTION

1. E. Hill, *American Scene,* 122.

2. *NYT,* June 30, 1932; *ADS,* July 1, 1932; *Chicago Tribune,* June 30, 1932.

3. IF to SBS, Jan. 6, 1911, and Dec. 25, 1915, all SC.

4. E. Roosevelt, *This Is My Story,* 169–70.

5. *NYT,* Dec. 19, 1953.

CHAPTER ONE   *"Time of Gray Sorrow"*

1. Putnam, *Theodore Roosevelt,* 311.

2. JSG interview.

3. R. Miller, *Julia S. Dinsmore,* 15–20.

4. CEF to Patty Flandrau, Jan. 20 and Mar. 6, 1883, Fl.C; PS to JD, July 5 and Dec. 2, 1883, DC.

5. Morris, *Rise of Theodore Roosevelt,* 283.

6. TR to Anna Roosevelt Cowles, Aug. 8, 1886, quoted in McCullough, *Mornings on Horseback,* 356.

7. PS to JD, Mar. 18, 29, 1885; PS to Sally Flandrau, Apr. 3, 1885; PS to JD, July 25 and Aug. 17, 1885, all from DC.

8. CEF to PS, Feb. 1, 1886, DC.

9. JSG interview with Blake Brophy; CEF to PS, Mar. 28 and Apr. 22, 1886, Fl.C.

10. Robinson, *My Brother,* 137; TR to Anna Roosevelt Cowles, *Letters* I:101; PS memo dated May 18, 1904, GC.

11. McCullough, 356.

12. Putnam, 590; PS to JD, Nov. 4, 1886, DC; Hagedorn, *Works of Theodore Roosevelt*, 289–90.

13. PS to JD, Nov. 4, 21, Dec. 13, 19, 1886, DC; PS to SBS, Nov. 20, 1886, SC.

14. Putnam, 591–93; McCullough, 344–45; PS to SBS, Feb. 7, Jan. 15, 1887, SC.

15. PS to JD, Mar. 6, 1887, DC; McCullough, 345; Putnam, 312.

16. PS to JD, Mar. 22, Oct. 7, 1887, DC; PS to SBS, Feb. 7, 1887, SC.

17. JD to PS, Sept. 7, Oct. 8, Nov. 28, 1887, GC; PS to JD, Nov. 5, 1887, DC; PS to Sally Flandrau, Dec. 26, 1887, DC.

18. PS to SBS, July 18, 1888, SC.

19. PS to SBS, Feb. 2 and June 28, 1888, SC; CEF to JD, June 21, 1888, DC; IGK to Eugene Lyons, May 12, 1948, GC.

20. PS to SBS, May 25, 1889, SC; PS to JD, Nov. 21, 1888, DC; IGK to Eugene Lyons, May 12, 1948, GC.

21. Sally Flandrau to JD, Jan. 29, 1890; PS to JD, Mar. 6 and May 8, 1890; Apr. 6, 1891, all from DC.

22. PS to JD, May 8, Oct. 4 and 11, 1890, DC; RHMF to PS, Feb. 18, 1891, DC.

23. PS to JD, Dec. 11, 1891 and Jan. 26, 1892, DC; PS to RHMF, Feb. 18, 1892, FC; RHMF to PS, Mar. 18, 1892, FC.

24. PS to RHMF, June 17, 1894, FC; TR to RHMF, Oct. 16, 1894, FC; PS to RHMF, Mar. 17, 1895, FC.

25. PS to RHMF, Mar. 17, 1895, FC; PS to RF, Mar. 26, 1895, Fl.C; JD Diary, Mar. 25, 1895, DC.

26. JD Diary, Apr. 23, 1895, DC; TR to RHMF, Apr. 25 and May 4, 1895, FC; PS to RF, Aug. 18, 1895, Fl.C; PS to RHMF, Apr. 1, 1896, FC; SFC to CEF, May 29, 1895, Fl.C.

27. JL to SBS, June 4, 1895, SC; JD Diary, June 16, Aug. 1 and 3, 1895, DC; CEF to PS, Aug. 11, 1895, DC.

28. PS to RF, 1895, DC; TR to PS, Apr. 26, 1896, GC.

29. PS to RF, Aug. 8, 1895, Fl.C; JD to PS, Oct. 22, 1896, GC; PS to Charlie Flandrau [1897], Fl.C; Doar interview, 2001.

30. IGK to Eugene Lyons, May 12, 1948, GC; JD to PS, Mar. 24, 1897, GC.

31. TR to PS, Oct. 5, 1896 and Aug. 8, 1897, GC.

32. TR to RHMF, Apr. 25 and 29, 1898; JD to PS, Apr. 27, 1898, GC.

33. RHMF to CRR, June 20, 1898, FC; TR to PS, July 31, 1898, GC; Sgt. M. T. McHehee quoted in unidentified clipping, John C. Greenway scrapbook, GC.

34. IGK to Eugene Lyons, May 12, 1948, GC; IS to MS, Jan. 27 and Dec. 7, 1898, SC; PS to IS, Dec. 25, 1898, FC; RF to PS, Feb. 19, 1899, DC; JD to PS, Apr. 17, 1899, GC; IS to PS, Dec. 20 and 23, 1899, DC.

35. IS to PS, Jan. 22, May 17 and [June], 1900, FC.

36. PS to JD, Nov. 28, Dec. 25 and undated, 1900, DC.

37. IS to JD, Jan. 25, 1901, DC; RF to IS, May 13, 1901, FC; SFC to IS, June 23, 1901, FC; CEF to IS, Aug. 9, 1901, FC; IS to Blair Flandrau, Dec. 12, 1901, Fl.C.

38. IGK to Eugene Lyons, May 12, 1948, GC; FWMC to IS, July 7, 1902, FC.

39. PS to JD, Oct. 6, 1901; Jan. 7 and Apr. 24, 1902, DC; Edith Roosevelt to PS, Dec. 3, 1901, FC.

40. IS to PS, Jan. 7, 1902, FC; PS to IS, June 25, 1902, FC; PS to JD, June 1, 1902, DC.

41. PS to IS, July 2, 1902, FC; FWMC to IS, July 30, 1902, FC.

42. PS to JD, Apr. 23, Apr. 30, and June 4, 1903; IS to JD, Mar. 30, 1903, all DC.

43. PS to JD, Mar. 2, Apr. 11, May 8, 1903; JL to JD, May 10, 1903; CEF to JD, Feb. 11 and Apr. 18, 1903, all DC.

44. IS to SBS, June 7, 1903, SC; IGK to Eugene Lyons, May 12, 1948, GC; IS to JD, July 23, 1903, DC.

45. IS to JD, Sept. 23, 1903, DC; IS to SBS, Sept. 29, 1903, SC; PS to JD, Sept. 28, 1903, DC.

46. PS to JD, Jan. 1 and Feb. 20, 1904, DC.

47. E. Roosevelt, *This Is My Story,* 85; IGK to Eugene Lyons, May 12, 1948, GC; SFC to JD, Feb. 7, 1904, DC.

48. IGK to Eugene Lyons, May 12, 1948, GC; PS to JD, July 26, 1904, DC.

49. JD to IS, Dec. 2, 1904, DC; PS to JD, Dec. 10 and 12, 1904, DC; PS to SBS, Dec. 28, 1904, SC.

CHAPTER TWO   *"O'er the Border and Awa'"*

1. IS Diary, Jan. 2 and 3, 1905, GC.

2. IS Diary, Jan. 2 and 3, 1905, GC.

3. Unidentified clipping, Jan. 9, 1905, in letter from SFC to JD, Jan. 11, 1905, DC; JD to PS, Jan. 27, 1905, GC.

4. IS Diary, Jan. 15, 1905, GC; IGK to Eugene Lyons, May 12, 1948, GC.

5. JL to JD, Jan. 19, 1905; PS to JD, Feb. 19, 1905, all DC.

6. ER to IS, Oct. 24 and Dec. 27, 1904, FC.

7. Lash, *A World of Love,* 202–5; IS to RHMF [Apr. 1905]; RHMF to IS, Apr. 11, 1905, FC.

8. RHMF to IS, Apr. 12, 1905, FC.

9. IS to RHMF, Apr. 12, 18, and 20, 1905, FC.

10. PS to RHMF, Apr. 19, 1905; RHMF to IS, Apr. 24, 1905, all FC.

11. PS to RHMF, Apr. 21, 1905, FC; IS to RHMF, Apr. 25, 1905, FC; RHMF to IS, June 7, 1905, FC; PS to JD, June 2, 1905, DC.

12. JL to IS, May 25 and June 1, 1905; JD to IS, May 20, 1905; Anna R. Cowles to RHMF, various letters, Mar. 7, 1905, to Sept. 3, 1905, all FC.

13. PS to IS, June 23, 1905, FC; *The Scotsman,* 1922, FFD.

14. IS to RHMF, undated; IS to PS, June 25, 1905; PS to IS, July 1, 1905, all FC.

15. RHMF to IS, July 3 and 5, 1905, FC.

16. IS to RHMF, July 5, 7, 10, 1905, FC; RHMF to IS, July 11, 1905, FC; Geoffrey Ward to Brophy, Jan. 26, 1986, FFD.

17. PS to SBS, July 20, 1905, SC; SFC to JD, July 15 and 27, 1905, DC; RHMF to SFC, July 23, 1905, FC; PS to IF, July 15, 1905, FC; JSG interview with Brophy.

18. JD to PS, July 13, 1905, GC; IF to MS, July 14, 1905, SC; PS to SBS, July 20, 1905, SC; JD to PS, July 23, 1905, GC; JL to IF, Aug. 13, 1905, FC.

19. Hector Ferguson to Mary Goodrich, Aug. 18, 1905, FC; JSG interview with Brophy; IF to PS, undated, FC.

20. IF to PS, undated, enclosing clipping of *Northern Weekly,* Aug. 17, 1905, FC; Hector Ferguson to Mary Goodrich, Aug. 18, 1905, FC; RHMF to Dave Goodrich, Aug. 25, 1905, FC; IF to JD, Aug. 30, 1905, DC; Cook, *Eleanor Roosevelt, Vol. 1,* 173–74.

21. Ward, *A First-Class Temperament,* 26–34; E. Roosevelt, *This Is My Story,* 105.

22. PS to SBS and MS, Nov. 1, 1905, SC; IF memo [Feb. 1906], DC; Edith Roosevelt to IF, Jan. 10, 1906, FC.

23. JL to JD, May 14, 1906, DC; PS to JD, May 12, June 7, and Aug. 12, 1906, DC; PS to IF, Feb. 25, 1906, FC; JD to PS, June 24, 1906, GC.

24. PS to JD, Sept. 6, 1906, DC; JL to JD, Feb. 4, 1907, DC; JL to PS, undated, FC.

25. IF to JD, Mar. 3, 1907, DC; PS to JD, Nov. 30, 1906, DC; JD to PS, Dec. 9, 1906, GC; TR to RHMF, Feb. 2, 1907, FC.

26. FWMC to IF, Mar. 15, 1907, GC.

27. PS to IF, July 5, 1907, FC; JD to IF, Sept. 4, 1907, DC; JL to IF, July 30, 1907, FC.

28. JD to PS, Mar. 5 and 13, 1908, GC; PS to IF, Aug. 16, 1908, FC; IF to JD, July 27, Aug. 7 and Sept. 1, 1908, DC.

29. RHMF to IF, Sept. 5 and 24, 1908; IF to RHMF, Sept. 30, 1908, all FC.

CHAPTER THREE   *"A Heart for Any Fate"*

1. JD to IF, Sept. 29, 1908, FC; FWMC to Ronald Ferguson, Nov. 21, 1908, FC; TR to RHMF, Nov. 27, 1908, FC; SFC to JD, Nov. 24, 1908, DC.

2. FWMC to Ronald Ferguson, Nov. 21, 1908, FC; Ronald Ferguson to FWMC, Dec. 3, 1908, FC; FWMC to IF, Dec. 11, 1908, GC; RHMF to FWMC, Feb. 27, 1916, FC; PS to JD, Nov. 11, 1908, DC.

3. SFC to JD, Nov. 30, 1908, DC; IF to OC, Dec. 5, 1909, GC; IF to FWMC, Jan. 16, 1909, GC; PS to IF, Dec. 25, 1908, FC; JL to IF, Jan. 2, 1909, FC; ER to IF, June 6, 1909, FC.

4. IF to OC, Apr. 7, 1909; IF to OC, undated [autumn 1921]; JCG to RHMF, Apr. 13, 1909, all GC.

5. PS to IF, Mar. 1, 1909, FC; FWMC to IF, July 4, 1909, GC; RHMF to IF, July 19, 1909, FC; PS to IF, Nov. 8 and 11, 1909, FC.

6. IF to SBS, Jan. 4, 1910, SC; FWMC to Ronald Ferguson, Jan. 7, 1910, FC.

7. ER to IF, Oct. 26 and Nov. 12, 1909, FC.

8. IF to RHMF, Mar. 15 and 18, 1910, FC.

9. PS to CRR, Apr. 7, 1910, GC; JD to PS, Mar. 22, 1910, GC; IF to RHMF, Apr. 1 and 2, 1910, FC.

10. IF to RHMF, Apr. 7, 1910, FC; IF to PS, July 1, 1910, FC; JCG to Dave Goodrich, Aug. 8, 1910, GC.

11. Higby, "The Burro Mountain Homestead," 1; FWMC to Ronald Ferguson, Oct. 22, 1910, FC; Breasted interview with Brophy.

CHAPTER FOUR *Cat Canyon*

1. Higby, 1; *Silver City Daily Press,* Aug. 4, 1987.

2. IF to ER, Nov. 21, 1910, FDRL; JL to JD, Dec. 30, 1910, DC.

3. JL to JD, Dec. 30, 1910, DC; IF to SBS, Jan. 6 and Feb. 14, 1911, SC; IF to RHMF, June 30, 1911, FC.

4. IF to SBS, May 16, 1912, SC; IF to OC, Nov. 16, 1911, GC.

5. JCG to RHMF, Feb. 7, 1911, FC; IF to OC, Apr. 30, 1911, GC; R. Miller, chapter 4, p. 9; PS to CRR, Mar. 13, 1911, GC; TR to RHMF, Oct. 20, 1911, FC.

6. ER to IF, Nov. 26 and [Dec. 29], 1910, FC; IF to ER, Aug. 11, 1911, FDRL.

7. IF to RHMF, June 22 and 24, 1911, FC.

8. IF to RHMF, June 27, 1911; JCG to RHMF, June 26, 1911; RHMF to IF, June 24 and 27, 1911, all FC.

9. RHMF to IF, June 28, 1911, FC; IF to RHMF, June 29 and 30, and July 2, 1911, FC; JCG to IF, Mar. 19, 1923, GC.

10. FWMC to IF, July 16, 1911, GC; JCG to TR, Oct. 11, 1911, GC; JCG to RHMF, Dec. 2, 1911, FC; IF to SBS, Oct. 16, 1911, SC; IF to ER, Aug. 11, 1911, FDRL.

11. IF to ER, Aug. 11, 1911, FDRL; IF to OC, Nov. 16 and Dec. 6, 1911, GC.

12. PS to CRR, Mar. 7, 1912, GC.

13. IF to OC, Apr. 5 and [June], 1912, GC; IF to SBS, May 16, 1912, SC; Doar interview, 2002.

14. IF to OC, Apr. 25, 1912, GC.

15. TR to RHMF, Mar. 26, 1912, FC.

16. ER to IF, Jan. 29, 1912, FC; IF to OC, May 13, 1912, GC.

17. IF to OC, May 13, 1912, GC; ER to IF, May 11, 1912; FC; E. Roosevelt, *This Is My Story,* 140–41; IF to SBS, May 16, 1912, SC.

18. IF to ER, July 17, Aug. 24 and undated, 1912, FDRL; IF to OC, July 14, 1912, GC.

19. IF to ER [Sept. 1912], FDRL; IF to SBS, July 25, 1912, SC; JCG to Dave Goodrich, Aug. 31 and Nov. 2, 1912, GC.

20. FWMC to IF, Nov. 3, 1912, GC.

21. ER to IF, Jan. 28 [1913] and Apr. 11, 1913, FC.

22. IF to OC, Aug. 26, 1912; IF Notebook, Aug. 20, 1912; JCG to Dave Goodrich, Aug. 31, 1912, all GC.

23. TR to RHMF, Oct. 29, 1912, FC.

24. IF to ER, Aug. 24, 1912, FDRL; FWMC to IF, Nov. 3, 1912, GC; IF to RHMF, Dec. 4, 1912, FC.

25. IF to RHMF, Dec. 10, 1912; RHMF to Edith Ferguson, Dec. 18, 1912; RHMF to IF, Dec. 18, 1912; IF to RHMF, Dec. 19 and 22, 1912; RHMF to IF, Dec. 19, 1912, all FC.

26. JCG to IF, Dec. 21, 1912, FC; Belle Eckles to IF, Dec. 26, 1912, FC; IF to JCG, Jan. 8, 1913, GC; IF to ER, Feb. 7, 1913, FDRL.

27. IF to SBS, undated [1913], SC; IF to ER, Feb. 7, 1913, FDRL; RHMF to OC, Mar. 17, 1913, GC.

28. IF to OC, Feb. 10, 1913, GC; RHMF to IF, Mar. 10, 1913, FC; M. Breasted interview with Brophy; JSG interview with Brophy.

29. IF to ER, July 14, 1913, FDRL; IF to OC, Apr. 24 and June 29, 1913, GC.

30. IF to OC, June 29, 1913, GC; RHMF to IF, May 20 and 28, 1913, FC.

31. RHMF to IF, June 11 and undated [May and June], 1913, FC; Breasted interview with Brophy; Brophy, *Isabella,* 274.

32. IF to OC, July 14, 1913, GC; TR to RHMF, Sept. 29, 1913, FC.

33. Breasted interview with Brophy.

34. IF to ER, July 14 and 24, and Oct. 1, 1913, FDRL.

35. IF to OC, Dec. 10, 1913, GC; PS to IF, Dec. 3, 1913, FC; IF to PS, Dec. 2 and 5, 1913, FC; IF to OC, Dec. 10, 1913, GC.

36. RHMF to OC, Dec. 27, 1913, GC; IF to OC, Dec. 29, 1913, GC; RHMF to FWMC, May 23, 1914, FC.

37. IF to OC, June 5, 1914, GC; IF to RHMF, July 24, 1914, FC.

38. IF to RHMF, undated; RHMF to FWMC, Aug. 3, 1914; RHMF to IF; IF to RHMF, Aug. 4, 1914, all FC.

39. IF to ER, Aug. 4, 1914, FDRL.

40. RHMF to IF, Aug. 14 and Sept. 3, 16, and 30, 1914; FWMC to RHMF, Aug. 26, 1914; IF to RHMF, Sept. 18 and undated, 1914, all FC.

41. IF to RHMF, Sept. 27, 1914, FC; JL to IF, Dec. 25, 1914, FC; IF to MS, Dec. 10, 1914, SC; Brophy, *Isabella,* 295.

42. IF to OC, Oct. 31, 1914, GC; Fransen, "Burro Mountain Homestead," 4–5; Higby, 2–6; E. Roosevelt, *This Is My Story,* 224; Breasted interview with Brophy.

43. Breasted interview with Brophy; Higby, 5–6; IF to ER [Feb. 1915], FDRL.

44. IF to ER, Aug. 19, 1914, and [Jan. 1915], FDRL; IF to OC, Oct. 31, Nov. 22, Dec. 14, 1914, GC; IF to FWMC, Nov. 10, 1914, GC.

45. IF to FWMC, Jan. 20, 1916, GC; IF to OC, Mar. 1915, GC; IF to ER [early Feb. 1915], FDRL.

46. E. Roosevelt, *This Is My Story,* 169–70; IF to ER, Apr. 7, 1915, FDRL; ER to IF, Apr. 30, 1915, FC.

47. IF to SBS, Dec. 25, 1915, and [Sept. 1916], SC; IF to ER, July 14, 1913, FDRL; Breasted interview with Brophy.

48. Miss Thorpe to IF [1915], FC; IF to ER, July 15, 1915, FDRL; IF to SBS [June 1915], SC.

49. IF to ER, July 15, 1915, FDRL; TR to RHMF, Aug. 6, 1915, FC; IF to SBS [late June 1915], SC.

50. IF to ER, July 15, 1915, FDRL; IF to OC, June 23, GC; PS to IF, undated, FC; PS to CRR, undated [1915], GC.

51. IF to ER, Nov. 9 and [late Dec.] 1915, FDRL.

52. IF to FWMC, Jan. 20, 1916, GC.

53. IF to ER, Jan. 22, 1916, FDRL.

54. IF to FWMC, Feb. 17 and undated, 1916; PS to FWMC, Feb. 10 and 14, 1916, all FC.

55. Walter James to E. S. Bullock, Feb. 25, 1916, FC; PS to FWMC, Feb. 13 [1916], FC.

56. R. Miller, chapter 4, 12; Brophy, *Isabella,* 313; IF to SBS, Nov. 16, 1916, SC; IF to RHMF, undated, FC.

57. IF to ER, undated, FDRL.

CHAPTER FIVE *"Potato Patriotism"*

1. Breasted interview with Brophy; J. Hill, *Burro Mountain Homestead;* IF to PS, July 24, 1916, FC; FWMC to IF, Dec. 5, 1916, GC; *Silver City Enterprise,* Oct. 21, 1916; IF to ER, Sept. 15, 1916, FDRL.

2. IF to OC [Dec. 1916], GC; PS to CRR, Sept. 15 [1916], GC; PS to FWMC, Jan. 11, 1917, FC; RHMF to IF, Feb. 2, 1917; RHMF to FWMC, Jan. 20, 1917, FC; IF to ER [summer 1916], FDRL.

3. IF to FWMC, Jan. 12, 1917, GC; PS to FWMC, Dec. 17, 1916, and Jan. 11, 1917, FC; RHMF to FWMC, Jan. 20, 1917, FC; RHMF to IF, Jan. 20, 29, and undated, and Feb. 2, 1917, all FC.

4. JD to PS, Feb. 10 and 25, 1917, GC; RHMF to FWMC, Mar. 1, 1917, FC; IF to RHMF, Feb. 28, 1917, FC.

5. IF to RHMF, Feb. 17, and Mar. 1 and 4, 1917, FC.

6. IF to MS, May 11, 1917, SC; FWMC to RHMF, Mar. 19, 1917, FC; FWMC to IF, Apr. 16 and Mar. 6, 1917, GC.

7. IF to MS, May 11, 1917, SC; RHMF to ER, July 9, 1917, FDRL; IF to OC, Aug. 22, 1917, GC.

8. IF to FWMC, July 20, 1917, GC; IF to OCJ, Aug. 22, 1917, GC; Ivy Lay to IF, Dec. 12, 1918, FC; RHMF to ER, July 9, 1917, FDRL; IF to SBS [Aug. 1917], SC.

9. Byrkit, *Forging the Copper Collar,* 1, 9, 165, 188–90, 204, 288; Boese, *John C. Greenway,* 1975, 200–205.

10. FWMC to IF, Sept. 11 and Dec. 15, 1917, GC; JCG to IF, Mar. 22 and 23, 1918, and Jan. 2, 1919, FC; JCG, "A Soldier's Diary, 1917," GC; IF to JCG [Sept. and Oct. 1923], GC.

11. IF to RHMF, Oct. 18, 27, and Nov. 7, 1917, FC; JCG to IF, Nov. 17, 1917, FC; JSG interview.

12. JCG to IF, Nov. 10 and Dec. 9, 1917, FC; IF to JCG, Dec. 16 and 31, 1917, GC; Breasted interview with Brophy.

13. IF to OCJ, Dec. 15, 1917, GC; IF to FWMC, Dec. 14, 1917, GC; IF to MS, Feb. 17, 1918, SC; IF to ER, Mar. 12, 1918, FDRL; ER to RHMF, Jan. 23, 1917, FC; ER to IF [Apr. 2, 1918], FC; Caroline Phillips to IF, Apr. 27, 1918, FC.

14. JCG to IF, Jan. 11 and 26, Feb. 10, Mar. 3 and 29, Apr. 10–23, 1918, all FC.

15. JCG to IF, Apr. 19, May 12, June 12 and 22, 1918, all FC.

16. Breasted interview with Brophy; RHMF to FWMC, June 1, 1918, FC.

17. *Silver City Enterprise,* June 28, 1918; W. E. Lindsey to IF, June 3, 1918; Maude Pritchard to IF, July 1, 1918, FC; Henriette L. Heyman, "The Women's Land Army in New Mexico," undated [1918]; IF to Mr. Gonzales, undated draft; J. Mueller to IF, July 6, 1918; Lois Fuller to IF, July 21, 1918, all FC.

18. Heyman, "Women's Land Army"; IF to Mrs. J. R. Kinyon, July 8, 1918, FC; PS to CRR, July 22, 1918, GC; IF to MS, Nov. 6, 1918, SC.

19. IF to MS, Nov. 6, 1918, SC; Dorothy Kayser to IF, Nov. 9, 1918, FC; Mrs. Charles Elders to IF, Nov. 11, 1918, FC; Breasted interview with Brophy.

20. RHMF to ER, Oct. 14, 1918, FDRL; IF to RHMF, Oct. 10, 1918, FC; JD to PS, Oct. 4, 1918, GC; IF to MS, Nov. 6, 1918, SC; A. Heyman to IF, July 30, 1918, FC; Kathryn Steward to IF, Dec. 3, 1918, FC; RHMF to FWMC, Dec. 19, 1918, FC.

21. JCG to IF, Aug. 28, 29, July 11, 31, Aug. 4, 8, 1918, all FC.

22. TR to RHMF, Aug. 9, 1918, FC.

23. JCG to IF, Oct. 20, Aug. 28, 1918, FC; IF to JCG [1923], GC; *New York Sun,* Apr. 1, 1919.

24. JCG to IF, Aug. 17, Nov. 22, and undated, 1918, FC; JCG to PS, Oct. 15, 1918, FC; IF to JCG, Dec. 29, 1918, GC.

25. IF to JCG, Dec. 29, 1918, GC; JCG to IF, Jan. 12, 1919, FC.

26. JCG to IF, Jan. 12, 1919, FC.

27. IF to PS, Mar. 25, 1919, FC; PS to MS, July 11, 1919, SC.

28. IF to MS, Feb. 17, 1919, SC; IF to RHMF [early Apr.] and Easter Sunday, 1919, FC; IF to OCJ, June 22, 1919, GC; JCG to Dave Goodrich, May 23, 1919, GC.

29. RHMF to IF, May 5 and 9, 1919, FC; IF to FWMC, June 4, 1919, GC.

30. IF to RHMF, Easter Sunday and May 24, 1919, FC; IF to ER, Oct. 15, 1919, FDRL.

31. IF to ER, Oct. 15, 1919, FDRL; ER to IF, July 11 and Sept. 16, 1919, FC.

32. IF to ER, Oct. 1 and 15, 1919, and Jan. 6, 1920, FDRL; IF to MS, Dec. 19, 1919, SC; ER to IF, Oct. 26 [1919], FC.

33. IF to ER [Jan. 1920], FDRL; IF to RHMF, Feb. 1, 1920, FC; RHMF to FWMC, Mar. 31, 1920, FC; IF to MS, Apr. 13, 1920, SC; IF to RHMF, Jan. 27, 1920, FC; IF to FWMC, Mar. 16, 1920, GC; FWMC to IF, Mar. 23, 1920, GC.

34. FWMC to IF [early Apr. 1920], GC; IF to RHMF, Apr. 11 and May 1, 1920, FC; IF to MS, June 19, 1920, SC.

35. IF to MS, June 19, 1920, SC; Robert Tally to JCG, May 12, 1920, GC; JCG to Andrew Baumert, Aug. 23, 1920, GC; Harold L. Ickes to JCG, Aug. 24, 1920, GC.

36. IF to ER, Jan. 6 and July 29, 1920; Dec. 29, 1921, FDRL; RHMF to FWMC, July 29, 1920, FC.

37. IF to ER, July 29, 1920, FDRL; IF to RHMF, Sept. 25, 1920, FC; RHMF to FWMC, Sept. 24 and Nov. 22, 1920, FC; IF to RHMF, Oct. 1 and Nov. 27, 1920, FC.

38. IF to RHMF [Jan. 1921], FC; IF to FWMC, Jan. 17, 1921, GC; IF to RHMF, Apr. 26, FC; RHMF to "Cousin Evelyn," Dec. 24, 1921, FC; IF to ER, Dec. 29, 1921, FDRL.

39. IF to PS, July 21 and 29, Aug. 8 and 10, 1921, FC.

40. IF to PS, Sept. 14, 1921, FC; IF to ER, Dec. 29, 1921, FDRL.

41. RHMF to ER, Nov. 5, 1921, FDRL; RHMF to FWMC, Jan. 3 and July 17, 1922, FC.

CHAPTER SIX   *"The Most Splendid Rainbow after the Storm"*

1. IF to FWMC, Apr. 24, GC; FWMC to IF, Apr. 24 and 27, 1922, and July 2, 1925, GC; IF to JCG, Apr. 29, 1922, GC; IF to ER, May 5, 1922, FDRL; IF to RHMF, Aug. 10, 1922, FC; PS to CRR, Dec. 2, 1922, GC.

2. Doar interview, 2001; IF to MS [winter 1923] SC; IF to FWMC, Oct. 24 and Nov. 14, 1922, GC; IF to ER, Dec. 2, 1922, FDRL.

3. Ronald Ferguson to FWMC, Dec. 24, 1922, FC; IF to OCJ, Dec. 1, 1922, GC.

4. IF to ER, Dec. 2, 1922, FDRL.

5. JCG to IF, Mar. 19, July 16, 1923, and Feb. 15, 1924, all GC.

6. IF to JCG, Feb. 17, Mar. 27, and undated 1923; JCG to IF, Feb. 22, Mar. 25, and June 7, 1923; FWMC to IF, Mar. 20, 1923, all GC.

7. IF to JCG [Apr. 7], Mar. 7 [10] and 20, June 28 and undated, 1923; IF Journal, Apr. 11–18, 1923, all GC.

8. PS to CRR, Mar. 9 and May 27, 1923; IF to JCG, Apr. 3 and 30, May 3; JCG to IF, May 7, 1923, all GC.

9. JCG to IF, May 4, Apr. 25 and 29, May 16, 1923, GC; JCG to Winifred Coombs, May 24, 1922, GC; *Arizona Labor Journal* clipping, GC; Boese, 212.

10. IF to JCG, May 5, June 1 and [14], 1923, GC; JCG to IF, May 13 and 18, June 2, 1923, GC; Breasted interview with Brophy.

11. JCG to IF, June 5 and 6, 1923; IF to JCG, undated and May 16, 1923, all GC.

12. Breasted interview with Brophy; PS to JD, July 7, 1923, DC; IF to JCG, Aug. 4, July 7, 1923, GC; JCG to IF, Aug. 21, and undated, 1923, GC.

13. IF to JCG, July 7, 1923, GC; IF to Blair Flandrau, Aug. 17, Fl.C; IF to FWMC, July 17, 1923, GC; JCG to FWMC, July 17, 1923, GC; FWMC to Miss Milliken, Nov. 7, 1923, GC.

14. IF to Grace Flandrau, undated, Fl.C; IF to CRR, July 24, 1923, GC; IF to JCG, July 28, 1923, GC.

15. IF to JCG, July 27, 28, 30, 31, and Aug. 4, 16, 1923; JCG to IF, Apr. 19, July 23 and undated, 1923, all GC.

16. IF to JCG, July 28, Aug. 3 and 5, 1923, all GC.

17. IF to JCG, Aug. 5, 25, Sept. 29, 1923; JCG to IF, Aug. 21, 23, and 31, 1923, all GC.

18. JCG to IF [mid-Sept.], Oct. 3, Sept. 28 [Oct. 18], 1923, GC; IF to JCG [Sept. 20] Oct. 7, 1923, GC; Boese, 212.

19. JCG to IF, undated, 1923; "Maria" to IF, Oct. 13, 1923; "Pauline" to IF, undated, 1923; Walter James to IF, Oct. 24, 1923, all GC.

20. Breasted interview with Brophy; IF to JCG, Oct. 19 and 22, 1923, GC; FWMC to Miss Milliken, Nov. 7, 1923, GC; Mariquita Martin to IG, GC; Mary Eckles to IG, undated, GC; OCJ to JCG, Sept. 7, 1923, GC; Ronald Ferguson to FWMC, Nov. 23, 1923, GC.

21. IG to self, undated and Aug. 30, 1926, GC; Agnew Holt to IG, Nov. 1, 1935, GC; IG to FWMC, Nov. 20, 1923, GC; Boese, 191–96.

22. JCG to Jim Greenway, Jan. 10, 1924, GC; IG to ER, May 9, 1924, FDRL; JCG to IG, Jan. 22, 1924, GC; IG to FWMC, Feb. 11, 1924, GC.

23. IG to FWMC, Apr. 4, 1924; IG to self, undated [1926], all GC.

24. IG to ER, Dec. 2, 1922, and June 11, 1924, FDRL; Boese, 209; *Arizona Cattleman and Farmer,* July 21, 1924, in GC.

25. IG to ER, May 9, 1924, FDRL; IG to FWMC, Jan. 10 and 11, 1924, GC; *Arizona Cattleman and Farmer,* July 21, 1924, in GC; JCG to Will Greenway, Aug. 12, 1924, GC; JCG to IG, Oct. 21, 1924, GC.

26. JCG to IG, Sept. 1, 1924, GC; IG to FWMC, Aug. 29 and Sept. 17, 25, and Oct. 11, 1924, GC; JSG interview with Brophy; JCG to FWMC, Oct. 11, 1924, GC; IG to JCG, Oct. 18 and 20, 1924, GC; JD to IG, Oct. 22, 1924, GC.

27. IG to JCG, Nov. 1 and Oct. 20, 1924; IG to OCJ, Jan. 11, 1925, all GC.

28. JCG to IG, Nov. 2, 4, and Oct. 28, 1924; IG to JCG, Nov. 1, all GC.

29. IG to FWMC, Jan. 14, 1925, GC; JD to MS, Mar. 15, 1925, SC; FWMC to Martha Ferguson, Apr. 3, 1925, GC; JCG to IG, undated, 1925, GC; IG to JCG, June 8 and May 23, 1925, GC.

30. JCG to Jim Greenway, May 22, 1925; IG to JCG, [May 1925], all GC.

31. *Bisbee Daily Review,* June 5, 1925; unidentified clipping, June 5, 1925, GC; JCG to Wirt Bowman, Aug. 6, 1925, GC; Boese, 212.

32. IG to JCG, Oct. 1, 1925, GC; JSG interview with Brophy.

33. Martha Ferguson to Robert Ferguson, Oct. 9, 1925, GC; IG to JCG, June 13, 1925, GC; JD to MS, Oct. 13, 1925, SC.

34. William Keller to IG, Nov. 11, 1925; IG affidavit [1926]; IG to William Keller, draft [late Nov. 1925], all GC.

35. Martha Ferguson to Robert Ferguson, Oct. 9, 1925, GC; IG to Robert Ferguson, Nov. 22, 1925, GC; Dr. W. Laurence Whittemore memo, Dec. 3, 1925, GC; James Greenway to JCG, Dec. 5, 1925, GC; JCG to Peck, Dec. 26, 1925, GC; Breasted interview with Brophy.

36. IG Journal, Jan. 7, 1926, GC.
37. IG Journal, Jan. 7, 1926, GC.
38. IG Journal, Jan. 8, 1926, GC.
39. IG to self, Aug. 30, 1926, GC.
40. Brophy, *Isabella,* 474–76.
41. Hannah Baird interview.

CHAPTER SEVEN   *"The Life of You in My Veins"*

1. Boese, 214.
2. Various letters, GC; JD to IG, Feb. 1, 1926; IG to B. Case, Jan. 31, 1926; IG to M. M. Carpenter, Feb. 15, 1925, all GC.
3. IG to self, July 15, 1926, GC.
4. IG to self, undated; IG to Hermann Hagedorn, June 1, 1926, GC.
5. Unidentified clipping, GC.
6. IG to JCG, Nov. 4, 1924, GC; Mildred Milton to IG, Jan. 22, 1926, GC; Mary Harkness to IG, Feb. 25, 1926, GC; W. B. Kelley, editorial in the *Stafford Guardian.*
7. IG to Robert Ferguson, Feb. 14 and Mar. 4, 1926; IG to C. T. Knapp, Feb. 19, 1926, all GC.
8. IG to FWMC, Mar. 22 and Feb. 22, 1926; IG to U.S. Forest Service, Apr. 22, 1926; MS to IG, Feb. 21, 1926; IG to self, July 15, 1926, all GC.
9. IG to FWMC, Apr. 1 and Mar. 22, 1926; IG to self, Aug. 30, 1926; IG to Robert Ferguson, Apr. 21, 1928, all GC.
10. Breasted interview, Dinsmore Farm.
11. Doar interview, 2001; IG unsigned letter fragment, GC; IG to self, July 15 and 16, 1926, GC.
12. IG to Mr. Case, May 21, 1926; IG to Thomas Robins, Dec. 6, 1926; IG to self, Aug. 30 and undated, 1926, all GC.
13. IG to self, Sept. 1, 2, and undated, 1926, GC.
14. IG to Dr. L. D. Ricketts, Nov. 17, 1926; IG to self, undated and Dec. 26, 1926, all GC.
15. Boese, 213.
16. C. Emmett Newton to IG, Feb. 25, 1927, GC; *Benson News,* Feb. 26, 1927; *ADS,* Mar. 8, 1927; IG to J. W. Strode, Jan. 29, 1927, all GC.
17. *ADS,* May 1, 1930.
18. *ADS,* May 1, 1930; *TC,* unidentified clipping, GC; *TC,* Feb. 23, 1927; Brophy, "Arizona Inn," 11–12.
19. Cook, *Eleanor Roosevelt,* 1:324.

20. IG to self, Mar. 17 and undated, 1927, and Aug. 30, 1926; IG to Robert Ferguson [Feb. 1927], all GC.

21. FWMC to IG, Sept. 18, 1927, GC.

22. FWMC to IG, Oct. 5, 1927, GC.

23. IG to self, undated, GC.

24. IG to RHMF, undated, GC; *ADS,* Apr. 11, 1928; unidentified clipping, Feb. 26, 1928, AHS; *ADS,* May 1, 1930; Probst, *Isabella Greenway,* 24.

25. Probst, 27–28; E. Roosevelt and Hickok, *Ladies of Courage,* 38.

26. IG to Robert Ferguson, Apr. 21 and May 27, 1928, GC.

27. IG to "Molly and Austin," June 24, 1928, GC.

28. Gertrude Bryan Leeper to IG, July 7, 1928; IG to Thomas Maloney, July 17, 1928; IG to F. A. Nathan, July 17 and 28, 1928; IG to C. T. Knapp, July 23, 1928; Oliver Patton to IG, July 24, 1928, all GC.

29. F. A. Nathan to IG, July 30, 1928; Oliver Patton to IG, July 24, 1928; IG to Thomas Maloney, July 30, 1928; IG to F. A. Nathan, Aug. 8, 1928, all GC.

30. FWMC to IG, Aug. 6, 1928, GC.

31. IG to self, Aug. 26, 1928, GC.

32. IG to Mrs. W. V. Whitmore, Aug. 16 and 17, 1928; IG to Mrs. Shepherd, Aug. 18, 1928, all GC.

33. John J. Raskob to IG, July 23, 1928; IG to John J. Raskob, Aug. 16, 1928, all GC.

34. IG to Mr. Dillingham, Oct. 2, 1928; IG to Mrs. Shepherd, Aug. 27, 1928, all GC.

35. Arthur Curlee to Fred Johnson, Sept. 9, 1928, GC; Smith headquarters to IG, Sept. 11, 1928, FDRL; IG to FDR, Sept. 6, 1928, GC.

36. IG to Robert Ferguson, Oct. 24, 1928, GC; *Nogales Daily Herald,* Oct. 26, 1928; *ADS,* Oct. 13, 1928.

37. IG to June Hamilton Rhodes, Nov. 2, 1928, FDRL.

38. IG to ER, Oct. 10 and 24, and Nov. 7, 1928, FDRL; ER to IG, Oct. 24, 1928, GC. See also K. Miller, "A Volume of Friendship," 121–56.

39. Unidentified letter, Oct. 30, 1928, GC; George Hunt to IG, Nov. 7, 1928, GC; Mrs. Sarah Crutchfield to IG, Nov. 14, 1928, GC; IG to FDR, undated, 1928, FDRL; IG to Mrs. A. H. Hammer, Mar. 1, 1929, 39/f477, GC.

40. Bridgie Porter to IG, Nov. 6, 1928; Russ Tatum to IG, Nov. 10, 1928; IG to William L. Rigney, Nov. 24, 1928; D. C. Babbit to IG, Nov. 22, 1928, all GC.

41. Christmas card in GC; Carter, *Gutzon Borglum,* 47; IG to self, June

19, 1928, GC; IG to FWMC, Mar. 1, 1929, GC; unidentified clipping, GC; *ADS,* Mar. 24, 1929.

42. FWMC to IG, Aug. 19 and Jan. 27, 1929; IG to FWMC, Mar. 1, 1929, all GC.

43. IG to FWMC, Mar. 1, 1929, GC.

44. IG to FWMC, Mar. 1, 1929; Robert Ferguson to Martha Ferguson, undated, all GC.

45. Nellie Tayloe Ross to IG, Jan. 12, 1929; IG to Mrs. J. C. Lindemann, Feb. 4, 1929; W. P. Stuart to IG; Eula Mae West to IG, Aug. 10, 1929, all GC.

46. W. L. Barnum to FDR, Sept. 24, 1929, FDRL; Probst, 36; FDR to IG, Oct. 21, 1929, and Jan. 22, 1930, FDRL.

CHAPTER EIGHT   *"More Women and More Money"*

1. IG to Mrs. T. S. Kimball, Mar. 20, 1930; IG to Mr. Moore, Mar. 24, 1930; R. C. Stanford to Dodd L. Greer, Mar. 10, 1930; IG to Dodd L. Greer, Mar. 10, 1930; IG to Mary E. Carrow, Oct. 20, 1930, all GC; unidentified clipping, Mar. 30, 1930, AHS.

2. W. L. Neel to IG, Mar. 13, 1930, GC; ER to Clarence Gunter, Mar. 10, 1930, FDRL; IG to George Babbitt, Mar. 11, 1930, GC; IG to Mrs. Murchison, Mar. 26, 1930, GC; Probst, 36–37.

3. IG to Dr. Clarence Gunter, Mar. 26, 1930; IG to R. C. Stanford, Apr. 7, 1930, all GC.

4. IG to Mary [Harriman Rumsey], Apr. 21, 1930, GC.

5. Charles Hardy to IG, Mar. 13, 1930; FWMC to IG, Mar. 22 and 27, 1930, all GC.

6. IG to "Stuart," Apr. 11, 1930; IG to Mr. and Mrs. Webb, May 11, 1930, all GC.

7. Unidentified Associated Press clipping, May 25, 1930, GC; IG to Louise Dillingham, May 27, 1930, GC; *ADS,* July 13 and 16, 1930.

8. IG to R. C. Stanford, Aug. 10 and Sept. 8, 1930, GC; Kennedy, *Freedom from Fear,* 34–35; IG to Mrs. Munds, Sept. 20, 1930, GC; Opal Le Baron Whitmore to IG, Oct. 14, 1930, GC.

9. Kennedy, 34–35; FWMC to IG, Aug. 19, 1929, GC; Brophy, "Arizona Inn," 28, footnote 19; Holmstrom, "Isabella Greenway and Gilpin Airlines," footnote 3, quoting *ADS,* Apr. 25, 1965.

10. Application, National Register of Historic Places, GC; Doar interview, 2001; Brophy, "Arizona Inn," 16.

11. Brophy, "Arizona Inn," 16–17, 28, footnote 21; Probst, 36–37.

12. *TC,* Mar. 26, 1931; Fred Gibson to IG, Jan. 26, 1931; IG to C. R. Whitaker, Jan. 27, 1931; draft article by Marguerite C. Rand to IG, May 21, 1935, FFD.

13. Unidentified clipping, Mar. 31, 1931; Abby Aldrich Rockefeller to IG, Mar. 23 [1931], all GC.

14. FDR to IG, Mar. 4, 1931, FDRL; *TC,* Feb. 12 and Mar. 26, 1931.

15. *TC,* May 9, 1931; OCJ to IG, June 1, 1931; IG to Mr. Coxon, Jan. 30, 1931, all GC.

16. IG to John B. Rawlings, Oct. 21, 1931; IG to Mrs. Foster, Nov. 8, 1931; William B. Mershon to IG, Apr. 29, 1931; J. W. Strode to IG, Nov. 5, 1931; *TC,* Nov. 25, 1931, all GC.

17. Billie Warner to IG, Dec. 7, 1931, GC.

18. IG to Louis Howe, Nov. 27, 1931; IG to John T. Gibbs, Dec. 15, 1931, all GC.

19. Mary W. Dewson to IG, Dec. 17 and [29], 1931, GC.

20. Martin, *Ballots & Bandwagons,* 279–80; Oulahan, *1932 Democratic National Convention,* 45; ER to IG, Jan. 23, 1932, GC.

21. Martin, 281–82; IG to ER, Feb. 4, 1932, GC.

22. Martin, 304–9; Russ Tatum to IG, Apr. 5, 1932, GC; ER to IG, Apr. 12, 1932, GC.

23. IG to Mary W. Dewson, Apr. 22, 1932, GC; Mullen, *Western Democrat,* 263.

24. IG to James A. Farley, May 7 and Aug. 9, 1932; IG to Mr. Rice, Apr. 21, 1932; IG to Mary W. Dewson, Apr. 22, 1932, all GC; Martin, 292.

25. Martin, 300; IG to Thomas J. Walsh, May 13, 1932, GC.

26. Farley, *Jim Farley's Story,* 265; *Chicago Tribune,* June 30, 1932; FWMC to IG, June 21, 1932, GC.

27. Martin, 311; Roper, *50 Years of Public Life,* 256; Kennedy, 91.

28. Hill, E., 124–25; *NYT,* June 28, 1932.

29. Martin, 305, 325; Mullen, 258–59.

30. *NYT,* June 30, July 1, 1932; *ADS,* July 1, 1932; *Chicago Tribune,* June 30, 1932; Mencken, *Making a President,* 2.

31. Quoted in Martin, 332–33.

32. Martin, 333; IG speech ms in GC.

33. *ADS,* July 1, 1932.

34. Martin, 333–34.

35. Martin, 334–36, 338–40, 346–47; Farley, 21.

36. Martin, 346–47.

37. Farley, 13; Martin, 348–50; Storke, *I Write for Freedom,* 106–7.

38. Martin, 349–54; Oulahan, 119–20; Storke, 108–11.

39. Storke, 115; Martin, 354–56.

40. Martin, 371; Oulahan, 117; Farley, 11; Storke, 123.

41. Martin, 356–57.

42. Martin, 359–62; Oulahan, 125.

43. Martin, 364–65; *ADS,* July 3, 1932.

44. Oulahan, 135–37; "HFB" to IG, Aug. 30, 1932, GC; IG to Lavinnia Engle, Aug. 30, 1932, GC.

45. Kennedy, 88–89; IG to Horace T. Lyons, Aug. 30, 1932, GC.

46. IG to James A. Farley, Aug. 24, Sept. 5 and 9, 1932, GC.

47. *ADS,* Sept. 27, 1932; unidentified clipping, all GC.

48. *ADS,* Sept. 27, 1932; ER to IG, Oct. 17 [1932], GC; Hickok, *Eleanor Roosevelt,* 37–38.

49. *ADS,* Nov. 6, 1932; Probst, 58–59.

CHAPTER NINE   *Lady of the House*

1. Unidentified clippings, Nov. 6 and 17, 1932; IG to J. F. Dietrich, Nov. 25, 1932; IG to Mrs. W. H. Woodin, Nov. 24, 1932, all GC.

2. JSG to IG, undated; IG to May Whitworth, Dec. 30, 1932, all GC.

3. IG to Anna Mae Griggs, Nov. 28, 1932; IG to J. S. Culliman, Mar. 4, 1932; Bill Mathews to IG, July 17 [1933], all GC.

4. A. W. McMillen to Henry Morgenthau, Feb. 2, 1933, 59/707; IG form letter, Feb. 2, 1933, all GC.

5. *ADS,* Feb. 10, 24, 1933, GC; IG to Sidney Osborn, Feb. 6, 1933, GC; FDR to IG; Feb. 24, 1933, FDRL; typescript of IG speech, 11/157, GC.

6. John Towles to IG, Feb. 25, 1933; C. M. Graves to IG, Feb. 25, 1933; IG to John Towles, Feb. 27, 1933, 311.

7. IG to Mr. Cauning, Feb. 28, 1933, GC.

8. W. R. Wayland to E. C. Grasty, Mar. 31, 1933, GC; press releases quoting *ADS,* 45/536, GC; Probst, 70, 75–76.

9. Unidentified clipping, 61/736, GC; *ADS,* Mar. 17, 1933, and undated clipping, 61/736, GC; E. W. Montgomery to IG, Mar. 28, 1933, GC; IG to S. Speare, Mar. 20, 1933, GC.

10. IG form letter, Mar. 22, 1933; Memo, Mar. 27, 1933; undated form letter, 61/737; IG to J. C. Rickman, Mar. 28, 1933; IG to R. R. Leary, Apr. 10, 1933, all GC.

11. Mattie Y. Meyer to IG, May 31, 1933, GC; Cott, *Grounding of Feminism,* 209–10; IG to W. E. Lutz, Apr. 11, 1933, GC.

12. On women competing against other women, see Robyn Muncy, "'Women Demand Recognition': Women Candidates in Colorado's Election of 1912," in Gustafson, Miller, and Perry, eds., *We Have Come to Stay,* 44–54; Joe Gnau to IG, Mar. 18, 1993, GC; IG to Nellie Bush, Aug. 22, 1933, GC; Grace Sparks to IG, Apr. 15, 1933, GC; IG to Grace Sparks, Apr. 20, 1933, GC.

13. IG to FWMC, Mar. 31, 1933; FWMC to IG, Apr. 3, 1933, all GC.

14. IG to Grover A. Miller, Apr. 12, 1933, GC; Katrina McCormick interview; Peter Riley to IG, Apr. 12, 1933, GC; IG to Charles F. Dittmar, Apr. 10, 1933, GC.

15. IG to Lewis Douglas, May 22, 1933; IG to FDR, May 22, 1933; Carl Hayden to IG, June 1, 1933, all GC.

16. B. B. Moeur to FDR, June 2, 1933; George Vensel to FDR, June 1, 1933, 61/736, all GC.

17. *TC,* Oct. 5, 1933; IG to ER, June 14, 1933; ER to IG, June 15, 1933, all GC.

18. *ADS,* June 25, 1933; *TC,* June 24, 1933, and unidentified clippings, AHS; IG to JSG [June 1933], GC.

19. Press release, 45/537; typescripts of radio address, July 17 and Aug. 4, 1933, 45/537; IG to Harold L. Ickes, July 9, 1933, GC.

20. IG to Mr. Bowland, July 18, 1933; IG to Charles Whitlow, July 18, 1933; IG to Frances Simonson, July 11, 1933, all GC.

21. Folder 45/537, GC.

22. IG to JSG [early June 1933], GC.

23. *NYT,* July 23, 1933; unidentified clipping, 45/537, GC.

24. *ADS,* July 30, 1933; IG to Clara Osborn Botzum, Aug. 3, 1933, GC; *TC,* July 20, 1933; press release, 45/537, GC; Probst, 95–96.

25. Unidentified clipping, 43/516; IG to Mrs. Baylor Shannon, Aug. 8, 1933; Mrs. E. V. Shaw to IG, Aug. 9, 1933, all GC; *NYT,* Aug. 9, 1933.

26. *ADS,* Aug. 18, 1933; *Time,* Aug. 21, 1933, 8; *Tucson Weekender,* Sept. 29, 1933, GC.

27. IG to OCJ, Sept. 1, 1933; IG to Nellie Bush, Aug. 22, 1933; IG to JSG, Sept. 2, 1933, all GC.

28. Lois J. Kronholm to Henry Coleman, Aug. 5, 1933; IG to Mrs. R. G. Carmell; IG to FDR, Sept. 26, 1933, all GC; *El Paso Herald,* Oct. 29, 1933; IG to Phil Merill, Sept. 25, 1933; IG to Samuel Morris, Sept. 30, 1933, all GC.

CHAPTER TEN   *Copper, Cattle, and Constituents*

1. IG Diary; *NYT,* Oct. 5, 1933; *Chicago Tribune,* Oct. 5, 1933; form letter; unidentified clipping; Jerrie Lee to IG, Oct. 7, 1933, all GC.

2. IG to Harold L. Ickes, Oct. 3, 1933, GC; *Chicago Tribune,* Oct. 11, 1933; *ADS,* Oct. 18, 1933; JSG interview.

3. "About Washington," unidentified clipping, AHS; IG to Chamber of Commerce, Oct. 21, 1933, 57/687; IG to L. M. Lawson, Oct. 25, 1933, all GC.

4. IG to I. P. McBride, Oct. 20, 1933; Cleveland Dodge to IG, Oct. 20, 1933, all GC.

5. *ADS,* Nov. 14, 1933; IG to Sidney Osborn, Oct. 26, 1933; Dorothy de Corse to IG, Nov. 4, 1933; Arizona Democratic Association, 54/644, all GC.

6. IG to Fred McCalley, Nov. 7, 1933; IG to Miss Goodwin, Harry Hopkins' secretary, Nov. 10, 1933, all GC.

7. Harold L. Ickes to FDR, Dec. 15, 1933, 16/211; IG to Gladys Lytle, Dec. 18, 1933, all GC.

8. "About Washington," unidentified clipping, AHS.

9. *TC,* Jan. 3, 1934; *ADS,* Jan. 4, 1934.

10. *ADS,* Jan. 5 and Feb. 4, 1934; Mrs. J. M. Keith to IG, Jan. 16, 1934; Arizona Cattle Growers' Association, Jan. 22, 1934, 20/255; IG to Howard Smith, Feb. 14, 1934; IG to Thomas Peters, Feb. 6, 1934, all GC.

11. IG to A. E. Schlink, Jan. 11, 1934; IG to Col. J. T. Keegan, Jan. 30, 1934, all GC.

12. Carl Hayden to Walter P. Taylor, Jan. 14, 1934; IG to Walter P. Taylor, Jan. 12, 1934; IG to Joseph W. Alexa, Jan. 30, 1934; unidentified clipping, "News of the Veterans," 61/736, all GC.

13. IG to Elmer Graham, Jan. 5 and 18, 1934; HOK to IG, Jan. 30, 1934, all GC.

14. *ADS,* Apr. 6, 1934.

15. IG to Victor Morowitz, Jan. 11, 1934, GC; *ADS,* Feb. 1, 1934.

16. Wade Hammond to IG, Mar. 5, 1934; IG to Walter Taylor, Feb. 3, 1934; IG to R. L. Whitlow, Feb. 12, 1934, all GC.

17. IG to FDR, Apr. 30, 1934, GC; FDR to IG, May 1, 1934, FDRL; IG to Mrs. J. B. O'Connell, Mar. 23, 1934, GC.

18. *Pittsburgh Post-Gazette,* Feb. 23, 1934; IG to G. Watson French, Feb. 28, 1934, GC; IG to Rodman Griscom, Mar. 21, 1934, GC; *Buffalo Courier-Express,* June 8, 1934.

19. Memo, 59/710, GC; *Congressional Record,* Feb. 28, 1934, 3494.

20. *Congressional Record,* Feb. 28, 1934, 3494; IG to Robert Evans, Feb. 24, 1934, GC; for legislation, see folders 59/710–11 and 61, GC; Cook, *Eleanor Roosevelt, Vol. 2,* 144.

21. Chris Johnson to IG, Feb. 19, 1934; L. T. Baswitz to IG, Jan. 26, 1934, all GC.

22. IG to William Wayland, Jan. 30, 1934; Evan Stallcup to IG, Mar. 20, 1934; IG to Russ Tatum, undated, 22/277, all GC.

23. IG to ER [Apr. 1934], FDRL.

24. IG to JSG, Mar. 29, 1934, GC; Associated Press, Apr. 9, 1934, clipping, GC.

25. IG to Mrs. Cabot Stevens, Mar. 22, 1934; IG to W. L. Howe, Apr. 4, 1934, all GC.

26. IG to E. W. Coker, Feb. 23, 1934; IG to Harold L. Ickes, Apr. 11, 1934; IG to Thomas Peters, June 27, 1934, all GC.

27. *Washington Post,* Jan. 8, 1934; Joseph Harsh, *NYT Magazine,* Apr. 11, 1934, 7; IG to FDR, Apr. 30, 1934, GC; other clippings and correspondence, 25/302. GC.

28. *ADS,* Mar. 13, 1934; IG to Mr. and Mrs. J. H. White, Apr. 21, 1934, GC; IG to W. H. Balch, Feb. 19, 1934, GC.

29. IG to Hugh Johnson, Feb. 13, 1934; IG to Sen. Joseph O'Mahoney, Mar. 9, 1934; IG to John Eager, Mar. 21, 1934; IG to Michael Curley, Mar. 30, 1934; IG to Gladys Penrose, Mar. 31, 1934, all GC.

30. IG to Cpt. William Mershon, Apr. 20, 1934; IG to Lewis Douglas, Apr. 17, 1934; IG to James Peers, Apr. 21, 1934; C. M. Roberts to IG, Apr. 20, 1934; IG to C. M. Roberts, Apr. 27, 1934, all GC.

31. *Congressional Record,* May 11, 1934, 8889; IG to T. S. O'Donnell, May 12, 1934, GC; *Yuma Sentinel,* June 26, 1934; IG to Aron B. Cammerer, Feb. 27, 1934, GC; IG to F. A. Silcox, May 5, 1934, GC; Grace Brewer to IG, Mar. 2, 1934, GC; IG to Grace Brewer, Mar. 21, 1934, GC.

32. IG to Nathan Margold, Mar. 12, 1934; IG to Dean G. M. Butler, June 17, 1934; Howard E. Caffrey to Carl Hayden, June 15, 1934; IG to Al Condron, June 16, 1934; IG to Anna Sullinger, June 20, 1934; IG to Oscar de Priest, May 11, 1934; IG to D. B. Morgan, May 19, 1934; IG to *Arizona Blade Tribune,* June 5, 1934; IG to FDR, June 7, 1934, all GC.

33. J. W. Hill to IG, May 9, 1934; Charles N. Sims to IG, June 19, 1934; IG to Eugene Hannum, May 26, 1934, all GC.

34. IG to Mr. Knorpp, June 26, 1934, GC; *Arizona Fax,* June 29, 1934;

IG to Robert Redwine, July 10, 1934. GC; IG to Mrs. Mark P. Blaemire, May 8, 1934, GC.

35. *Washington Post,* July 1, 1934; IG to Vernon F. Foy, July 3, 1934, GC.

36. Mattie Hussey to IG, July 3, 1934; IG to JSG, June 26, 1934; Msgr. William Hughes to IG, July 13, 1934; IG to Msgr. William Hughes, July 15, 1934, all GC.

37. IG to May W. Berry, July 29, 1934, GC; IG to Bill Mathews, July 27, 1934, GC; *Chicago Tribune,* July 30, 1934; *Washington Post,* July 1, 1934.

38. HOK to IG, July 21, 1934, GC.

39. Gutzon Borglum to IG, undated, GC.

CHAPTER ELEVEN   *"The Lonely Goal"*

1. IG to J. V. M. Goldsmith, July 25, 1934; IG to Thomas H. MacDonald, Aug. 22, 1934; Thomas H. MacDonald to IG, Aug. 23, 1934, all GC.

2. Hilgeman leaflet, 46/543; W. S. Powers to IG, July 20, 1934; IG to R. A. Campbell, Aug. 13, 1934; IG to Mrs. J. Lee Loveless, Aug. 5, 1934; IG to Ben Benchoff, Sept. 22, 1934, all GC.

3. IG to James A. Farley, Sept. 22, 1934, draft marked "not sent," GC.

4. IG to Harold L. Ickes, Sept. 23 and Oct. 6 and 7, 1934, GC; *Arizona Republic,* Oct. 14, 1934.

5. IG to John Phebus, Nov. 14, 1934; IG to John McManus, Oct. 18, 1934; IG to Mr. McKinney, Oct. 1, 1934; IG to FDR, Oct. 27, 1934, all GC; *ADS,* Oct. 14, 1934.

6. HOK to IG, Oct. 25, 1934, GC.

7. Brooks Davis to IG, Nov. 3, 1934; IG to various, Nov. 2, 1934, 45/540; IG to Ina Reed, Nov. 3, 1934, all GC; Harry Carr, "The Lancer," unidentified clipping, 45/540; IG to J. Leo Cannon, Nov. 15, 1934, all GC; IG to ER, Nov. 15, 1934, FDRL.

8. IG Diary, GC.

9. Office memo, Jan. 30, 1935, GC; Duncan Aikman, *NYT Magazine,* 9,11, Apr. 21, 1935; Critchell Rimington to IG, Apr. 25, 1935, GC; IG to Ernest Jaquo, Feb. 11, 1935, GC.

10. F. M. Warner to IG, Jan. 21, 1935; Ellen Woodward to IG, Feb. 2 and [Mar.] 1935; memo, Mar. 29, 1935, 21/268, all GC.

11. B. B. Moeur to IG, Feb. 1 and 16, 1935; Thomas H. MacDonald to IG, Feb. 20, 1935, all GC.

12. *ADS,* Mar. 10 and 22, 1935; IG to A. L. Sweitzer, Mar. 28, 1935; IG to John Collier, Apr. 13, 1935; IG to Edna O'Dowd, Mar. 27, 1935; IG to

Kenneth C. Miller, Mar. 13, 1935; IG to Maude Howard, Mar. 14, 1935, all GC.

13. Kennedy, 247, 258–70; John T. Ambert, Mar. 5, 1935, 35/452, GC.

14. IG to ER, undated, GC; IG form letter, Apr. 17, 1935, 36/455, GC; *NYT* clipping, undated, 36/458, GC; "JM" to IG, Apr. 10, 1935, GC; *Congressional Record,* Apr. 18, 1935; unidentified Associated Press clipping, Apr. 18, 1935, AHS.

15. IG to James A. Farley, Apr. 25, 1935; IG to G. F. Gibson, Apr. 15, 1935, all GC.

16. IG to ER, undated, GC.

17. Office memo, May 18, 1935; IG to I. E. Moore, May 30, 1925; IG to Charles Maphis, May 31, 1935, all GC.

18. *Congressional Record,* 6359; Gladys Lytle to Frank Vesley, Sept. 11, 1935, GC.

19. *Phoenix Republic and Gazette,* July 15, 1935; Charles Collins to IG, July 23, 1935, GC; IG to W. J. Jameison, July 25, 1935, GC; memo, July 27, 1935, 11/159, GC.

20. IG to JSG, July 29, 1935; JSG to IG, July 31, 1935, all GC.

21. IG to Paul Shoup, Aug. 1, 1935, GC; IG to A. E. Taylor, Aug. 7, 1935, GC; IG to Mr. Totten, undated, 3/65, GC; *ADS,* Sept. 1, 1935, AHS.

22. IG to W. J. Jameison, Oct. 29, 1935; IG to FDR, Sept. 10, 1935; HOK to IG, Nov. 12, 1935; IG to James C. McNary, Nov. 15, 1935, all GC; *ADS,* Nov. 24, 1935; unidentified clipping, Nov. 26, 1935, AHS.

23. JSG to IG, July 2, 1945, and Jan. 18, 1936, GC.

24. IG to Gertrude Franzen, Jan. 17, 1936, GC; *Newsweek,* Feb. 29, 1936.

25. IG to T. W. B. Anderson, July 16, 1935; press release, Mar. 23, 1935; Associated Press advance, Mar. 29, 1936; undated draft, all GC.

26. *TC,* Mar. 23, 1936.

27. *Arizona Republic,* Mar. 23, 1936; Associated Press, Mar. 29, 1936, AHS; JSG interview.

28. Abbie Crabb Keith to IG, Apr. 11, 1935; IG to Frank E. Keiming, June 4, 1935; unidentified woman to IG, Mar. 23, 1936; William Coxon to IG, Apr. 6, 1936, all GC.

29. "Bro' Noah" to IG, May 26, 1936, GC; Saranne King Neumann interview.

30. Grace Sparkes to IG, Jan. 2, 1936; Harry Hopkins to IG, Feb. 20, 1936; F. M. Warner to IG, Mar. 9 and 28, and May 6, 1935; H. P. Davis to IG, Feb. 7, 1936; IG to FDR, June 6, 1936, all GC.

31. Social Security Board memo, Feb. 14, 1936, 57/681; IG to Ward

Twitchell, Mar. 17, 1936; IG to Arvelia B. Sadler, June 10, 1936; memo, Apr. 29, 1936, 59/710; undated memo, 10/148, all GC; *Coolidge News,* May 8 and June 26, 1936; IG to R. M. Harrington, Apr. 1, 1936, GC; IG to "JJD," May 6, 1936, GC.

32. IG to E. F. Sanguinette, Feb. 5, 1936; IG to J. G. Scrugham, Apr. 21, 1936; IG to J. L. R. Dickson, Apr. 21, 1936, all GC.

CHAPTER TWELVE   *"At Home with the Right to Stay There"*

1. IG to MS, May 30, 1936; IG to Mrs. Fred Johnson, Dec. 21, 1936, all GC.

2. HOK to IG, undated, GC.

3. IG to A. N. Zellmer, Aug. 25, 1936; "LK" to IG, July 16, 1936; JL to IG, Mar. 9, 1936; "Mary" to IG, Sept. 30, 1936; JSG to IG, Sept. 30 and Oct. 2, 1936; IG to JSG, Oct. 9, 1936, all GC.

4. Cremation certificate, Nov. 13, 1936; JSG to IG, Nov. 14, 1936, all GC.

5. IG to Mayela McKinney, Feb. 18, 1937, GC.

6. IG Diary; IG to Mayela McKinney, Feb. 18, 1937; JSG to IG, Jan. 30 and May 16, 1937, all GC.

7. *Washington Star,* Feb. 14, 1937; IG to Mayela McKinney, Feb. 18, 1937; IG to Joseph Otis, May 11, 1937; IG to Gladys Lytle, July 31, 1937; IG Diary, all GC.

8. *TC,* Jan. 31, 1938.

9. Howard Caffrey to IG, May 16, 1938; IG Diary, GC.

10. IG Diary, June 1938; HOK to IG, Aug. 3 and 5, and undated, 1938, all GC.

11. IG Diary, Sept. 8, 1938, GC.

12. HOK to JSG, May 30, 1938, and Aug. 2, 1937; JSG to IG, Feb. 6, 1938; Edward Fay to IG, June 6, 1938; Joseph Handley to IG, July 17, 1938; Claude Fuess to IG, Nov. 3, 1938, all GC.

13. Katrina Barnes interview; Elizabeth Lindsay to IG, Mar. 16, 1939, GC.

14. IG to SFC, Apr. 1939, GC; Neumann interview.

15. HOK to IGK, Mar. 26, 27, and 31 and Apr. [20], 1940, all GC.

16. *TC,* July 10, 1940.

17. Unidentified clipping, AHS; *ADS,* Oct. 20, 1940; Neumann interview; "Family Newsletter," no. 19, June 8, 1945, GC.

18. JSG interview.

19. *ADS,* Oct. 20, 1940.

20. IGK to ER [Aug. 1940], GC.

21. ER to IGK, Aug. 22, 1940, GC; ER to Lorena A. Hickok, quoted in Lash, 478; Kennedy, 463.

CHAPTER THIRTEEN *"She Was Unique"*

1. Associated Press, July 9, 1941; AWVS memo, May 10, 1941, and undated memos, GC.

2. Undated speech [1942]; memo, all GC.

3. C. Vann Woodward, preface to Kennedy, xv; AWVS memo, Oct. 8, 1942, GC; *New Yorker* clipping GC; AWVS memo, May 12, 1941, GC; Anne Berenholz to IGK, Sept. 18, 1942, GC.

4. AWVS reports, July 20 and Sept. 8, 1942, GC.

5. IGK to Emily Newell Blair, June 13, 1942; IGK to Alice McLean, June 15, 1942; Alice McLean to Joseph Davies, July 30, 1942; IGK to J. H. Rosenbaum, Aug. 15, 1942; invitation, Dec. 19, 1942; Alice McLean memo, Sept. 15, 1942, all GC.

6. Neumann interview; Mildred Bliss to IGK, Oct. 23, 1942, GC; Paul Fitzpatrick to IGK, Mar. 13, 1943, GC.

7. Memos Jan. and Feb. 1942; AAA minutes, Oct. 13, 1942; Paul Fitzpatrick to IGK, Mar. 13, 1943; IGK to Alice McLean, Jan. 7, 1943, all GC.

8. HOK to IGK, Feb. 24, 1943; Paul Fitzpatrick to IGK, Mar. 13, 1943; Frances Kellor to IGK, Feb. 2, 1945, all GC.

9. IGK to JSG, Oct. 11, 1945; JSG to IGK, July 2, 1945, and various letters, 1945, 194/2682, all GC.

10. JSG to IGK, Jan. 24 and June 21, 1945, GC.

11. "Family Newsletter," no. 21, June 26; no. 24, July 16; no. 12, Apr. 10, GC.

12. "Family Newsletter," no. 12, Apr. 17, 1945, GC.

13. "Family Newsletter," no. 21, June 26, 1945; JSG to IGK, June 29, 1945, GC; David Breasted interview.

14. "Family Newsletter," no. 28, Aug. 23, 1945, GC.

15. IGK to JSG, Aug. 23 and Sept. 16, 1945, GC.

16. IGK to JSG, Sept. 29 and Oct. 25, 1945, GC.

17. IGK to JSG, Oct. 11 and Nov. 11, 1945, GC; Deezy Manning Catron interview; David Breasted interview.

18. James, *Letters of Elizabeth Sherman Lindsay,* 227, 230.

19. Brophy, "Arizona Inn," 22; Emma Brady Rogers interview.

20. IGK to John L. Lewis, Jan. 28, 1948; IGK to Clifton Anderson, Feb. 15, 1948; IGK to Harry S Truman, Apr. 2, 1948; Clifton Anderson to IGK, Feb. 25, 1948; IGK to Clifton Anderson, Mar. 19, 1948, all GC; *ADS,* Mar. 26 and 31, 1948.

21. JSG interview; *ADS,* Dec. 12, 1953; HOK to IGK, Apr. 18, 1949, GC.

22. IGK to JSG, Oct. 25, 1950; JSG to IGK, Oct. 31, 1950; IGK to JSG, Nov. 3, 1950, all GC; Emma Brady Rogers interview.

23. *TC,* Sept. 15, 1995.

24. *ADS,* Dec. 19 and 21, 1953.

25. Morris Udall to JSG, Dec. 24, 1953; Carlos Ronstadt, Dec. 18, 1953; Corinne Roosevelt Alsop [Dec. 1953], all GC.

CHAPTER FOURTEEN   *Isabella's Legacies*

1. Doar interview, 2002; Patty Doar to author, July 16, 2003.

2. Richmond interview; IGK to Eugene Lyons, May 12, 1948, GC.

3. Condé Nast *Traveler,* Jan. 2003, 132; *Travel & Leisure,* Jan. 2003, 116.

4. ER to Lorena A. Hickok, quoted in Lash, 478.

BIBLIOGRAPHY

INTERVIEWS WITH THE AUTHOR

Hannah Baird, September 4, 1998
Katrina Barnes, June 15, 2000
David Breasted, May 27, 1999
Deezy Manning Catron, February 25, 1998
Frances Ferguson "Patty" Doar, July 12, 2001; July 26, 2002
John S. Greenway, July 28, 1995
Saranne King Neumann, March 10, 1998
Peg Richmond, March 26, 1998
Emma Brady Rogers, September 4, 1998

OTHER INTERVIEWS

Martha Ferguson Breasted interview April 13, 1990, Dinsmore Farm
Martha Ferguson Breasted with Blake Brophy, undated, FFD
John S. Greenway with Blake Brophy, undated, FFD

PUBLISHED SOURCES

Berry, Susan, and Sharman Apt Russell. *Built to Last, an Architectural History of Silver City New Mexico,* 2nd ed., Silver City Museum Society, Silver City, N.Mex., 1995.
Boese, Donald L. *John C. Greenway and the Opening of the Western Mesabi.* Grand Rapids: Itasca Community College Foundation, 1975.

Bibliography

Brophy, Blake. "Tucson's Arizona Inn: The Continuum of Style," *Journal of Arizona History*, 24, no. 3 (autumn 1983): 255–82.

———. *Isabella: An American Original*. Unpublished manuscript in Doar Collection.

Byrkit, James W. *Forging the Copper Collar: Arizona's Labor-Management War of 1901–1921*. Tucson: University of Arizona Press, 1982.

Carter, Robin Borglum. *Gutzon Borglum: His Life and Work*. Austin: Eakin Press, 1998.

Chamberlin, Hope. *A Minority of Members: Women in the U.S. Congress*. New York: Praeger, 1973.

Cook, Blanche Wiesen. *Eleanor Roosevelt, Volume One: 1884–1933*. New York: Viking, 1992.

———. *Eleanor Roosevelt, Volume Two: The Defining Years 1933–1938*. New York: Viking, 1999.

Cott, Nancy. *The Grounding of Feminism*. New Haven: Yale University Press, 1987.

Ehrenreich, Barbara, and Deidre English. *For Her Own Good: 150 Years of the Experts' Advice to Women*. New York: Doubleday, 1978.

Farley, James A. *Jim Farley's Story: The Roosevelt Years*. New York: McGraw Hill, 1948.

Fransen, Annie, "Burro Mountain Homestead 1800–2000." Unpublished manuscript, Silver City Museum Society, Silver City, N.Mex.

Gustafson, Melanie, Kristie Miller, and Elisabeth Perry, eds., *We Have Come to Stay: American Women and Political Parties 1880–1960*. Albuquerque: University of New Mexico Press, 1999.

Hagedorn, Hermann, ed., *The Works of Theodore Roosevelt,* National Edition. New York: Charles Scribner's Sons, 1926.

Hickok, Lorena A. *Eleanor Roosevelt: Reluctant First Lady*. New York: Dodd, Mead and Co., 1962.

Higby, John. "The Burro Mountain Homestead," Grant County History, no. 5. Silver City Museum Society, Silver City, N.Mex., 1970.

Hill, Edwin C. *The American Scene*. New York: Witmark Educational Publications, 1933.

Hill, Janaloo. *The Ranch on Whitewater Creek: A One Hundred Year History of the Burro Mountain Homestead and the Surrounding Area*. Unpublished manuscript, Silver City Museum Society, Silver City, N.Mex.

Holmstrom, Betty. "Isabella Greenway and Gilpin Airlines." Unpublished manuscript, Greenway Collection, Arizona Historical Society, 1990.

James, Olivia, ed. *The Letters of Elizabeth Sherman Lindsay: 1911–1954.* New York: Privately printed, 1960.

Kennedy, David. *Freedom from Fear: The American People in Depression and War, 1929–1945.* New York: Oxford University Press, 1999.

Koller, Edith, "A Brief History of the New Mexico Cottage Sanatorium." Unpublished manuscript, Silver City Museum Society, Silver City, N.Mex., 1979.

Lash, Joseph P. *A World of Love.* New York: Doubleday, 1984.

Martin, Ralph G. *Ballots & Bandwagons.* Chicago: Rand McNally, 1964.

McCullough, David. *Mornings on Horseback.* New York: Simon & Schuster, 1981.

Mencken, H. L. *Making a President: A Footnote to the Saga of Democracy.* New York: Alfred A. Knopf, 1932.

Miller, Kristie. "A Volume of Friendship: The Correspondence of Isabella Greenway and Eleanor Roosevelt, 1904–1953," *Journal of Arizona History,* 40, no. 2 (summer 1999): 121–56.

Miller, Robert E. *The Private Writings of Julia S. Dinsmore: Farmer, Poet, and Old-Time Country Gentlewoman, 1873–1926.* Unpublished manuscript, Dinsmore Farm, Burlington, Ky.

Montoya, Denise. "The Woman's Land Army of Grant County, 1918, or Farmerettes to the Rescue." Unpublished manuscript, Silver City Museum Society, Silver City, N.Mex., 1979.

Morris, Edmund. *The Rise of Theodore Roosevelt.* New York: Coward, McCann and Geoghegan, 1979.

Mullen, Arthur. *Western Democrat.* New York: Wildred Funk, Inc., 1940.

New Mexico Cottage Sanatorium. Pamphlet in Silver City Museum Society, Silver City, N.Mex.

Oulahan, Richard. *The Man Who . . . : The Story of the 1932 Democratic National Convention.* New York: The Dial Press, 1971.

Probst, Avan. *Isabella Greenway: Arizona's 1933 Congresswoman.* M. A. thesis, Northern Arizona University, 1994.

Putnam, Carleton. *Theodore Roosevelt: Volume One: The Formative Years 1858–1886.* New York: Charles Scribner's Sons, 1958.

Robinson, Corinne Roosevelt. *My Brother Theodore Roosevelt.* New York: Charles Scribner's Sons, 1921.

Bibliography

Roosevelt, Eleanor. *This Is My Story*. New York: Doubleday, 1937.

Roosevelt, Eleanor, and Lorena A. Hickok. *Ladies of Courage*. New York: G. P. Putnam's Sons, 1954.

Roosevelt, Theodore. *Letters from Theodore Roosevelt to Anna Roosevelt Cowles, 1870–1918*. New York: Charles Scribner's Sons, 1924.

Roper, Daniel C., with Frank H. Lovett. *50 Years of Public Life*. Durham: Duke University Press, 1941.

Storke, Thomas M. *I Write for Freedom*. Chicago: McNally & Loften, 1963.

Ward, Geoffrey C. *A First-Class Temperament: The Emergence of Franklin Roosevelt*. New York: Book-of-the-Month Club, 1998.

ILLUSTRATION CREDITS

Illustration Credits

INDEX

Index

ABOUT THE AUTHOR

Kristie Miller is an independent scholar, author of the award-winning biography of her grandmother, *Ruth Hanna McCormick: A Life in Politics 1880–1944* (University of New Mexico Press, 1992), and co-editor of *We Have Come to Stay: American Women and Political Parties 1880–1960* (University of New Mexico Press, 1999). She has written more than two dozen articles for encyclopedias including *American National Biography, American First Ladies, Women in World History, Women Building Chicago,* and *The Eleanor Roosevelt Encyclopedia.* She co-edits the Women's Biography Series for the University of New Mexico Press. She writes a weekly column on women, history, and politics for her hometown newspaper, the La Salle, Illinois, *Daily News Tribune.* She holds a B. A. from Brown University and an M. A. from Georgetown University. She lives in McLean, Virginia, with her husband.

LIBRARY OF CONGRESS CATALOGING-IN-PUBLICATION DATA
Miller, Kristie, 1944–
   Isabella Greenway : an enterprising woman / Kristie Miller.
      p. cm.
   Includes bibliographical references and index.
   ISBN-13: 978-0-8165-1897-5 (cloth : alk. paper)
   ISBN-10: 0-8165-1897-1 (cloth : alk. paper)
   ISBN-13: 978-0-8165-2518-8 (pbk. : alk. paper)
   ISBN-10: 0-8165-2518-8 (pbk. : alk. paper)
   1. King, Isabella Greenway, 1886–1953. 2. Legislators—United States—
Biography. 3. Women legislators—United States—Biography. 4. United States.
Congress. House—Biography. 5. Democratic Party (U.S.)—Biography.
6. Arizona—Politics and government—To 1950. 7. New Deal, 1933–1939
—Arizona. I. Title.
   E748.K53M55 2004
   328.73'092—dc22
   2004002842